The Compleat Social Worker

Also by David Howe

Social Workers and their Practice in Welfare Bureaucracies
An Introduction to Social Work Theory
The Consumers' View of Family Therapy
Half a Million Women: Mothers Who Lose Their Children by Adoption
(with P. Sawbridge and D. Hinings)
On Being a Client: Understanding the Process of Counselling and
Psychotherapy
Attachment Theory for Social Work Practice*
Attachment and Loss in Child and Family Social Work
Adopters on Adoption: Reflections on Parenthood and Children
Patterns of Adoption: Nature, Nurture and Psychosocial Development
Attachment Theory, Child Maltreatment and Family Support * (with M.
Brandon, D.Hinings and G. Schofield)
Adoption. Search and Reunion (with J. Feast)
The Adoption Reunion Handbook (with L. Trinder and J. Feast)
Contact in Adoption and Permanent Care (with E. Neil)
Child Abuse and Neglect: Attachment, Development and Intervention*
The Emotionally Intelligent Social Worker *
A Brief Introduction to Social Work Theory*
Attachment Across the Lifecourse: A Brief Introduction*
Empathy: What It Is and Why It Matters*

* Also published by Palgrave Macmillan

The Compleat Social Worker

David Howe

 palgrave

First published 2014 by
PALGRAVE

Palgrave in the UK is an imprint of Macmillan Publishers Limited, registered
in England, company number 785998, of 4 Crinan Street, London N1 9XW.

Palgrave Macmillan in the US is a division of St Martin's Press LLC,
175 Fifth Avenue, New York, NY 10010.

Palgrave is the global imprint of the above companies and is represented
throughout the world.

Palgrave® and Macmillan® are registered trademarks in the United States,
the United Kingdom, Europe and other countries

ISBN 978–1–137–46946–5

This book is printed on paper suitable for recycling and made from fully
managed and sustained forest sources. Logging, pulping and manufacturing
processes are expected to conform to the environmental regulations of the
country of origin.

Typeset by Cambrian Typesetters, Camberley, Surrey

Printed in China

For Catherine Gray

Contents

Acknowledgements

Catherine Gray has been the publisher for my Palgrave Macmillan books for the last twenty years. I owe her a huge debt of gratitude for two decades of wonderful advice, support and encouragement. So a big thank you, Catherine. Stretching back even further in time, I owe my career in social work, as a practitioner and an academic, to two people in particular. In the late 1960s I was interviewed by Brian Stimpson, Derby's Children's Officer, for a job as a child care officer. My first degree was in science. After graduating, I spent a couple of years teaching sciences in East London. So, given my provenance, I was surprised, to say the least, when Mr Stimpson offered me the job. During my time working as a child care officer, and a few years later as a social worker, I met many, many remarkable people from whom I learned so much. And then in 1976 I found myself being interviewed again, this time for the post of Lecturer in Social Work at the newly established MA in Social Work degree at the University of East Anglia, Norwich. The interview panel was altogether more intimidating than the cosy affair that was my experience in Derby. It was not until I had arrived back home the next day that I learned I'd been successful. Dr Martin Davies, then Director of the new programme, and now Emeritus Professor, 'phoned to tell me the news. I was thrilled and daunted in equal measure. But Martin proved a great colleague, a stimulating mentor, and a consummate scholar. As both friend and fellow academic, he has taught me so many things over more years than I care to remember about the value of research and the craft of writing. Thank you, Martin. And while we're on the subject of writing, many thanks to Nick Brock who has copy-edited this book with great speed, accuracy and sympathy. Thanks, too, for the comments and advice of the three anonymous reviewers of this book. Honestly, I have tried to follow your suggestions whenever and wherever I could, but probably not always to the degree or extent your insights deserved. And when, occasionally, one of you said one thing and another said the opposite, I've generally stood frozen in the middle and done nothing. However, I'm always struck by the wisdom and generosity of social work colleagues who take the time and interest to read and think about each other's efforts. Although I am not presuming for one second that my fellow social workers will agree with all that I am saying in this book, nevertheless the idea of the *compleat* social worker is my way of saying thank you to the profession I have worked in for the last 46 years and which has given me the opportunity to meet so many kind, able and extraordinary people.

David Howe
Norwich

1

The Individual and Society

Looking Both Ways in Social Work

Looking both ways

People, as individuals, take note of what is expected of them by society. They have responsibilities to raise children safely and well, to work if they are healthy and fit, to care for those who are vulnerable and dependent. Most people behave within the law.

People also have rights. They have the right to be treated fairly, to be supported when they are old and ill, to enjoy a basic standard of living. There is therefore a balance to be struck between individual conduct and social living. Valuing the freedom of the individual has to be weighed against the good of the community. Societies don't work unless people are prepared to accept some social duties and obligations.

Society and its agents also take an interest in the individual. Those who break the law will be sought and punished. Those who are *troublesome* will be identified, assessed and dealt with – by the police, the courts, probation officers, child protection agents, mental health specialists. People who are a problem for society therefore become subject to treatment and control.

Those who are *troubled* will also be of concern to the state and its agents. The troubled might include parents who struggle to raise their children, individuals who suffer mental illness, people who have a learning disability, old people who can no longer care for themselves, and families who get into debt and become homeless. Those who find living in society a problem are likely to become the subject of care and protection, support and guidance, or, again, treatment and change.

Social workers are one of the groups whose activities take place within this busy area between the individual and society. Social

workers therefore find themselves looking two ways as they represent the individual to society *and* represent society to the individual.

In the nineteenth century, worries about people's wellbeing as
well as the risks of social unrest began to colour political debates and
social policy. Calls for something to be done about both the plight of
the poor and the risks they posed to social stability were one of the
factors that led to social work's early formation. The profession began
to take shape and grow in the space where the 'respectable' classes
brushed up against the 'dangerous' classes (Parton and O'Byrne
2000: 37). Social workers began to represent the strong to the weak
but also the weak to the strong. In early charity work, for example,
social workers 'represented the humanity of the privileged to the
poor and the essential "goodness" and social nature of the poor to the
privileged' (Philp 1979: 94).

Modern social work formed as the relationship between the individual and society, the private and the public became more complex.
And as the personal and the political began to meet, an area, a space
was defined which became known as 'the social' (Donzelot 1979). One
of the main occupational groups who worked in this 'space' eventually became known as 'social' workers.

It was in this social space that the public face of personal behaviours
began to be identified, labelled, and classified. Experts and policy
makers moved in, offered explanations and made laws. There was a
gradual shift in approach from simply punishing wrongdoers and poor
performers to demanding their return, both body and mind, to a better
life, one of social usefulness and value. Social workers were one of the
professions charged with keeping the vulnerable safe, the dangerous
controlled, and the distressed and unhappy calm and content.

To help social workers do these things, many in the profession
turned to the social sciences for ideas and suggestions about how
best to explain and understand, cure and change, treat and train, care
for and control those whose behaviours lay outside and beyond what
was seen as socially acceptable or morally defensible.

Thus, people's minds, and the behaviours these minds prompted,
became the objects of professional attention. Social workers, doctors
and educationalists began to treat the actor and not the act, change
the doer rather than punish the deed (Cohen 1985: 139). More and
more behaviours became subject to surveillance, monitoring, and
assessment (Donzelot 1979).

For example, it seemed that if the state was to function and thrive, it mattered how children were raised. Parents and their families became the subject of scientific as well as political interest. Parents and families not performing well became a matter of concern. And as so many of these problems arose in the context of poverty and inequality, it was not lost on many social workers that much of their work emerged as the rich were obliged to take note of the poor.

Thus, from the outset, social workers found themselves thinking about clients in relation to society and society in relation to clients. For example, parents who have learning disabilities and whose own childhoods were blighted by abuse and neglect seem good candidates for society's compassion and care. When social workers assess such families, in part they are making the case – to the welfare authorities, schools, courts – that if the parenting is poor, then the problems are understandable and perhaps worthy of concern. But by the same token, to the extent that the parenting is also seen as deficient and neglectful, these same families are asked to recognise that they are not meeting the standards that society requires and expects.

In one and the same case, the social worker presents the family to society, and presents society to the family. It is therefore difficult to separate issues of care *and* control, change *and* concern.

It seems unavoidable therefore that social workers find them-selves being pulled in opposite directions. They exist in a state of tension. But here we must note something important. Social work's character and very being are shaped by this self-same tension. Herein lies much of the profession's make-up and spirit, strength and vulnerability.

Not surprisingly, then, social work is viewed with ambivalence – by both clients and society. It is all too easy for failing families to see the social worker as an interfering agent of the state. It is all too easy for the state to see the social worker as a gullible, do-gooder, hope-lessly naïve as he or she is taken in by dangerous families and ne'er-do-wells.

This leads to the familiar dilemmas in which social workers regularly find themselves: they are damned when they do and damned when they don't. They are castigated in the press as unfeeling bureaucrats when they remove children from supposedly loving families, and ridiculed as credulous fools lacking all common sense when they leave vulnerable children with hopeless parents.

None of this is to say that social workers don't sometimes get it wrong, but the point of this book is to recognise social work's deeper nature. Social work is an occupation forged in the heat of the middle ground. It arises out of the tensions between society as it struggles with matters of care on the one hand and issues of control on the other. Little wonder, then, that social work is so often viewed with mixed feelings. Its origins make this inevitable.

However, this should not be a cause for despair or regret. Rather, it should be embraced as a defining feature of social work's essential make-up. This doesn't always make the job easy or comfortable. But it does make the work dynamic. So although social work can be many things, as we shall conclude, it is never dull.

By embracing the pushes and pulls of the job, and by celebrating the richness and diversity of what social workers need to know to do their work, we might talk of the fully rounded practitioner and recognise the idea of the 'compleat' social worker who we shall shortly meet at the end of this chapter.

Agency and structure

Societies are made up of individuals interacting. But it is also possible to argue that individuals, as psychological selves, only come into being in the context of the society in which they find themselves. Putting society first means that the political, spiritual, and economic nature of the society in which the individual finds himself or herself will have a profound impact on the kind of psychosocial being an individual self will become. Collections of interacting individuals make up society which in turn shapes individuals and the way they interact. Relationships and social action therefore both produce society and are themselves a product of society.

It is immediately apparent from the circularity of this insight that trying to think about the individual and society, which is what social workers have to do all the time, is not easy. The two are difficult to separate. It's like looking at an eddy in a stream. The eddy has its distinct qualities, but it cannot be understood apart from the swirling waters in which it takes form. Of course, one way to think about individuals and society is for one group, psychologists, to look at individuals and their behaviour, and another group, sociologists, to look at societies and their make-up.

We shall certainly be touching on this classic division in some of the following chapters, but before we do, it is worth staying for a moment with the sociologists. They have useful things to say about the relationship between the individual and society and to help them do this they employ two concepts, *agency* and *structure*.

Put rather simply, from one viewpoint, individuals are seen as free *agents* who act and interact on a voluntary basis and in so doing bring about society. People can and do take charge of their own lives. Social changes occur because people make them occur.

> Social interaction and therefore social relationships arise from the fact that the satisfaction of need and the pursuit of interests requires the co-operation, collaboration or control of other individuals in a similar position. This leads to the development and construction of mutual forms of the regulation and organization of relationships between individuals that are based upon reciprocity of understanding and expectations which then licence and control their interactions with one another. (Walsh 1998: 12)

Those who are impressed with the ability of individuals to determine their own actions and produce relationships according to their own needs and agenda see social life as the sum of all these individual actions and relationships. This view encourages social workers to help clients recognise their own strengths and take charge of their own destiny.

From the other perspective, social *structures* and society's institutions exist *prior* to any one individual. We are born into society. The individual is shaped, both mentally and culturally, by the world in which he or she finds himself or herself – the world of language, laws, customs, institutions. For *structuralists*, our beliefs, values, interests, expectations, and understandings derive from the culture, class, and social norms in which we are raised and have to live. It is inside these social realities that we learn to think, feel, believe, and act in a culturally distinct way. We become socialized. Thinking this way encourages social workers to recognise the political and economic realities that shape our lives, and that for many clients, if life is to improve then change has to be sought and fought at the structural level of politics, economics and ideology.

So, social structures result from the actions and interactions of individuals but these interactions and relationships also produce an independent emergent social reality which exists apart from, and prior to, each of us as individuals. An early version of this was given by Karl Marx (1852) who said that human beings indeed do make their own history, but not in circumstances of their own choosing. There is no escape from the idea that the personal is political and the political is always personal, and that individual experience can only be understood in the social and structural context in which it is to be found.

Either–or, and–both

Being caught in the middle between the individual and society explains why social work has such a wide knowledge base. Practitioners need to know something of psychology, sociology, the law, human nature, social behaviour, ethics and values, roles and relationships, welfare and justice, policy and politics, art and science.

And herein lies the rub. Many of the things that social workers need to know and understand are pitched in binary opposites. They are polarized into 'either/or', as we have already seen with ideas about agency and structure, and the personal and political. It seems as if the practitioner is being invited to take sides (Dickens 2013, Healy 2000). The social, psychological, and political sciences are rife with debates about nature and nurture, freedom and equality, quality and quantity, professionals and bureaucrats, and it seems that as social workers we are forever caught up in these arguments.

But like social work itself, polarizing the debates, and arguing for one side or the other, ignores not only the richness and complexity of life but also the deeper dynamics that underpin and define a thing, a person, a circumstance, or an event. This is true of human growth and development, social behaviour and the demands of living together, what people do and why they do it, as well as social work itself. This is what C. P. Snow thought of split, dichotomous thinking:

> The number 2 is a very dangerous number: that is why dialectic is a dangerous process. Attempts to divide anything into two ought to be regarded with much suspicion. (Snow 1959/1964: 10)

In the following chapters, we shall present some of these debates in polarized, binary form, particularly as they have influenced and informed social work. Each side of each debate will be reviewed in brief, before a more rounded, integrated picture is drawn in which the two sides of the debate will be seen, more often than not, to be two sides of the same coin. Or different takes on the same thing.

The world of people and things is extraordinarily diverse. And so about any one thing we will find 'multiple discourses' with many voices saying many things (Fook 2012: 13; Sands and Nuccio 1992). So, rather than speak of *either–or* approaches, we shall favour a *both–and* approach. For example, we no longer speak of nature *or* nurture, but nature *and* nurture. Nature and nurture interact in ways that are both wonderful and complex, helping us to understand the subtlety of human development so much better than nature or nurture could ever do on their own.

Grasping the full and rounded picture, not being afraid to embrace the tensions and conflicts, grappling with division and uncertainty not only makes the subject under study more complete but also makes the social worker who recognises how these subjects inform and underpin her own knowledge base and practice more complete. Social workers who can embrace the whole and who can live with the pulls and pushes, ambiguities and uncertainties of their work might therefore be described as *complete* social workers. So a quick word, then, about the title of this book and why complete is being spelled archaically as *compleat*.

The word is borrowed from the title of Izaak Walton's famous book on fly fishing, *The Compleat Angler*, first published in 1653 and still in print today. It celebrates the art, science, and spirit of fishing. Walton recognises that, like 'mathematicks' fishing can never be fully learnt, but for those willing to study and practise the 'recreation', he or she will be on the road to becoming a *compleat* angler. And so it is with social work. Those willing to ponder, pursue and enjoy the practice of social work in all its fraught glory will be on their way to becoming *compleat* social workers. I'll be sticking with the old spelling throughout the book, partly to stay true to Walton's spirit and meaning, and partly for the fun of it, so bear with me.

Each of the following 13 chapters follows a set pattern. The subject or topic about which there is debate and divide is introduced. Each side of the debate is then presented. The final section of each chapter seeks to find merit in the arguments of both sides in an attempt to resolve some of their differences. However, more ambitiously this final section goes on to suggest that a dynamic relationship between the two sides can also be found out of which emerges a much more plausible, energetic, and exciting understanding of the subject under study. This is the first sense in which the social worker's understanding of who she is and what she does might be said to be *compleat*.

The second sense takes matters one stage further. It distils the major themes of each chapter into six key elements which, in the author's personal view make up the *compleat* social worker. So as you read the following pages, you will recognise the importance I give to being simply interested in people and remaining forever *curious*. You will understand that making judgements and reaching decisions is part and parcel of doing social work. If the judgements made and decisions taken are to be sound, you will need to be clear about the *values* you hold and the principles you espouse. You will appreciate the therapeutic significance of *empathy* and the need to practise in ways that are structured, ordered, and clear. You will then be in a strong position to establish a good relationship with those with whom you work. *Relationship-based practice* is the platform on which all other interventions need to operate if they are to be successful. The interventions chosen should, whenever possible, have some *evidence* to support their use and effectiveness. However, much of what social workers do stretches beyond the scientific compass of evidence-based approaches. This invites you to be pragmatic and craftful, philosophical and political, reflective and *critically reflexive*. And so you find yourself back at the beginning – being curious, maintaining your interest, fuelling your passion, asking questions, and challenging assumptions.

The book is not designed as a blueprint or manifesto. Rather, read it for ideas and understandings. Allow it to trigger discussion, debate and disagreement. But most important of all, use it to make you think and feel, savour and celebrate what it is to be a good practitioner, a *compleat social worker*.

2

Order and Change

The Purpose of Social Work

Introduction

Much of the legislation and policy that underpins social work is the result of people who have felt bothered, even outraged about some injustice, unfairness, or deprivation. These are people who have turned private troubles into public concerns.

Campaigners who recognise the difficulties that disabled people have negotiating steps and narrow doors, the discrimination suffered by those with a mental illness, or the poverty experienced by many old people even after a lifetime of hard work have helped bring about changes in policy and legislation. Improvements in access for disabled people, equal opportunities in the job market for those with a mental illness, and the provision of state pensions for older people are the result of campaigning individuals and groups defining problems and recognising needs, and then shouting long and loud about them. These welfare reformers demand change. They challenge assumptions and the status quo. They pursue *causes*.

But when the cause has been won and there is recognition that the situation is unacceptable, the collective will demands that things have to change. When governments bring in new laws, change policies, and provide fresh resources, different social work talents are required. Welfare organizations have to be created to deliver the new services. Social workers have to learn about disability and old age, legal requirements, and pension rights, children's development and mental illness. They become agents of the Welfare State delivering care, exerting control, providing cures. Their *function* is to sustain personal wellbeing and maintain social order.

Personal temperaments and ideological outlooks generally determine whether social workers are more likely to pursue causes or carry out functions (Lee 1937). This division reflects similar splits in the social sciences.

Modern society emerged in the late eighteenth and early nineteenth centuries. Rapid changes were taking place in technology and industry. Cities were growing at breakneck speed as people left the countryside to work in factories. The belief in reason and rational thought that was powering the natural sciences began to inform the social sciences. If science could order, tame, and improve nature then surely the social sciences could bring order, stability, and improvements to the social world as populations grew and urbanization spread.

So, debates in the social sciences in general and social work in particular have often been pitched in terms of either conflict or order, change or regulation.

Conflict and radical change

Many social and political theorists continue to be impressed by society's more restless qualities. They are struck by the constant presence of tension and conflict in human affairs. These conflicts are usually driven by inequalities in the distribution of resources, or injustices in how people are treated (Pease 2013). Whenever the gap between rich and poor, the strong and weak, the powerful and the powerless becomes too wide, tension and conflict arise. Instability sets in. Societies begin to break down. The only way to ease these tensions is to reconfigure the social order and narrow the gaps. Money should be shared more equally. Wages ought to be fair. The powers of the privileged should be reined back.

However, there is a tendency for the rich and powerful to organize the world to suit their interests. The way they frame the laws, control the media, assert social values, and allocate resources makes it difficult for most of us to see that we live in a world defined by the powerful for the powerful. To the extent that the weak, vulnerable, and disadvantaged get anything out of society, it is only to keep them quiet and subdued, and in the case of workers, compliant and productive.

It is only when the differences between the rich and poor, the powerful and the powerless become too great that dissatisfaction and anger are likely to erupt. Extreme inequalities and blatant injustices fuel personal problems, desperation, and social unrest. It is the threat of instability which prompts the privileged to concede, albeit reluctantly, some rights, some wealth, some power. Social change only occurs when tensions threaten breakdown and conflict.

Some social observers are more alert than others to the vast differences that exist between people in terms of power and wealth. For example, in the UK the richest 1 per cent of the population hold as much wealth as the poorest 55 per cent of the population put together (ONS 2014). Similar inequalities of wealth are found in most advanced neo-liberal capitalist societies, and the gap is getting wider (Piketty 2104).

Critical and radical observers are not only more likely to be alert to these massive differences in wealth distribution, they are also more likely to be bothered by them. They offer a radical analysis of society's ills and propose radical solutions – that is, solutions that get to the root cause of things.

For radical, structurally oriented social workers and reformers, the only long-term answers lie in changing society and its laws, policies, economics, and social structures (Bailey and Brake 1975; Lavalette 2011). It is therefore the job of the radical analyst to identify and expose misuses of power, unfair laws, unjustified wealth, social injustice, and the degrading effects of poverty. If the analyst happens to be a social worker, she will campaign for change; she will fight, as Porter Lee (1937) said, a *cause*.

Radicals therefore campaign for reform, advocate people's rights, and encourage people to see how their views about themselves, typically negative and pathologizing, have been shaped by those in power. 'Consciousness-raising' is an attempt to get those whose lives are ones of oppression and disadvantage to see how the strong and powerful have organized things to suit their interests at the expense of others. Such critical analyses help empower the poor and emancipate women. They help radicalize those who have been ill-treated because they are old, who have been misunderstood because they have a mental illness, and who have suffered discrimination because of their race, gender or physical ability.

The history of social work throws up many fine examples of people who have spotted injustices and fought for change. In pursuit of causes, they seek fairness. They expose self-interest and greed.

They fight prejudice and oppression. They are driven by anger every bit as much as by compassion. For example, the recognition that women who were the victims of domestic violence were ill-served by the law, police and welfare services led to the establishment of women's refuges and demands that policy, resources, and legislation be changed to protect women from violent men. These early radical feminists recorded many successes.

In the 1980s, Wolf Wolfensberger (1983) developed what became known as Social Role Valorization. His analysis of how certain people were treated unfairly based on some socially irrelevant difference led him to develop ideas about how society values and devalues individual citizens. Individuals and groups given low social value by the powers that be and their ideologies are at high risk of being treated poorly. They miss out on the everyday things that make life pleasant – friends, freedom, money, services, travel, even work. They have fewer rights. They lose out on basic freedoms. They are denied opportunities.

For example, in the 1980s, many people with a learning disability would end up living a segregated life in some large, medically based institution, often on the edge of town. They would be removed from the community, no longer visible, no longer valued. This was hurtful, demeaning, and undermining. Challenging the assumption that people who had a learning disability were not fit or able to live a normal life in their local community helped bring about profound changes in social policy. All it took to support adults who had a learning disability to live in the community was a change in attitude, a shift in policy, and the transfer of resources from institutional provision to community care.

Social Role Valorization theory played a key part in the early community care movement which began to take shape in the 1980s, although the idea of supporting people in their home environment had been around for several decades before then. The belief was that people should be able to direct and lead their own lives whenever possible (Kendrick and Hartnett 2005). As a result of this change in social philosophy, many large institutions were shut down as people were moved back into their local communities to live a normal life.

The analysis and the practices such ideas encouraged saw many social groups being revalued. As well as people with a learning disability, the default assumption for those with a mental illness or physical disability also shifted. With the right help and support, they, too, could and should lead a normal life in the community.

Leece (2012: 20) describes how a number of strands came together to bring *personalization* – the belief that clients and service users should have control over how their needs ought to be met – to the forefront of adult social care. These strands included: (i) campaigns by the disabled people's movement demanding the right to 'independent living and control over their social support'; (ii) market economy and neoliberal ideas reducing the state's involvement in social welfare provision while increasing consumer power and choice; (iii) the need for governments to find more cost-effective ways of providing social care; and (iv) feminist research highlighting the part that informal carers play in supporting their relatives usually without financial support or recognition (Leece 2012: 20).

With the idea of personalization and *person-centred planning*, it is now accepted that people with sensory impairments, physical impairments, and learning disabilities should be able to live their lives as they choose, including the choice to live independently. Individuals and not institutions should determine what kind of care suits them (Department of Health 2010a). Social workers have to tailor their responses to each case (Thomas 2013: 260). Their tasks will include helping individuals: (i) overcome the problems of their disabilities as they experience them; (ii) access direct payments and individual budgets; and (iii) secure personal assistance, equipment, and employment. Direct payments, for example, involve giving clients the cash to choose and buy the supports and services that they feel will best meet their needs. In general, definitions of independence for disabled and older people involve the ability to make decisions about their own life and exercise control over any help needed (Oliver 1989).

However, Rabiee (2013) goes a step further and sees independence as more relative and multidimensional. For some clients it does mean the ability to do things on their own, or indeed live on their own. For others it is the more general principle of feeling in control of their own lives, including making decisions. And for yet others, *inter*dependence is just as important as independence. Many disabled and older people are caregivers as well as care receivers.

The book *Social Work with Adults*, edited by Martin Davies (2012), is packed with examples of person-centred planning and personalization

in practice. Bamber et al. (2012: 77) describe the case of 78-year-old
Mary, a summary of which is given here:

> Mary was recently widowed and suffering bipolar disorder and
> dementia. She had two sons, neither of whom live close by. Mary
> was not comfortable being looked after by people she didn't know.
> Finding the right kind of care for her was not easy. However, she
> did have a next-door neighbour, Kathy, in her fifties, whom she
> had known a long time. Although Kathy had some health prob-
> lems of her own, to Mary delight, she became her carer. Kathy was
> able to pop in throughout the day to prepare food, chat, take Mary
> to the hairdresser, and organise other friends to help if Kathy had
> to be elsewhere herself. The sons, who also knew Kathy, felt free to
> phone her and discuss their mother's situation, becoming
> involved as and when necessary, and also supporting her in her
> caring role.
>
> 'The relationship continued for over three years and had many
> positive aspects for both women. For Kathy, it provided a sense of
> purpose, a part-time job… and satisfaction. Mary received the
> care she needed from someone she knew and trusted and could
> continue her life with very few changes. She and her family also
> felt secure knowing Kathy would respond rapidly in an emergency
> at any time of day or night. The relationship had a synergy that
> nobody had anticipated and only ended when Mary's health began
> to deteriorate and she went to live with her son in Scotland, where
> she died a year later.' (Bamber et al. 2012: 78)

Theories of social change and conflict are the ones most likely to inspire
campaigning social workers, those who believe that only radical
shifts in the ways in which societies are organized and structured will
lead to better lives for the disadvantaged, deprived, and vulnerable.

Order and regulation

In contrast, there are other social scientists who are fascinated by the
ability of social groups to organize, maintain, and develop themselves into well-functioning wholes (Parsons 1951). They believe there
is an underlying unity and cohesiveness that holds societies together
(Burrell and Morgan 1979: 17). These social scientists study human

cooperation and social order. They are impressed by people's ability to live and work together. They see societies generating social norms, laws, and expectations and most people, most of the time keep to them. Our behaviour is socially regulated.

The emergence of social structures helps complex societies to function and tick along reasonably smoothly. This allows food and goods to be produced, circulated, and exchanged. Governments monitor and aim to maintain stability and social order. Social agencies deliver services and resources. Families and schools help socialize new members of society into how to behave socially, economically, and ethically. Ideally, everyone works for the common good.

When individuals or groups do not function well in society they are described as *dysfunctional*. Parents fail to socialize their children. Children don't go to school. People steal from others. Men are violent to women. One race discriminates against another. When these behaviours are drawn to the attention of the state and its agents, social interventions take place. Social workers get involved. Police officers are called. Psychologists are allocated.

Implicit in the belief that societies work best when there is order is the idea that societies tend towards social stability and balance. They have self-equilibrating properties (Tonkiss 1998: 41). Everyone and everything is interdependent. As we all go about our business, whether we are growers of food, makers of steel, carers of children, builders of boats, healers of the sick, drivers of buses, or appliers of the law, so society forms and functions.

The name 'functionalist' is, in fact, given to those who are concerned with the processes that maintain stable social systems. So as one element of the social system changes, others adapt in response to keep things working. For example, modern factory-working, city-dwelling families tend to be smaller and more geographically mobile in a way that wasn't true when generations of families grew up in the same place working the land.

Although most of us get angry and distressed when we meet inequality and injustice, we also need to feel secure. We need to feel that life is stable and reasonably predictable. Too much uncertainty is stressful (see chapter 5). Those who mount campaigns recognise that the vulnerable and disadvantaged lack the power and resources to control the content and meaning of key areas of their own lives. So if the radical social worker *is* correct in her analysis *and* successful in her aims, the social changes she will have brought about will be permanent, established, and resourced. New laws will be introduced and fresh resources allocated. Old people will be given pensions when they retire. It will be illegal to discriminate against someone on grounds of sex, age, or ethnicity. All buildings should be accessible to people with a physical disability. These beliefs and practices aim to empower groups who would otherwise be disadvantaged, all too easily finding themselves politically and economically on the margins.

However, to ensure the successful delivery of these services and resources, society has to employ a whole range of people and agents, including social workers. The virtues and talents of social workers who deliver services and carry out statutory duties are not the same as those possessed by the radical campaigner (Lee 1937; Howe 1979). The policy and philosophy underlying the practices of agency-based social workers is that social order is good and should be maintained. Societies are at their best when they are running smoothly. They are at their most stable when people feel safe, supported, recognised, and valued. Welfare policies in this political outlook value cohesion and stability.

In this welfare approach, social workers are employed to help those who are struggling to get back into everyday society. The aim 'is for integrated services to integrate people back into mainstream social and economic life, but not to change society' (Dickens 2010: 47). The methods of choice tend to be ones that value support, treatment, and re-socialization. Much of what social workers do and deliver therefore involves keeping people safe (children, old people, homeless families), competent (parents, adults with learning disabilities), and in order (young offenders, abusive partners). In these ways, social workers contribute to the smooth running of society. They 'are the maintenance mechanics oiling the interpersonal wheels of the community' (Davies 1994: 28). They help society to work better (Bartlett 1970).

Davies's 'maintenance theory' eloquently expresses the idea that the two key roles of social workers are 'to enable individuals to maintain their own role in society, and, by so doing, to maintain society in a state of social equilibrium' (Davies 2013: 449). Public monies support social workers to the extent that they continue to maintain vulnerable adults in the community, protect children from harm, and look after the long-term wellbeing and development of the young, disabled, and elderly. Social competence and the ability to cope are valued. The theory explains why social work, in spite of some bad press and the problems it has had trying to be an evidence-based practice, continues to play a key and wide-ranging role in the lives of those who live on society's margins.

Sheppard (2006) also argues that one of the key characteristics of social work is its commitment to working with the socially excluded to help them re-engage with society and, once more, feel socially involved and included. The socially excluded lie outside the normal 'give and take' of society. Their ties with the moral fabric are loose. They are marginalized. They feel alienated. The socially excluded therefore represent a threat to social stability.

It is the state of being socially excluded that defines which people become clients of social workers. Helping clients cope better and improve their social functioning then becomes the purpose of social work (Sheppard 2006). Stable societies are ones in which everyone feels they have a stake. A sense of community and togetherness binds people, socially and morally. And, in turn, children raised in such communities learn to play their part as full and active citizens. Their sense of worth and value is bound up with a sense of belonging. They become socialized. This partly explains why the state takes so much interest in children's upbringing and the quality of parenting. If children are to become 'good citizens' they must be raised by committed, competent parents (Sheppard 2006: 17).

Theories of social order and regulation are therefore the ones most likely to be employed by social workers wanting to understand the role they play in caring for those who are vulnerable, controlling those who are 'out of order', and treating those who find it difficult to function in today's complex world.

Changing and maintaining the order

In practice, most social workers most of the time are, in Davies's sense, 'maintenance workers' (Davies 1994). They work with people who have social problems or who are social problems.

For example, for those who *have* social problems, social workers either provide services to make life better or they help them develop the skills to function more effectively. Old and frail clients might receive packages of social care. Stressed parents might be offered a place at a family centre or classes in how to raise their children.

For those who *are* social problems, social workers have powers to intervene. Abused children can be removed from their parents. With the support of other mental health colleagues, a mentally ill patient can be compulsory admitted into psychiatric hospital. Social workers might also attempt to change people's problematic behaviours by treating them therapeutically.

But mindful of the idea that society can be a problem for the individual just as often as the individual can be a problem for society, the social worker as state functionary can also argue for change as well as the maintenance of order. The well-rounded social worker should feel comfortable with maintaining order *and* promoting change, pursuing a cause *and* carrying out a function, challenging norms *and* asserting control.

The imaginative social worker might support a woman to report her violent partner to the police. Or because domestic violence and coercion thrive in isolation and behind closed doors, the worker might develop a support group for abused women (Mullender 2009). But the same worker might also decide to organize a group for abusive men to help them change their violent and coercively controlling behaviour (Westmarland and Kelly 2013). For example, Stanley et al. (2012) describe a pioneering programme working with fathers who were also perpetrators of domestic violence.

In another example, it was noticed that for many years young people in foster and residential care were finding it difficult to make the transition to independent living. These are young people at high risk of becoming homeless or unemployed, and suffering mental health problems (Stein et al. 2000). Unlike their peers who continue to enjoy the supports of home life, young people leaving care all too often have to face the challenges of independent living at a young age and in a short space of time. Stein (2006) describes their journey into adulthood as both accelerated and compressed. Without devaluing foster and residential care, critical social workers have been passionate advocates of better resourced, more sensitive leaving care services that offer more gradual, that is, normative transitions from substitute care to independent living with better advice and support, and more money, skills training, and education (Stein 2004).

In these examples, social workers are intent on keeping people safe and promoting good citizenship, but at the same time they are critically constructive of existing practices. Law abiding and socially competent behaviours are encouraged but when society's responses fail to support and maintain them, change is in order.

Changing as well as maintaining the social order captures the mind and practice of the social worker who recognises the need for people to feel secure and safe, valued and included but a social worker who is also not afraid to expose failure, identify tension, argue for change, and pioneer new practices.

3
Care and Control
The Tasks of Social Work

Introduction

As we saw in the previous chapter, since its beginnings in the nine-teenth century, social work has been concerned with, on the one hand, people's quality of life, and on the other, their social behaviour.

The welfare and wellbeing of the vulnerable and young, the dependent and old, the weak and defenceless invites a caring, protec-tive response by society. It leads to welfare services in which old people receive help to live independently in the community. It sees resources being provided to support single parents raise young chil-dren. This is social work as *care*.

In contrast, the conduct of those who are a danger to themselves or others requires social workers to take notice and intervene. People who put themselves in harm's way because of their mental illness might need to be taken to a safe place. Some children have to be protected from their abusive parents. Backed by the law, this might involve removing them from danger and placing them with new carers. This is social work as *control*.

Care and control continue to be two of social work's most basic activities. They are not the most comfortable of bedfellows but they have both been around from the profession's earliest beginnings.

Care

Social welfare includes the reduction of poverty and distress. It addresses those who find living happily in society difficult because they have no work, they are old and dependent, or they can't manage roles and relationships.

Caring for people has two strands. The first involves caring and being concerned about people's welfare and wellbeing. Social work as care occurs when practitioners attempt to meet clients' needs or interests. The relief of misery, providing accommodation for the homeless, making aids and adaptations available for the old and frail, organizing support in the community, offering a listening ear for the distressed and depressed might be examples of providing a caring response.

Caring responses can also include less tangible services. Social work responses that help clients feel more independent, for example, can be seen as caring in the sense that they help clients to make their own decisions, feel more in control, and therefore feel less stressed.

Caring for someone can also mean physically, practically, and emotionally looking after them. Helping them to have a bath. Feeding them. Holding their hand when they remember with fondness the many years of happy marriage they enjoyed before their partner died. To care *for* someone can therefore also mean to care *about* them (also see chapter 14 on care ethics).

To care for the other is to be open to their thoughts, feelings, hopes, and fears. It involves communication and talk. Unlike cure and control which demand outcomes that can be measured, counted, and costed, care is simply a good to be valued in its own right. It doesn't fit neatly into modern ideas of accountability and performance-rated outcomes. Bureaucracies, whether health or welfare, are not always sure how to recognise it, value it, reward it, or promote it.

Care work is all too easily dismissed as low-grade, low-skilled work that rarely attracts the kudos or status of the high-tech, science-based interventions associated with cure and control. And because caring traditionally has been viewed as women's work and because it has so often been seen as unskilled, it is poorly paid and underrated. This is extraordinary given the personal value we give to feeling loved and being cared for. The absence of care and compassion denies nursing its humanity, social work its sensitivity, medicine its respect (Gilbert 2010). Without care the personal social services become impersonal, and that is deeply ironic and desperately sad.

As we saw in the previous chapter, the idea of community care took shape in the 1980s as social care agencies were encouraged to move their focus from one of residential care, with the attendant loss of independence, to one of community care with its emphasis on individuals retaining as much independence as possible. Community care involves the allocation of health and welfare resources to those assessed as dependent and vulnerable.

Putting community care into practice in the late 1980s and early 1990s gradually gave rise to the concept of *care management*. Care management is a needs-led approach to welfare. It is a process which assesses, tailors, and delivers services in response to an individual's needs. Whenever appropriate, the client is encouraged to be an active partner in the assessment and delivery of the service. Client choice and independence underpin the care management approach (Hutchinson 2013: 325).

Clients are recognised as active partners in the care management process. In effect, the individual is volunteering to be a client and in theory always has the choice not to become involved in the community care ethos. However, paradoxically, in order to retain as much independence and freedom as possible, the majority of vulnerable adults have little practical choice but to become involved in the care management process.

In reality much of the care provided for vulnerable adults still rests with family and friends acting as informal carers. Nevertheless:

> ...the care management process has been an essential part of making care in the community possible, ensuring that care needs are properly established and that service provision reduces risks and increases levels of independence. (Hutchinson 2013: 326)

Control

If social order is to be maintained, it is essential that states have ways of dealing with those who behave in a disorderly and antisocial manner. Laws are framed that define which behaviours are socially unacceptable. Agents of the state are then appointed to deal with the misconduct. In the case of criminal behaviour, police officers respond. In the case of mental illnesses which lead people to behave in ways that are either a danger to themselves or others, psychiatrists and social workers become involved. And in the case of social behaviours that adversely affect the way parents raise their children, social workers react.

As we noted in chapter 1, in the nineteenth century, social work became one of the professions given the job of judging and controlling some social behaviours. And to support them in their work, more and more laws were passed giving social workers powers which allowed them to intervene in people's private lives and personal conduct. This was especially true in the area of family life.

Again, we meet a familiar split in social work's psyche. As welfare workers and applied social scientists, social workers have always been keen to explain people's behaviour psychologically and socially. And once the behaviour has been assessed and explained, it becomes ripe for treatment and change. In part, the welfare model holds out the prospect of changing behaviour by treating people's minds. Social order and social control are maintained by getting people to behave well and function better.

But as pursuers of justice, social workers often find themselves dealing less with the person and more with what they have done. Social order and social control are maintained by legal retort rather than therapeutic intervention. The neglectful parent is taken to court. The disruptive student is threatened with exclusion from school.

This shift in ideology from welfare to justice sees social workers dealing with *what* people do rather than *why* they have done it. As we noted in the opening chapter, the response is to deal with the act rather than treat the actor, to punish the offence rather than reform the offender (Cohen 1985). A 'justice' model believes that the best way to maintain social order is not through increasing psychological insight but by demanding social compliance (Smith 2005). It doesn't matter what you think so long as you behave in a socially acceptable way. Control and social order are maintained when everyone is absolutely clear about what will happen if social norms are broken and behaviour is bad. If you abuse and neglect your children, they will be removed and you'll be sent to prison. If you steal or racially attack other people, you'll be taken to court and punished.

For example, for a long time, much of post-war child and family welfare work was based on psychologically trying to understand abusive parents and why they maltreat their children. If you could understand them, then you could change their behaviour by treating their minds. As a result, they would become safer and better parents. But the alleged failures of social workers to protect children from dangerous parents cast doubt on the effectiveness of these welfare-based, psychologically inspired, therapeutically oriented practices.

Throughout the 1980s and 90s, child abuse enquiries continued to feed politicians and the media with the idea that social workers as therapists was a hopeless basis on which to keep children safe. Social workers seemed to lack common sense. It was therefore time to remove the profession's therapeutic ambitions and replace them with much tighter, obligatory, rule-bound procedures. Social workers had to learn to react to *what* parents did and did not do rather than investigate *why* they did or did not do it. They needed to deal with the *act* of maltreatment and not the *actor* who maltreats.

In this attitude, the rules and expectations are clear. Break the rules and fail to meet expectations, and clear, unequivocal social sanctions follow. The sustained political critique of the 'gullible' and 'over-optimistic' social worker caused many child care practices to shift from a welfare to a justice model, from one of care to one of control (also see chapter 5). And because a justice outlook no longer took much interest in why the parent was failing, social workers lost interest in taking social histories and making psychosocial assessments. It was the abusive event and not the narrative build-up to that event that had to be addressed. These changes also saw changes in the language being used. Social workers became involved in protecting and safeguarding children rather than supporting and rehabilitating families (Parton and Parton 1989). Politicians, influenced by the media, and not social workers, began to determine what was to be seen as appropriate and effective practice (Marston and McDonald 2012: 1031).

Social workers as agents of social control are therefore encouraged to ask 'what' and 'who' and 'how many' rather than 'why' and 'how come'. This change in professional practice has also been matched by changes in the theories that social workers adopt. Theories which concentrate on changing behaviour rather than changing minds are preferred. Out go psychodynamic theories and in come task- and behaviourally-based models. And with these theoretical clearouts, we also see the loss of professional discretion and the increase in rules and procedures, checklists and guidelines to keep the wandering social work mind firmly in check and 'on message'.

Care and control

Care and compassion help define a civilized society. Societies that look after the vulnerable and weak are ones in which people feel safe. They are societies in which it feels good to belong. In their delivery of services and support for those who no longer find it easy to support themselves, social workers play a key caring role.

Concern for order and social wellbeing also mean that the state has to keep on eye on those who threaten other people's safety and peace of mind. As we saw in chapter 1, social work emerges as society organizes care for the distressed and seeks control of the difficult. Indeed, Foucault (1975) went so far as to suggest that over time social workers and their agencies do not arise simply in response to problems, they help constitute the problems and how we understand them. As scientific ideas about what is normal began to look at more and more areas of social life, so the idea of things not being normal – that is, abnormal and pathological – took hold of the social professions.

> While normalcy became measured by statistical means which acted to describe difference, it was also associated with being right and healthy. As a consequence, the abnormal was not merely different but wrong and diseased. (Parton 1998: 9)

Thus, Donzelot (1979) describes social workers along with medics, educationalists, and mental health professionals as 'technicians in human relations' whose domain is the 'social', that area where, on the one hand the political penetrates the personal, and on the other the private erupts into the public.

As they set about their work, these technicians in human relations perform two acts, simultaneously, whenever they deal with children and their parents, the mentally ill, the old, and the disabled. They judge *and* they treat. Social workers therefore have a hybrid make-up. They are law enforcers and they are therapists. They have duties to judge and assess (in acts of monitoring and surveillance) but also expectations to care, cure, and change (in acts of support, education, and treatment). While much of their work is defined by statute, many of social work's methods are based on the clinical applications of psychological theory.

The family, for example, is judged to be the cause of many problems, but it is also the place where the problems must be resolved. The parent, argues Donzelot (1979: 225), is called upon continually to fight an enemy that is none other than himself or herself. And so the private space of family life becomes politicized. The ultimate trick, therefore, is that having taught bad parents how to be good parents, the social worker can bow out, for 'there is no need for the state to act as parent and teacher if parent and teacher can be made to act like the state' (Cohen 1985: 136).

However, as they practice, it is usual for social workers to begin to feel that many of those seen as socially troublesome can also be understood as socially troubled. Many abusive and neglectful parents themselves suffered abuse as children. Most violent men report violent, loveless childhoods. In practice, social workers realize that it is difficult in fact to separate the two defining components of care and control in their professional make-up. It is clearly wrong for parents to neglect their children but it is difficult to ignore their poverty, their own troubled histories, the stresses under which they live, and the difficulties they have regulating their own thoughts and feelings.

It is also the case that poverty and deprivation increase stress (Frost and Hoggett 2008). We all function less well and less reasonably under stress. It is, therefore, not some simple class bias that accounts for the fact that most children compulsorily removed from their parents live in families in which social and economic deprivations are particularly high (Dickens et al. 2007; Featherstone et al. 2014). It is generally true that the parents with the fewest resources – material and psychological – have to cope with the greatest number of stresses. For them, raising children is never going to be easy.

In this analysis, today's abused child might well become tomorrow's abusive parent. There is no clear dividing line between the neglect suffered when you are young and the neglect you cause a few years later when you have children of your own. And yet the media and politicians live in a simple world of black and white with no shades of grey. They demand care and protection for children at risk, and control and punishment of those same children who, only a few years later, become risky parents. However, it is social work's fate to straddle these two worlds of care and control. Indeed, social work practice can sometimes find itself at its best and most creative when care and control are unable to be prised apart. Here is an example that I came across during and after presenting an independent witness court report (the names have been changed):

Josie was in court. While in her care, her two young children had suffered long-standing and extreme emotional abuse and neglect. This was the view of the paediatrician and the psychologist, the health visitor and the social worker. The recommendation was that the children be removed from her care and placed for adoption. The judge accepted this recommendation. As the judgement was being read out, Josie stared ahead of her with a blank look. Then she broke down in tears.

In her report, the social worker agreed with other professionals that it was in the children's best interests for them to be placed for adoption. Nevertheless, in her assessment, the social worker recognised that Josie's own bleak, loveless, often violent childhood meant that she found it difficult to give her children what she had never received herself. The social worker could see that Josie was both angry and in pain about the loss of her children, but she was also clear that there was little prospect of Josie changing in the near future to become a safe, responsive parent within the critical window of developmental time still left open for her children. It was when she was reading the bit of the social worker's report about her own unhappy childhood that Josie again cried. The worker noticed her response and made the decision to return to the matter once the court hearing was over.

A local group of social and adoption workers recognised that mothers who had lost their children to adoption (birth mothers) were themselves in need of support and understanding. They were aware of Neil's (2007; Neil et al. 2010) work on adoption which recognised that many adopted children benefited from continued contact with their birth parents. But contact could only be contemplated when the birth parent had accepted the placement and was able to see the situation from the adoptive parent's and adopted child's point of view. Only by caring for the troubled, hurt, and often angry birth parent could that parent be helped to accept and support her child in the placement. *Control* meant the removal of Josie's children to a safe place and a secure future. *Care* and compassion for her gave Josie time to reflect and heal. And

when she had reached a place where she could begin to understand and accept what had happened to her, even though she
could never have her children back, she could begin to play an
important and meaningful part in their young lives. With open-
minded adopters, Josie could be allowed back into her children's
story, sometimes directly, sometimes indirectly, so that they could
know her and her limitations, but also experience her as strong
enough to love and support them in their new lives.

Social work can be at its best when the tensions between care and
control are accepted and embraced. This idea has parallels with
Baumrind's (1967) views of the ideal parent as *authoritative* – one who
is firm and fair, loving and just. When parenting is too *permissive*, there
is no structure and no discipline. Children raised by these parents feel
incoherent and anxious, unable to self-manage or self-regulate. In
contrast, when parenting is too controlling and *authoritarian*, the
room for manoeuvre and exploration is limited. Children raised by
these parents find it difficult to be curious, initiate, and be themselves. Like authoritative parents, the most effective social workers
tend to be those who create relationships in which clients feel
contained but accepted, and in which there is firmness as well as fairness, honesty as well as warmth, realism as well as respect, control as
well as care.

We shall revisit some of these elements in later chapters when we
consider the part that thoughts and feelings (chapter 8), relationships
and process (chapter 12), and values and virtues (chapter 14) play in the
life and practice of the *compleat* social worker. But, more immediately,
we need to look at the way social workers organize themselves professionally and the way they are organized by others bureaucratically.

4

Bureaucrats and Professionals

How Social Workers are Organized and Operate

Introduction

To be told you are being bureaucratic is not usually meant as a compliment. Being professional, on the other hand, carries more than a hint that you are behaving intelligently, independently, and well. Social workers aspire to be professionals but very often find themselves dismissed as bureaucrats. Much of what social workers do hovers interestingly, even awkwardly between following the rules and thinking on your feet. To be a good bureaucrat is to follow the rules. A good professional has no problem thinking on her feet.

Most professionally qualified social workers are employed by large bureaucracies. It is therefore interesting to explore how these two occupational organisations, bureaucracies and professions, might affect the lives of social workers and what they do.

Bureaucracies

Students of the German sociologist Max Weber (1964) will, of course, know that he recognised bureaucracies as an effective way of rationally delivering complex services and running large organizations. Bureaucracies are excellent ways of organizing, directing, and controlling human behaviour in the workplace. They help individuals carry out their allocated purposes and functions in a rational, efficient, and systematic manner. Bureaucratic organizations have become the dominant institutions in modern societies.

If a social worker is to carry out her statutory duties and role functions efficiently and effectively it is important that she acts rationally. Her behaviour in the workplace should not be governed by emotion, caprice, or tradition. The goal of each action should be clear. The ways in which that goal is to be achieved should be spelled out. Any worker pursuing that same organizational goal should pursue it in an identical way. A bureaucracy represents rational action at the organizational and institutional level.

The more complex the bureaucracy, the more likely it is that the overall purposes of the organization will be achieved by breaking down large tasks into many smaller, more discrete, and manageable parts. Each official specializes in carrying out one, or a small number of these parts. He or she therefore has a clearly defined role, set of duties, and area of responsibility. The consistent application of the rational rules and explicit regulations of the organization applied to particular cases reduces personal initiative, discretion, idiosyncracy, and error. Officials at each level in a bureaucracy are governed by the rules.

To make sure that individual workers in the bureaucracy are acting rationally, it is necessary to introduce various organizational controls. The supervision of staff ensures that workers keep to their task by following procedures. This eliminates the need for discretion. The supervision and bringing together of these front-line tasks generally requires several layers of management. This means that most bureaucracies are hierarchical. Those at the top of the hierarchy need to keep the organization's overall purposes and functions clearly in mind. This means that every lower office is under the control and supervision of a higher one. Each individual in the hierarchy is accountable to their immediate superior. Weber therefore defined a bureaucracy as a hierarchical organization designed rationally to coordinate the work of many individuals in the pursuit of large-scale administrative tasks and organizational goals (Weber 1964).

All of this might make bureaucracies sound rather robotic, inflexible, and dull. But the fact is that bureaucracies represent an extraordinarily precise, efficient, and effective way for organizations to carry out their purposes and achieve their goals. Bureaucracies are found everywhere – in organizations of the church, government, the military, commerce, health, education, and, of course, local authority departments, including those of adult social care and children's services.

Bureaucracies work well when needs are tightly defined, eligibility for services established, rules made clear, and guidelines put in place.

By following the rules, social workers play their part in helping the organization pursue its purposes and achieve its goals. Bureaucracies celebrate impartiality, specialization, and the rational application of expert practices. Prescribed tasks are carried out in defined situations. This form of organization is most appropriate in environments which are stable and settled.

The downside of bureaucracies is that officials can lose sight of the true function and purpose of the organization. There is the ever-present danger that workers at all levels become trapped in a mindset that sees obeying the rules and following the procedures as *the* purpose of what they do. When challenged for being rigid and inflexible, they say that they are only doing their job. Individual customers and clients with their unique needs become crushed by the weight of the organization's rules and procedures. And that's when workers are pejoratively accused of being bureaucratic.

Professions

When practitioners have the power and ability to make independent decisions, on the spot, according to the needs of the situation, they are said to be acting professionally. Professions have a body of knowledge and they bring this know-how and expertise to bear on the work in hand. Professionals make independent assessments. Accountability for what they do lies at their feet. This means that the organization of professionals tends to be non-hierarchical with limited managerial control. Society licences professionals to be their own authority on matters of illness and health (in the case of doctors), statute and law (in the case of lawyers), and theology and religion (in the case of priests).

Professional responses are most appropriate when the work is inherently complex and unpredictable. When each fresh case presents a new problem or unique set of needs, bureaucratically fixed and procedurally driven responses don't work. By knowing and understanding a lot about their area of concern, professionals profess to know better than the layperson or the client what is the matter, what is the need, what is the solution, and what is the right response.

Such is the power and prestige of some professions that they are able to define how the rest of us recognise, understand, and think about particular problems and needs. Doctors control the meaning of illness and disease. Lawyers shape the law and so determine what is legal and not legal. Professionals claim a mandate that says that only they are fit and proper persons to pronounce on what is legitimate conduct in their field of expertise. They argue for autonomy and control over the terms of their own work. Only their professional body can licence who is allowed to practise.

Thus, the success of the established professions, and what Macdonald (1997) calls their 'professional project', is based on their ability to gain control over key areas of everyday life which are seen by the rest of us as critical to the maintenance of our personal and social wellbeing. The most successful professions claim that only they have the right to pronounce on matters over which they are the accredited and licensed experts.

The rise of the professions is most marked in those areas of everyday life in which there is uncertainty and irregularity, where fixed rules and invariant responses don't work. The professional practitioner is someone who says that he or she has the ability to reduce uncertainty, and bring about order and wellbeing by dint of applying their hard-won expertise. The anxiety and uncertainty in the mind of the patient or client is relieved by handing over the power to resolve the problem to the professional. In power terms, this makes the client weak and the professional strong. The history of the professions, says Johnson (1972), is a story in which particular occupational groups gain control over crucial areas of life, including health, justice, and general welfare.

The strongest and most established professions are those which define both the needs and problems of their clients *and also* the manner in which these needs are met and problems are solved (Johnson 1972). Control rests with the professional. Historically, this has been true of doctors, priests, and lawyers. But because most professions claim that their practices are inspired by public service rather than personal reward, their autonomy is not always challenged. The fact that the market power and control their professional autonomy grants them also puts them in a good position to bargain for high rewards is seen as incidental to their self-proclaimed public service ethos.

In some practices, although clients retain control over defining their wants and needs, the manner in which the wants and needs are met lie with the professional. In these cases, the professionals don't have much say about what *is* the problem, but they do have the skills to deal with it. They are employed or commissioned by their clients to carry out the work. Architects, accountants, and engineers fall into this category.

But unlike medicine, law, or accountancy, social work, for example, has not entirely convinced the public that it possesses skills that are highly valued, hard to learn, or difficult to acquire. The media and politicians frequently suggest that social work is just 'common sense'. Because many problems dealt with by social workers are problems in everyday living and most people feel that they, too, are also experts in everyday living, then the job of social work doesn't carry the same kudos or authority granted to the traditional professions. There can be no special competence in an area of life in which everyone claims to be an expert. Social workers have therefore found it difficult to wrest control from politicians and the public to determine the content of their own practice and thereby gain full professional status.

In this sense, other people (politicians, the media, lawyers), that is 'third parties', mediate the relationship between the practitioner and the client (Johnson 1972). The third party defines both the need of the client *and* the manner in which that need is to be met. In the case of social work, the state and its welfare legislation define who is to count as a social work client. In many cases, it also says how that need is to be met. This limits social work's discretion, autonomy and power.

However, in spite of the state's efforts, some uncertainty remains surrounding clients, their needs and behaviour, and what social workers do and with whom they do it (we shall explore this further in chapter 5). This leaves social workers with a certain amount of freedom and independence about which the state can do little. To this extent, and given the nature of what they do, social workers find themselves possessed of some power to determine the content of their own practice. They might therefore be described as a semi-profession – not quite the full-blown thing like a surgeon, but neither a simple cog in the bureaucratic machine. The occupational status and rewards of social workers are therefore similar to other semi-professional groups such as nurses and teachers.

Stepping back, there is a tendency by the state to try and rein in the powers held by professionals, particularly if the state is paying them their wages. The work of doctors is increasingly subject to government control. Their performances are measured, their costs counted. Some of their pay depends on meeting set targets. Lawyers working on legal aid cases continue to lose much of the professional freedom and choice they once had. These political moves represent attempts to de-skill the professional, decrease their power, and reduce their costs.

But to the extent that clients and patients remain unique, unpredictable, and frustratingly intractable, the state has little choice but to leave the professions with some control, power, and autonomy to determine who is seen and how they are to be treated. Only when the state is told by professionals that society is to blame for some health or social problem do they court political censure and control. Any professional analysis, for example, which suggests that the unequal distribution of wealth and the extreme poverty in which some people continue to live is one of the biggest causes of disease and ill-health, criminal behaviour, and social problems is that professional likely to receive short shrift from politicians, rich entrepreneurs, and the right-wing press.

Nervous about losing too much power and pay, this tends to make most professionals a little conservative. Social workers, like doctors, have an occupational bias towards placing failure in the client more often than in society. But to its credit, social work does have a strong track record of encouraging independent thinking and reflective minds which continue to see that inequalities of wealth, power, and opportunity explain much of the stress and problems of living experienced by many clients (Gray and Webb 2013; Featherstone, White and Morris 2014; Mullaly 2007).

Street-level bureaucrats and welfare professionals

In most occupational groups there are three types of member: *practitioners, manager-administrators,* and *teacher-researchers* (Freidson 1986). Although each member clearly identifies with the profession, each has a different take on how the work should be done and what kind of knowledge best supports it.

The first type of member in any professional group are the managers and administrators. In the most positive sense, they think like bureaucrats. They like to render the profession's knowledge and skills into rules and regulations, procedures and guidelines. They are keen to ensure that the needs of clients and their problems are dealt with predictably, consistently, and in a standardized manner. For managers, formal knowledge should be 'simplified and rationalised' (Freidson 1986: 226). Thus, if you are a front-line social worker faced with this kind of need or that kind of problem then, according to the procedures laid down, this is what you do. Managers get bothered when practitioners don't follow the rules or deviate from guidelines. They also see themselves as the ones who have to put into organizational practice what the academics come up with in research and theory.

The second type of member within a profession are those who teach, train, and research. They tend to be academics who concern themselves with conceptual rigour, evaluation, and intellectual challenge. They are the keepers of the profession's knowledge base. They are the ones who pass on the profession's wisdom to the next generation. Teachers and researchers like practitioners and managers to keep as close as possible to the conceptually pure, empirically proven, ideologically sound, and the operationally proper.

The third type of member are practitioners. They occupy the profession's front line. They are in receipt of the strictures of both managers and trainer-researchers. But because they are the only ones who actually meet and work with clients, to make the job work they often find themselves having to bend the rules and adapt the theories to the realities of practice. The rank and file, says Freidson, have to take the formal rules into account but they also have to:

> ...cope with the practical exigencies of their work situation. Just as they are likely to take liberties with the formal knowledge they learned in school and read about in professional journals, so they are likely to take liberties with the guidelines promulgated by their supervisors and managers. (Freidson 1986: 216)

There is, in fact, a constant flow of knowledge between these three types of member. Researchers report findings. Managers, if they like the look of those findings, create and implement guidelines to operationalize the research. Practitioners are expected to know about the evidence which supports a particular practice as well as work within the organization's rules and procedures. And as knowledge flows round the profession, researchers might take another look at how the theories and research are being put into practice, and, in light of what they see, they might tweak things, develop them, or even have doubts about them. And so the profession's knowledge evolves, adapts, and progresses around the different professional member types and, as it does, it gets transformed into the interests, vocabulary, and methods of the particular type of member the knowledge just happens to be with at that time in that place.

However, the power held by each type of member over the expression of the profession's knowledge and practice principles varies. It is rarely equally distributed. The dominant type has the power to set the conceptual, political, policy, and resource agenda of the other two. This means that the most powerful of the three at any one time can exert some control over what the others think and do.

At the moment in social work, it looks as if managers hold the most power. This means that practitioners can't simply do what they like. Their discretion is curtailed. Guidelines, legislation, procedures, and resources constrain what can be seen, thought, and done. Similarly, researchers find that the questions they ask, the practices they observe, the resources they are allocated, and the access they are given have already, in a sense, been shaped and determined by the interests of managers, policy makers and politicians.

Nevertheless, when front-line social workers are out there with clients being buffeted by real life, managerial control and evidence-based injunctions get knocked about by particular people and every-day situations. It was Lipsky (1980) who pointed out that most professionals operating on the front line, whether they are social workers, teachers, or police officers, find themselves unable or unwilling to carry out to the letter the stiff biddings of managers or idealistic expectations of academics.

Lipsky called those who practise on the front line and in the real world *street-level bureaucrats*. They develop their own routines, under-standings, and devices to deal with the uncertainty and pressures they face. To this extent, front-line practitioners do retain a signifi-cant degree of discretion in what they do and how they do it. The real-ities of actual practice mean that it is just not possible for managers to be overly prescriptive or researchers too idealistic.

So, much of the discretion and creativity found on the front line is the result of practitioners finding that they need to be flexible and show some compassion and humanity when they meet real people.

These practitioners use their discretion to respond to the unexpected, the personal and the particular.

The changes and interpretations that 'street-level' workers have to make in order for the job to work in particular cases often requires them to bend, adapt, and embroider the organization's guidelines and procedures. Practitioners need coping strategies. Practitioners therefore come up with individual solutions to solve work pressures and meet case demands (also see chapter 5 on certainty and uncertainty in social work).

> Lipsky observes that public employees who interact with citizens behave in ways that are unsanctioned, sometimes even contradicting official policy, because the structure of their jobs makes it impossible to fully achieve the expectations of their work. (Hupe and Hill 2007: 280)

There is one other group who remain sufficiently close to the front line for them to have a hint of the street-level bureaucrat about them. Being that much closer to clients than senior managers, local managers do have a more realistic sense of what can and can't be done. Evans (2010) calls their approach 'discursive managerialism'. This is a hybrid position, 'beyond street-level bureaucracy', which recognises the need for both practitioners and local managers to retain discretion in order to make things work, albeit within an organizational context in which senior managers control resources, departmental systems, and staffing numbers. Clients, their needs, and the lives they live really are just too idiosyncratic and unpredictable to be dealt fully with by centrally generated, managerially controlled formulae.

As an addendum to this chapter, we shall take a quick look at a related binary. In order to be good street-level bureaucrats, should social workers be trained or educated?

Training and education

Organizations, including social work organizations, don't like uncertainty in what they do and how they do it. In chapter 5 we shall see that managers try to iron out uncertainty whenever and wherever possible. They do this by defining what is to be seen as a need or count as a problem. They try to define what services are appropriate in order to meet a particular demand. They attempt to determine which responses are allowable when faced with problems of this kind or that.

Thus, when the balance of occupational power shifts towards managers and favours bureaucracies as the best form or organization, the divide between who decides what is to be done and who actually does it increases. Under managerial, bureaucratic regimes, design and practice, conception and execution are carried out by different people. Most organizations try to increase the amount of control they have over what their front-line practitioners do. The more managers can predetermine how workers should respond, the more they value a *trained*, compliant, predictable workforce.

Training involves teaching someone to acquire certain skills in order for them to carry out a particular job. In a strict sense, the trained person is someone you know will carry out prescribed tasks in a set way in defined situations. When organizations have rules, procedures, and formulae about how workers should respond when faced with a particular need or problem, the best kind of worker to have is a trained worker, one who does not think too much outside the box, one who doesn't question what's going on, one who doesn't try to see things differently. If they are well trained and follow the rules, then the responses of trained workers will be predetermined and therefore predictable, invariant, and appropriate. For example, a trained benefits officer will know that a particular claimant with his or her characteristics will, according to the formulae, be entitled to a specified amount of benefits. Another worker dealing with exactly the same case will reach the same answer.

On the whole, bureaucracies prefer trained workers. To the extent that social work and social care organizations believe that what they do can be reduced to following a set of rules and procedures, then they would like their workforce to be trained in the sense being used here. They do not want their workers to have too much discretion. They do not want their employees to do too much independent thinking. They want workers to be consistent and systematic.

But what if the work to be done isn't so tractable? What if the work to be done is by its very nature unpredictable and uncertain? Problems that need practitioners to think on their feet and use their judgement don't respond well to workers who only know how to follow the rules. Dangerous parents and neglectful families do not follow a script. Clients with major mental health problems are rarely predictable. Older people who are distressed at the prospect of losing their independence might veer one way and then another as they try to think about what to do next. In each of these situations, practitioners constantly have to assess and reassess what is going on. Their responses cannot be fixed or based on simple rules. Training may tell you what to do and when to do it, but the ability to think creatively and constructively on your feet requires an *educated* practitioner. Such a worker, if she is to be a good problem solver, needs a certain amount of freedom and discretion in order to do her job.

Trained workers have a fixed repertoire of skills. An educated worker sees and understands matters in ways that are wider and deeper. An educated worker is able to enquire and understand the 'reason why' of things. 'Training,' says Peters (1966: 33), 'suggests the acquisition of appropriate appraisals and habits of response in limited conventional situations; it lacks the wider cognitive implications of "education."' In short, we *train* bureaucrats and we *educate* professionals.

Of course, in practice, social workers, as street-level bureaucrats, need to be both trained and educated. They need to know many things – laws and statutes, policies and procedures, resources available and services to which clients are entitled. They need to know when to bring this knowledge into play. Training helps them do these things.

But they also need to remain responsive to situations which don't stand still. It is no good social workers trying to squeeze clients into bureaucratic boxes if they don't fit. There is a danger that trained workers, as bureaucrats, only see and understand clients in terms of existing rules, resources, and administrative categories. Procrustes was a mythical Greek innkeeper. In order to get his guests to fit his bed exactly, he would either stretch or chop their legs. Getting people to fit beds rather than beds to fit people, or people to fit the rules rather than the rules fit people is rarely a good idea. Procrustes would not have made a good social worker. The idiosyncracies which many clients present either get ignored or trampled on by social workers who simply go by the book and follow the rules.

The best kind of worker to have in situations that are fluid, erratic, and out of the ordinary are educated professionals who can think laterally and respond imaginatively. In these cases, the professional practitioner retains control. She both designs and executes the content of her own practice. The problem and her understanding of it guide her assessment and her response. In this way, she remains connected to the reality of her clients and their world. As a result, her practice is likely to be more appropriate, sensitive, and effective. Clients feel understood and not just processed.

So, like creative artists, social workers need to understand and be trained in the materials with which they work (see chapter 11). They need to feel at home with the tools of their trade. Only when they are thoroughly versed in what makes people tick, and only when they are disciplined in the methods of their practice can they use their professional skills and imagination. Then they can be creative. In their training, social workers need a basic grounding in the nuts and bolts of the job. In their education, social workers have to learn to think flexibly, responsively, and creatively.

We have been playing around with the ideas of certainty and uncertainty in several of the previous chapters. It is now time to address the ideas head-on.

5

Certainty and Uncertainty

How Social Work Decisions are Made

Introduction

Increasingly, social work, along with most other professions, is having to account for its actions. There has also been a steady shift away from an immediate concern to meet client needs to a more general preoccupation with risk and protection (Cree and Wallace 2009). This has pushed the profession and its organizations towards practices which can be measured and accounted for. If a practice cannot be audited and measured, it has a hard time justifying itself. Even more perverse are the attempts by governments and organizations to improve effectiveness and efficiency by setting targets and measuring performance. 'A measure is a dangerous tool,' warns Skidelsky (2014: 7), 'for it tends to take the place of whatever it measures.'

In this climate of audit and quality control, performances that can be measured thrive. This climate therefore favours some social work interventions more than others. For example, behavioural, task-centred, and brief solution-focussed approaches are likely to enjoy organizational support.

In contrast, relationship-based practices, seemingly nebulous, can be dismissed as vague, too soft, and not easy to quantify. As a result, systems of accountability have contributed to social work's shift towards being more measurable, quantifiable, and procedural.

Traditionally, experts, including professionals, have been turned to when matters of doubt and uncertainty arise. As we discussed in chapter 4, their knowledge and authority promise to keep the world explicable and in order. Diseases can be diagnosed, explained, and cured. The law can be invoked and navigated. This is all very reassuring.

When dealing with cases in which it is not immediately clear what is the matter, professionals use logic and reason to try and make sense of what's going on. They then bring their professional skills and techniques to bear in order to bring about change. They follow formulae and protocols supported by evidence of what works to solve problems and meet needs.

In practice, social workers are often faced with situations that don't fit neat formula or respond to set practices. Clients and their lives tend to be complex and confused, idiosyncratic and unpredictable, turbulent and messy. Uncertainty and ambiguity are ever-present. 'Real world problems,' notes Parton (2003: 1) 'do not come well formed.' And so, observes England (1986), it remains 'a fundamental strain for social work that it must persistently strive for a certainty that is in fact inherently unattainable' (p. 6).

For example, 91-year-old Nancy's dog dies. Her latest loss feels like the final straw in a long line of recent losses. Nancy is inconsolable. She stops eating and begins to neglect herself. What to do?

Jason, unemployed and the father of three young children, attempts to steal gas by tapping into the outside pipes before they arrive at the meter. There is an explosion and the house collapses, although fortunately everyone escapes to safety. The family is homeless. Many needs and issues arise all at once.

Ruby's foster carer is suddenly taken seriously ill. The seven-year-old has been with her carer for over a year and the hope was that this could evolve into a long-term permanent placement. Overnight, the little girl finds herself with new foster carers. Her world is turned upside down.

When working with complexity and uncertainty, social workers, rather than reaching for an 'off-the-peg' solution, tend to engage the client in a collaborative process as together they work out ways of coping and getting from a bad-place here to a better-place there. The search for certainty in an uncertain world is understandable, but might have its limits.

Certainty

All occupational groups attempt to reduce the amount of uncertainty in what they see and do. They therefore try to increase control over what they see and do. As we discussed in chapter 4, organizations, politicians, and managers do not like unpredictable environments. They feel that they are not in control and that makes them nervous. This also makes them risk-averse.

One way to render the environment more predictable is to define its characteristics in terms of what the organization and its workforce can measurably do. Perrow (1972) noted that organizations which do this are dealing not with some actual state of their 'raw materials' (clients, in the case of social work), but with the way these raw materials are being viewed and defined by the organization. Social work organizations, therefore, have a tendency to define clients in such a way as to minimize exceptions (Perrow 1972: 51). Once clients and their problems have been defined according to preconceived criteria, procedures can be designed which determine how practice should be conducted in situations of that kind. And beyond bureaucratic management lies an even more subtle form of control, that of the market.

Throughout the 1990s, more and more areas of social work practice became subject to market-based thinking. What has become known as New Public Management was intent on:

> ...enhancing efficiency, effectiveness and economy through the application of performance management strategies that involve high levels of surveillance, inspection and regulation (Skinner 2010). Embedded within these foundational principles is an understanding of human behaviour that privileges cognition, rationality and predictability and pays less attention to the emotional, irrational and unpredictable dimensions of human beings. (Ruch 2012: 1317)

This way of delivering social work means that the decisions which practitioners are allowed to make have already been implicitly taken in the very way that the service is conceived. And so social workers become 'case managers' rather than 'case workers'. They identify and manage risk rather than meet needs and provide care. What they do becomes governed by 'new systems of audit, devolved budgets, codes of practice and citizen charters; and giving individuals new freedoms by making them responsible for their own present and future welfare and the relations they have with experts and institutions' (Parton 1998: 14).

In this sense, social work organizations prefer to see clients not as unique or endlessly variable but in terms of a limited number of potentially workable characteristics – this is a case of drug dependency, or a case that needs aids and adaptations to help a client remain independent in the community, or a case in which a parent is failing to get a child to school every day. Thus what the work means and how it is perceived and defined is not based on the intrinsic nature of the client and his or her situation, but rather on what the organization does and the way it does it. Clients are viewed through an organizational lens, through the resources available, the risks specified, and the options offered.

Implicit control can also be exerted by restricting what resources are made available. If workers are constrained by time or money or tools, then they may not be able to do what they would otherwise prefer to do if they had complete freedom and discretion. If your caseload doubles, then short-term interventions become more attractive. If the number of community support hours available is fixed, it might not be possible to argue that 86-year-old Ron continues to live independently. Assessments, decisions, and intervention strategies begin to be formulated in terms of what is available and not what ideally might be possible.

Almost without realizing it, over time, everyone in the organization begins to sing from the same hymn sheet. These politics of conception and policies of perception organize the way people think about and practice what they do. Who becomes a client and how they should be treated is defined by the systems and knowledge-based practices which support them. Alternative realities become difficult to imagine. So, for example, clients who fail to follow an agreed plan might be cast off as uncooperative, while those who are forever presenting themselves in a state of urgent need are seen as too dependent.

In his book on social work in a risk society, Webb (2006) beautifully and remorselessly shows how the focus of social work has shifted from nineteenth-century concerns with improvement, through post-war efforts to meet need, to current preoccupations with risk and protection. In making the case he uses some heavy-duty sociology as he looks at how social work has become more enamoured of control and technique and less moved by care and compassion.

We shall see in chapter 13 that in the final decades of the twentieth century, the political pendulum began to swing from left to right, from welfare to freedom, from viewing clients as passive victims of life's misfortunes to people responsible for their own actions, from sympathizing with the weaknesses of clients to promoting their strengths.

The political right began to argue that the Welfare State was failing on many key fronts. Children were still being killed at the hands of their parents. Old people were still found dying of cold and malnutrition. Mental health patients could still be left unsupervised, becoming a danger to themselves or other people.

Swept along on these political tides, rafts of social work practice moved from meeting need to preventing risk (Kemshall 2002). And to facilitate this change in outlook, social work was subjected to tighter definition and firmer control. Risks had to be reduced, targets set, performances measured.

This change of focus and practice philosophy had a profound impact on the relationship between social workers and their clients. In order to be seen to be reducing risk, social workers and what they did had to be accounted for. Practice became the subject of rational discipline. It was broken down into constituent bits, and delivered by different people for specified periods of time. This led to the setting of targets and the measuring of outcomes. Clients were identified by counting the number of risks present in their lives and calculating the probabilities of danger (Parton 1996).

The client was seen no longer as a unique individual but rather as an identifiable danger thrown up by a checklist of statistically based risk indicators. Clients began to be assessed by the use of manuals and tick boxes, computerized information systems and eligibility criteria. What social workers did with clients was governed by procedures, frameworks, and reviews.

> Risk and regulation are shown to be inter-dependent concepts in shaping social work. The rise of risk management in social work is considered as typically involving four major components: risk identification; risk analysis; risk reducing measures and risk monitoring. (Webb 2006: 9)

Webb (2006) describes these increasingly disciplined and limited interventions as 'technologies of care' to be delivered in organizations increasingly dominated by a focus on risk and controlled by managers. And with these changes, the vocabulary changes. The talk is of 'care management', 'risk assessment', 'evidence-based practice', and 'decision pathway models of practice' (Webb 2006: 141). Cases and their content are managed. So, rather than shape the work to fit the client, the client begins to be shaped by the resources available, the interventions preferred, and the procedures prescribed.

Webb (2006) continues his analysis, recognising that there is no longer any need for prolonged face-to-face casework or personally 'getting to know' the client. What takes place between the social worker and client is no longer left to the discretion of the practitioner. There is too much uncertainty there. By removing discretion and introducing the tools of the case manager and the actuary, there is the constant danger that the humanity of the relationship might disappear.

To help us explore the search for certainty and the illusion that risks in human affairs can be reduced, even eliminated, let's look at how social work with abused and neglected children changed from a policy of support, therapy, and the reduction of poverty and stress to one of surveillance, investigation and the avoidance of risk.

Many people have noted that every time politicians, the public, and the media look at cases in which children die at the hands of their parents, they respond by prescribing more rules and more procedures. The aversion to the idea that there could be inherent risks and uncertainties in child protection work has led to the bureaucratization of child and family social work.

The sociological ideas of 'translation' and 'actor–network theory' (Callon 1986; Law and Hassard 1999; Latour 2005) have been used as one way of trying to make sense of why there have been these repeated attempts to render child care work less uncertain and more safe. This is a subtle idea but one that has profound consequences for the way professionals in general, and social workers in particular practice.

Actor–network theory, well known for being difficult to summarize (Latour 2005; Ziemkendorf 2103), seeks to explore the complex interactions between people and the world of things, between views that emphasize social determinism and those that consider technological determinism. In other words, as human beings we relate and react to objects and things just as much as we do towards people.

Both people and things, roles and responsibilities, become potential 'actors' in any situation. When whole clusters of 'actors' are operating in a particular circumstance, we talk of an 'actor network' in which each 'actor' is dynamically affected by and affects every other 'actor', more or less. In the child welfare example we are exploring here, 'actors' might include court reports, case assessment tools, and organizational procedures as well as children, parents, police officers, health workers, and social workers.

In this analysis, children being abused or neglected by their parents are gradually redefined (that is, 'translated') as people in need of protection rather than members of families who need help. Bureaucratic approaches appear best suited to manage these practices (Howe 1992; Parton and Parton 1989). These managerially-based practices of risk assessment encouraged by society's increasing aversion to risk of any kind rule in some ways of seeing and thinking about cases and rule out others (such as, for example, poverty and parental stress).

The first 'moment' of translation is that of 'problematization'. This involves key people getting others to see and accept their understanding of what's really going on and how it should be dealt with (Callon 1986). In the case of child and family work, throughout the 1980s to the present, the main players in constructing matters this way (rather than any other) have been vulnerable children, potentially dangerous parents, social workers, health professionals, Inquiry reports into the death of children, Serious Case Reviews, social work managers, politicians, policy makers, legislators, and the media. As the problem of how to think about and view child abuse moved between these 'players' or 'actors', the key question to answer gradually crystallized into 'How can we protect children from being killed by their parents?' rather than, say, 'How can we support families in need and help them raise their children more optimally?'

The question represents a strategic success for approaches to problems that are administrative, managerial, and judicial in attitude rather than approaches that are economic, political, and preventative. Therapeutic approaches gradually dropped out of favour as being too naïve and missing the point. The caseworker's question 'How can we help parents to be more competent, less troubled, and less dangerous?' began to fall outside the emerging 'discourse' of 'How do we protect children?' Helping parents to become better carers, supporting families in need, and reducing stress by reducing poverty became increasingly difficult to justify as the protection of children at risk became the primary purpose of the child welfare services.

Today it is very difficult to think about child abuse and neglect in any other way except in terms of improved systems, more guidelines, better communication, tighter supervision, less optimism. All solutions to the problem and ways of studying it are couched in a certain way, one that continues to promote surveillance and increasingly structured investigations.

In turn, thinking about child abuse and neglect in this fashion sponsors a new knowledge base and expertise, one that is more procedural, guided, and judicial and less therapeutic, rehabilitative, and poverty-oriented. As the problem and the solutions to it are shaped and redefined in light of these new beliefs, each of the main players (or 'actors') finds himself or herself with a particular role to play in the shift from therapy and welfare to surveillance and control.

Children become victims. Parents are cast as dangerous. They are objects of enquiry and not subjects whose mental health, social skills, parenting capacities, and housing might be improved. Social workers become more like investigators and less like family caseworkers. Managers and policy makers design systems of surveillance and investigation. Social workers meet their managers for supervision and not case consultation. And although social workers still practice 'out there', they are controlled by managers through having to follow the guidelines and tick the boxes.

Law (1986: 15) has a nice turn of phrase to describe organizational practices that control people at a distance when they are 'out there' in the field. Through the use of 'documents, devices and drilled people' practitioners and operators acting away from the centre can nevertheless still be controlled and their behaviours predicted because they have to follow the rules, read the manuals, and fill in the forms. In this sense, social workers become 'passive agents' and the power flows towards the centre and the managers who produce the documents, devices, and drilled people.

Defining the problem of child abuse and neglect in this particular way encourages certain kinds of solution. The analysis of past failings in which children have died suggests that success in child protection work comes from: (i) knowing what information to collect about parents in order to determine whether or not they might be a danger to their children; (ii) systematically collecting that information by thoroughly investigating cases; (iii) processing and analysing that information to decide whether or not children are likely to be safe in the hands of their parents; and (iv) closely monitoring and re-assessing cases in which children are thought to be at risk (Howe 1992: 499).

The underlying belief is that situations which appear to be problematic and possessed of uncertainty yield to rational enquiry, analysis, and calculation. This renders them *manageable*. Risk and uncertainty, or so it was claimed, would be taken out of the equation by removing discretion from workers, downplaying the idea of a casework relationship, increasing control, exercising authority, emphasizing enquiry, tightening up procedures, and promoting systems.

In parallel, research should concentrate on producing findings that could tell us which family facts, when collected, predict danger, and which cases should therefore be defined as high risk. These facts, themselves born of a particular way of studying cases, then become the basis on which investigations are made, procedures designed, and managers monitor. Checklists and schedules based on risk factors that have been shown statistically to predict dangerousness become ways of allocating time and resources. Only cases that reach risk thresholds receive attention.

It appears, then, that the aversion to risk and the striving for certainty leads to ways of working that become increasingly proceduralized, performance-related, audit-governed, and managerial. This is true not just in child protection work, but also in adult care services for older people, the health services, schools, and health and safety. Risk has become the key criterion for making assessments, taking decisions and allocating scarce resources (Parton 1996: 104).

And once the world is cast in terms of risk, it then becomes possible to hold professionals responsible for failing to protect their clients from exposure to risk (Parton 1996). The expert should have seen the risk coming. The practitioner is accountable. He or she is to blame.

In risk-obsessed societies, we see shifts in professional practice from promoting good to preventing bad, from increasing wellbeing to avoiding danger, from meeting need to calculating risk. Old people should be safe in their homes rather than content in their communities. Children should be protected from parents rather than made happy in their families. In many countries it is the case that elaborate processes have been designed to manage institutional risk rather than promote strong and supportive networks in which families might flourish (Featherstone et al. 2014).

But what if risk is unavoidable? What if uncertainty is endemic in most situations where there is social strain? What if it is the human response to stress rather than weak surveillance and poor social discipline that makes prediction so difficult? Although the case for developing safer systems and evidence-based practices is strong, social work also needs to recognise that uncertainty and the human condition go together.

Uncertainty

Let's begin with floods. At face value, we might simply see them as forces of nature, acts of God. But let's think about them a bit more closely (Hinchliffe 2004). It is late summer, the heavens open, the local river rises rapidly, overflows its banks, and floods the market town through which it flows. Cars are swept off the street. A hundred shops and houses are flooded.

Who or what is to blame? Could the flood have been predicted? What should be done to prevent it happening again? Parallels with child deaths, old people being neglected in the community, and the high rates of mortality in some hospitals compared to others can be made. This is the world of risk.

Beck (1992) said we now live in a 'risk society.' It is not so much that we live in more dangerous times but we are made more aware of risks with the consequent expectation that we should be able to predict and prevent them. Blaming systems:

> …treat every death as chargeable to someone's account, every accident as caused by someone's criminal negligence, every sickness a threatened prosecution. (Douglas 1992: 14, quoted in Parton 1998: 20)

The presumption is that we should be able to anticipate, avoid, remove, and prevent risk. In all walks of life, we are risk-averse. We feel that experts should be able to anticipate and manage risks so that we can lead lives that are safe and untroubled. As we saw in the previous section, the practice of risk assessment and risk management in social work begins to change how practitioners see clients and how they work with them.

But as our awareness of disasters, disgraces, and tragedies increases so we also lose our trust in the experts and institutions set up to handle these risks. It seems that the more we know about the complexity of people and things, the more uncertainty we see, and the more anxiety we feel. There is less confidence and respect for the skills of the expert, whether he or she is an economist, public health official, social worker, teacher, climate researcher, or crop scientist.

Back to the floods. The most obvious culprit is the weather. An unusual, exceptional, and once-in-a-hundred-year storm event was the cause. It could not possibly have been predicted, although surely the meteorologists on the day, with all their science and big computers, might have been a little more specific about where the rain was going to be heaviest.

However, the people who live in the town centre remind those looking into the disaster that the river flood defence system maintained by the Environment Agency has not been upgraded and heightened for more than fifty years, in spite of warnings raised by the local townsfolk. The retort is that government cutbacks mean that the Agency has had to be much more prudent in the way it spends its increasingly limited resources. As the town has not been flooded in recent living memory, it seems unreasonable to blame them for failing to predict and respond to an event that no one foresaw.

The analysis then spins out in ever wider circles. More people have been paving their front gardens to park their cars. This has resulted in less rain soaking into the ground and, instead, it streams off down the street and overwhelms drains. In its eagerness to construct more houses, the local authority ignored advice and allowed a new estate to be built on the flood plain. Farmers have been merrily digging up hedgerows, stripping out woodland, planting single crops on a vast scale, and streamlining rivers and brooks, again resulting in less rain being absorbed and held up by dense vegetation. But the economic pressures on farmers to compete in a global market leaves them with little choice but to make their fields bigger and their businesses more efficient. And, of course, the burning of fossil fuels at an ever faster rate has led to an increase in greenhouse gases and global warming.

More energy and moisture in the atmosphere leads to more frequent and heavier rainstorms, so taking this view means that the ultimate cause of the problems of local flooding is a global industrial one.

So when Mrs Evans wants to know who is to blame for her house flooding, the answer is not quite as straightforward as she might think. Simple explanations, easy predictions, and common sense answers fail to account for the complex nature of risk and uncertainty. Hazards crop up repeatedly as people engage with their environment. In human affairs, prediction is far from an exact science. Thus, there are no absolute causes, although many 'actors' might be seen to be playing a small part in the overall drama.

Similar states of affairs exist in social work. For example, although it might be true that some social careworkers supporting older and disabled people in the community appear short on care and compassion, it might also be that the commercial interests of the private company which employs them has reduced the length of time each worker has for a home visit from 20 minutes to 15. Under pressure to tick the boxes of what she (for it is usually a she) must do on each visit, the personal relationship between worker and client suffers. But the care company itself only won the contract to carry out the service because it put in the most attractive bid under competitive tender to the local authority… whose central government budget allocation has been cut….in part because the banking failure led to a recession which reduced the tax flows into the Treasury… which also had to bail out the banks, leaving central government even more short of cash. Blaming front-line care workers, nurses, doctors, and social workers for the latest tragedy and a lack of common sense is generally too easy and simplistic.

None of this is to say that individual workers are never responsible for a death, an incompetence, a failure of care, a lack of compassion, or an injustice. It is just a reminder that, in many cases, the web of causes and effects is usually dense and complex. And because each web is so difficult to map, the certainty that people look for is rarely achieved.

Risk and uncertainty appear to be inbuilt properties of highly complex systems. Because these systems are open, says Hood:

…they are also sensitive to influences outside the system itself. Therefore, unlike 'classical closed systems, complex systems do not settle into an equilibrium determined by a finite set of rules; instead they continually adapt and evolve, organising themselves into a state of critical imbalance before shifting suddenly to new patterns of behaviour. (Hood 2013: 31)

Clients in their lives, in Hood's (2014) sense, are open systems. The behaviour of individual clients with their own unique psychosocial histories living in particular environments under varying levels of stress interacting with a range of different people is therefore never easy to predict. And being difficult to predict, it is never totally obvious what to do, what treatments to offer, what interventions to deploy, what decisions to make. Indeed, in some cases, it is only when the outcome is established that the wisdom of the decision can be known. For example, taking the risky decision to leave a child with a parent who has a mental health problem looks wise when things work out well, but foolish when the outcome is one of child neglect.

One-dimensional scientific studies on their own are unlikely to improve the social worker's ability to deploy a specific technique with a predictable outcome in a given case. Social work is rarely that kind of business. More often than not, social workers operate in non-standard environments. The everyday world of the social worker is one in which vulnerable people living in conditions of uncertainty are failing to cope. This makes social work an inherently risky business.

What an aggressive adolescent with a chaotic home life might do next is difficult to predict. How an 87-year-old woman might react to the sudden death of her only daughter on whom she was dependent for much of her care and support is hard to tell. Whether a toddler will be safe in the care of his mother now that she has begun a new relationship with a man with a known drug habit is a tough one to call. It always seems obvious with hindsight that things were bound to turn out the way they did, but it is much more difficult to be so clearsighted when you are in the middle of turbulence and uncertainty.

Thus, as Hinchliffe (2004: 146) notes, the laboratory model shouldn't be confused with reality. It has its value and can be helpful, but it offers a simplified and limited version of life as lived. The world, both physical and social, rarely behaves in a straightforward way. This therefore requires workers to be flexible and creative in their use of knowledge, practices and techniques.

So there are doubts about whether rigorously scientific, experimentally evidenced approaches translate well into all corners of social work (see chapters 6 and 7). During the course of a week any one social worker might find herself dealing with domestic violence, alcohol abuse, mental health problems, a child in foster care, suspicions of child neglect, school non-attendance, and a young person's offending behaviour. It is unrealistic as well as impractical to think that a front-line practitioner could keep up-to-date with the research and evidence across these many and varied areas of concern (Gray et al. 2009: 146). And even if a worker was determined to keep abreast of best practices, there isn't actually a lot of clear, translatable, adaptable evidence-based research out there. There isn't that much definitive advice to be found (Kirk 1999). If evidence-based guidelines are meant to produce uniform responses under given conditions, they haven't proved terribly successful.

Good practice in an uncertain world

Downie and Loudfoot, both philosophers, observed that the 'possibility of a science of human relationships with the certainty of the natural sciences does not exist, and hence there is serious doubt about the reality of a social work expertise based exclusively on it' (Downie and Loudfoot 1978: 119). They go on to add that if this is the case, then social workers have little choice but to make practical judgements in situations of uncertainty.

> No amount of knowledge of what is the case can ever establish for us what we ought to do about it. The need for practical judgement of what we ought to do, granted our knowledge, is inescapable; and therefore there are radical limits to the possibility of expertise… (Downie and Loudfoot 1978: 122)

Thus, the certainty that there will be uncertainty and the uncertainty that there will be certainty suggest the value of a more open and reflexive type of social work practice given the complexity of the situations with which they are faced and the fallibility of most predictions. Social workers can never remove risk entirely (Munro 2013).

Adams et al. (2009b: 1–2) also recognise that social work exists in a 'complex world', one in which there are many ambiguities. Answers are rarely simple or linear. Many of the problems which social workers face are, in fact, intractable. 'A mother with a mental illness may love her family and be loved by her children, but they may still be at risk from her instability' (Adams et al. 2009b: 5). The only kind of practice that makes sense in such a world, they argue, is one which is 'integrative', thoughtful, questioning, critical and imaginative.

So as well as minimizing risk, social work should be about maximizing welfare (Munro 2002). A reminder that social work is primarily about welfare and wellbeing means that risks can and should be taken. Yes, there will be risks in supporting a young severely disabled woman to live independently, but that's what she wants more than anything. Both the young woman and social worker know the risks, but higher values override organizational caution and defensive postures (see chapter 14 on values).

Experts are good at seeing patterns in the world in which they work (Fook 2000). And because their work is invariably complex and rarely straightforward, they also tend to be flexible and adaptive in their use of formal theories (Fook et al. 1997).

It is also the case that because everyday life is fluid, contingent, and evolving, bringing about change has to use the same elements that construct everyday social reality – talk, argument, 'give-and-take', attempts to understand and be understood, the search for meaning, efforts at interpretation (Schutz 1962–6; Berger and Luckman 1967; Parton 2003).

Front-line social work in the hands of experienced practitioners appears to be a skilled version of these everyday interactions. It is gifted with alertness and sensitivity, ideas and empathy, collaboration and negotiation, shared assessments and jointly agreed plans.

Talk and language create our realities. And so it is that as we talk with clients all of this possibility takes place. If we want clients to achieve a better life, talk and language are where we have to start, and if these are to be successful, social workers need to be in possession of considerable skill and craft (see chapter 11).

> This is far from an 'anything goes' approach, as it requires a critically reflective stance… This is a process of reflective and informed judgement that acknowledges the reality that social workers will not achieve definitive answers to many practice questions. The centrality of human relationships and the diverse and complex contexts in

social work practice mean that the integration of scientific, practical, political and interpretive evidence will generally require creativity and improvisation on the part of the practitioner (Graybeal 2007). (Gray et al. 2009: 71)

So, in social work, decision-making will always 'entail a complex mix of life experience, professional judgement, heuristics, political expediency and research knowledge' (Gray et al. 2009: 170). In their pragmatic approach to social work practice, Gray and her colleagues explore and explain why top-down attempts to advance evidence-based practices are unlikely to succeed. More realistic, and therefore more effective practices are likely to appear as social workers attempt, with their clients and colleagues, to understand the meaning of their experience, share ideas including research effectiveness studies, collaborate, form judgements, and work out ways to go forward that are realistic, revisable, resource-wise, legally informed, safety-conscious, and politically sensitive. Each case will conjure its own unique pathway with its own particular twists and turns. The more complex the case, the more likely it is that social workers will find it helpful to analyse and discuss matters with colleagues and arrive at decisions collectively (Hood 2013).

Best practice finds social workers creatively and flexibly working in ways that appeal to evidence-based research whenever appropriate or possible but always within clinical approaches that value the client–worker relationship. Here, clients become 'known' individually as opposed to being just examples of this type of behaviour or that category of problem. By channelling all our energies into the assessment of risk, suggest Cree and Wallace (2009: 53), 'we may lose sight of social work's traditional strengths and relationship values.'

And so if the idea of uncertainty in human affairs recognises that people can't simply be seen as objects or case categories, that they have personal experiences and an inner life, then we need to think a bit more about trying to understand them subjectively as well as objectively.

6
Objects and Subjects
People's Inner and Outer Worlds

Introduction

Although there are many examples of early civilizations trying to make sense of the world by approaching it rationally (the Greeks, medieval Arabic cultures), much human thought up until the Age of Enlightenment in the seventeenth century believed the world was preordained and God-given. The truth of things could be found in holy texts, which is to say the word of God, whomsoever your God happened to be. This meant that there wasn't much enquiry into the whys and wherefores of nature, or indeed human conduct. Neither objective enquiry nor subjective reflection would reveal the truth of human being and human behaviour. The world was just as it is, divinely ordained, and you accepted your place in it without question.

However, this settled, relatively unquestioned view of things was about to be upset in ways that were profound and far reaching.

Objective understanding

The seventeenth century witnessed a radical shift in thinking. There was a growing belief that Nature could be fathomed by the application of human reason. Rational thought, systematic enquiry, and mathematics were the way to make sense of things. The enquiring mind was a sceptical mind in search of universal truths. The result was what we now refer to as the Age of Reason, the European Enlightenment and the Scientific Revolution. These were times of great minds and original thinkers including Francis Bacon, René Descartes, David Hume, Immanuel Kant, and Isaac Newton.

The modern stance sees reality lying outside the human mind. Both the physical world and the social world exist independently of our appreciation of them. Their character and independent properties impose themselves on our senses and consciousness.

However, human reason was capable of discovering nature's laws and the universal principles upon which the world and everything in it were based. And, of course, if you could understand the world and what made it work, then you could increase your power to change it, manipulate it, and ultimately control it. Thus, the application of science lead to the Industrial Revolution.

Rather than passively accept the world and our place in it, men and women began to feel that they could change the world through their own efforts. They could be in charge of their own destiny and liberate themselves from nature and the divine will.

The rational, scientific mind believed that to all rigorous questions of fact and value, there is only one true answer, and that answers to such questions are in principle knowable by the application of human reason (Berlin 1991: 209). All things, including people, possess internal properties, which, if known and understood, can explain the character and behaviour of the thing, or person under study.

As scientists, therefore, we can make sense of, and explain nature, including human nature, by observing it, measuring it, examining it, probing it, experimenting on it, taking it to pieces, controlling it, manipulating it, changing it, and using it. The scientific mind stands outside the things it observes and wishes to explain. This is true of science's interest in people and human behaviour as well as its fascination with nature and things.

It follows, then, that if nature can be studied and if we are part of nature, then we must also be subject to its laws. We can be observed, explained, and changed as a result of being investigated and looked at scientifically. So whereas the natural sciences, including physics, chemistry, and biology, investigate things, the social sciences study people. The belief is that there are social facts just as there are physical facts, and social facts are just as real in their effects as any solid fact. For example, being young, male and long-term unemployed might mean you experience yourself as being without social value and that you are a personal failure. Such a state of mind might increase feelings of anomie and alienation. It might lead to depression or a 'couldn't care less' attitude. On this analysis, our behaviour is seen as the product of the kind of society in which we live.

Nineteenth- and early twentieth-century social scientists, including the sociologists Auguste Comte and Émile Durkheim, and the psychologists Wilhelm Wundt and William James, believed that by applying the scientific method to people and society, not only could people and societies be understood, they could be changed and improved. Herein lay the idea that there could be progress in human affairs as well as in technological and industrial matters. People, just like nature, could be *controlled* and *improved*.

As we saw in chapter 2, to the extent that social workers began to see themselves as applied social scientists, they, too, found themselves in the business of social control and personal improvement, maintaining social order and promoting social change, valuing progress and making predictions. By scientifically working out what made people 'tick', it became possible to think about ways in which those who were not functioning well could be improved or made better.

For example, the application of evidence-based, *psychologically inspired*, scientifically informed models of intervention has seen many social workers develop a strong interest in treatments arising out of psychology's attempts to be science-like. Behavioural modification and cognitive behavioural therapies (CBT) are good examples of social work's interest in science-based approaches to practice (see Sheldon 2011).

A practitioner might make careful observations which reveal a parent only reacts and takes notice of her toddler when he misbehaves. The rest of the time she ignores him. Learning theory tells us that that for most children some attention is better than no attention. Responding only to the boy's negative behaviour reinforces his misbehaviour and so he becomes more and more naughty. This way he gets some kind of reaction and attention from his parent.

A behavioural modification programme might advise the parent to ignore all the child's difficult behaviours, but respond positively to all behaviours that she sees as acceptable. Evidence-based research predicts that as a result of the parent changing her responses, the boy's behaviour will also change, and in this case improve. This reshaping of the child's behaviour has taken place without reference to what he thinks or feels. No interest has been taken in his internal world, his subjective experience.

On a grander scale, social workers have also been interested in changing and improving society. The application of *sociological under-standings* has encouraged many social workers to argue that we shouldn't be changing people to fit society, rather we should be changing society to fit the needs of people. Radical and structurally-based social work has been attracted to these more sociologically inspired practices (Lavalette 2011; Mullaly 2007). For example, if we improve people's wages, housing, educational opportunities, and ability to control their own lives, we are also likely to improve people's mental health and social behaviour more than any amount of behavioural modification.

But whether social work practice looks towards the psychological and evidence-based sciences, or the more sociological and economic based theories, there is the shared view that people and society can be objectively observed, scientifically examined, theoretically explained, rationally predicted, and systematically changed. Like any natural object, people and their society really can be studied objectively using the scientific method. We shall be examining these claims in more detail in chapter 7 when we look at social work research and the methods that it uses.

Subjective understanding

However, throughout the nineteenth century and into the beginning of the twentieth, it began to dawn on some social scientists that trying to understand people as we understand natural objects doesn't entirely work. Observing what people do, measuring their responses, and getting them to fill in questionnaires certainly provides informa-tion that's interesting, but it only takes you so far in trying to make sense of human action and individual behaviour. Social workers who take a scientific stance are liable to drift into the murky waters of treating social facts as objectively solid and true, chanting 'if it can't be measured, it doesn't exist' (White 1997: 741).

There is something fundamentally different about people compared to things. Whereas objects in themselves are meaningless, people are meaningful. Rocks, magnets, and trees have no sense of themselves as objects in the universe. But human beings do. They are self-aware. They have plans, hopes, worries, beliefs, interests, motives, and values. They think about and are affected by contemplating their past, present, and future. They live in different places, in different cultures with different traditions, at different times. So although people can be looked at and studied objectively in terms of what they say and do, they are also the *subjective* centres of a world of their own experience. This internal world of subjective experience affects what they say and do, as well as what they think and feel.

Thus, if we are to understand people, we need to understand them subjectively as well as objectively. Human behaviour needs to be thought about from the insider's perspective if it is to be understood at all. And this requires a different set of techniques to those employed by the natural sciences.

So although, like physical objects, people do possess some fixed properties and predictable behaviours, they also have ideas about themselves that shift and change as they reflect on what they think and feel, and ponder on what they have done and might do. If people are to be understood, we have to get a sense of what the world looks and feels like from their subjective point of view. This makes much of social science an *interpretive* discipline.

Matters are even more fluid when we realize that thought and meaning are carried, indeed constructed by language. And as we attempt to communicate and express ourselves meaningfully in language, the other, as he or she observes and listens, is trying to interpret what we say and mean. So whereas science looks for causes and effects and seeks to explain, human interaction involves language, and language carries meaning and conveys personal experience and requires interpretation.

We impose meaning on the meaningless world around us. We create our own realities and our own purposes. We are self-caused. There are no social facts 'out there'. There is nothing fixed. There is only what we create in our heads, our language, and our talk with one another. Language which carries meaning shapes experience, but language also changes over time, between cultures, across social groups, amongst friends. That is why the search for meaning and the need to feel understood is never-ending and a constant cause for delight, frustration, confusion, love, and hope. The interpretation of what we think other people might mean and might be trying to say lies at the heart of all our exchanges and communications.

To understand the experience of the other we have to see the world from their point of view. We can't see it, count it, or measure it.

The meaning that the other person gives to their experience can only be grasped as we try to connect with them, one meaningful self with another. It is in our relationships with others that we hope and struggle to be understood. But we 'can only "understand" by occupying the frame of reference of the participant in action,' write Burrell and Morgan (1979: 5). And because there are no social facts, and because there are only meanings that arise as we speak with and listen to others, our realities are in a constant state of change, flux and construction.

It is the human mind which therefore imposes order on the world. As our senses perceive, so our minds conceive. We construct our realities. We look for and find patterns and regularities within and between things, including our actions, behaviours and the people with whom we live, work and play.

For example, many acts labelled as deviant are only viewed as such because those in power have defined them to be so. The deviant act does not reflect an inherent quality of the individual. It is merely the consequence of those in power applying their rules to judge the behaviour of others (Becker 1963). And because laws change over time and between cultures, what is seen as deviant in one place at one time might not be seen as deviant in another place at a different time.

Depending on when and where you live, smoking cannabis, having sex outside marriage, or driving at eighty miles an hour can have very different consequences. Producing, selling, and drinking alcohol in many states in America during the 1920s and 30s was a criminal offence, but not today. Being male and gay in 1950s Britain was unlawful and punishable by imprisonment, but this is no longer the case. Having a baby and not being married carried a heavy social stigma right up until the early 1960s. The lack of support coupled with the social opprobrium of having an 'illegitimate' baby led many young women to give up their infants for adoption (Howe et al. 1992). But changes in social attitudes have seen a gradual decline in the number of babies being placed for adoption from a peak of over 12,000 in 1960s Britain to barely a few hundred today.

As we change society and its attitudes, so we change people's personal experience. As we alter the meanings we give to what we think and do, we change our sense of who we are and how we feel. Guilt and shame are replaced by celebration and acceptance; deceit and denial are dropped in favour of honesty and openness.

Objective outsides and subjective insides

In practice, social workers are interested in both what people do and how they experience themselves as they do it. Subject and object are interrelated; one affects the other.

> Rather than simply refer to their 'objective' label – the poor, mentally ill or criminals – social work is concerned with identifying the person, or people, who are labelled this way. Rather than simply talk about a young offender, they are concerned with *this* young offender, called John, who has lived this life, had these experiences and feels these feelings. They are interested, in other words, with *creating subjectivity (the person) out of objective states (the label, such as offender)*. (Sheppard 2006: 41, emphasis in original)

A mental health social worker observes the difficulties a young woman has leaving her house each morning. The client's life is becoming unmanageable as she obsessively and repeatedly washes her hands before compulsively checking and rechecking that the windows are shut, the cutlery is arranged in meticulous order of length, and that the cushions sit at either end of the sofa are in exact symmetry. If these rituals are not performed, the fear is that something terrible might happen – she will catch a disease, suffer harm, be punished, or lose a close relative. The rituals take anything up to an hour or more to complete. She probably knows as well as her mental health worker that these behaviours are irrational, but even though they are unwanted, they feel uncontrollable. The thoughts are obsessive; the behaviours compulsive. She can't get them out of her head.

The origins of such obsessions and compulsions can be many and varied. As a child, an overanxious, overprotective parent fussed excessively about germs and cleanliness in the house, and the dangers and risks which lurked outside. So the child washed her hands and rarely got ill. Or the young teenager who somehow imagined that when she had carried out her chores and tidied her room her uncle was less likely to visit, and if he didn't visit she would not be sexually abused that night. Obsessive order and tidiness somehow became caught up with feelings of not being hurt and staying safe.

Some treatments don't require too much reflection by clients on the behaviours themselves and what might have caused them.

Exposure treatments and response prevention require you to refrain from carrying out the compulsive behaviour. You then wait to see what happens. You shut the lavatory door and with gentle support your therapist prevents you from washing your hands. And nothing terrible happens. You don't get ill. The world doesn't fall around your ears. Such exposures and response preventions usually have to be repeated many times before the fears and anxieties begin to reduce. But gradually the urge to wash your hands fades. The ritual begins to lose its grip. You begin to have some control over your obsessive thoughts.

Another treatment might ask you to focus on your 'catastrophic' thoughts. Your subjective experience, and what you think and feel become the focus of attention. Using CBT, you are taught that your intrusive and obsessive thoughts are the result of your anxiety, your Obsessive Compulsive Disorder (OCD). You need to say to yourself, firmly and repeatedly, 'I really do not need to wash my hands and arrange the cutlery. I'm simply having a compulsive urge and I *can* resist it.' You learn that your brain has chemically organized itself to give you these urges, so you tell yourself 'It's not me but my OCD that's pressuring me to do these things. It's a false message and not meaningful.' The therapist then encourages you to focus on some other distracting behaviour. Schwartz and Gladding (2011) describe this treatment as a four-step model for dealing with OCD: re-label, re-attribute, re-focus, and re-value.

Social workers are constantly being made aware of the concerns that society has about what people do and can't do. Someone has a learning disability and finds shopping difficult. Someone abuses their child. Someone's husband has died and aged 83 they are left feeling grief-stricken to the point of self-neglect.

Behind these observed behaviours also lie subjective feelings and minds at work. There is agitation and distress because there is so much to think about when you are shopping. Deep, unresolved, and painful memories of a loveless, violent childhood leave you poorly equipped to deal with the emotional needs of your own children. Aching feelings of loss after sixty years of marriage sap the will to live.

Social workers have to address both the external and internal worlds of their clients. Practice based solely on objective concerns lacks warmth and compassion. But practices that only address what people are thinking and feeling might forget their more obvious behaviours and material needs – a support worker to shop, a nursery place for the child of a highly stressed and potentially dangerous parent, and a home help and meals-on-wheels for a grieving widow.

The 1998 paper by Gillian Schofield offers one of the best descriptions of the importance of the *inner and outer worlds* concept in social work. Schofield reminds us that social workers have to operate in both worlds simultaneously. They visit schools, organize home care, phone doctors, and contact housing departments. But at the same time they seek to understand their clients subjectively and psychologically, provide emotional support, and help change behaviour. Social workers listen and attend, but they also act and organize.

A depressed mother who neglects her children discloses that she was sexually abused as a child. The family live in an overcrowded high-rise flat, the mother suffers low self-esteem, and feels empty inside. She feels powerless and can hardly look after herself never mind her young children. Each of these inner and outer world elements is connected; neither can be ignored.

The social worker has constantly to see how the environment and the individual affect each other, for good or ill. Past experiences affect current events. Current events trigger past, often unresolved emotional memories. Anxiety and anger, shame and despair lie as embers of old hurts and traumas, easily fanned into fury by the slightest gust – of a thoughtless word, a deliberate taunt, a criticism, a rejection. To the outsider, many an outburst by a client looks like an overreaction; an inappropriate, unwarranted response. These behaviours only make sense when the client's past pains are recognised and understood.

Clients need to sense that their social workers are trying to see and understand their inner worlds. But social workers also need to sort out problems in the outer world. Usually it is not until the stresses of the external world are resolved that people can tackle their inner world problems and worries. When the outer world begins to feel safe it then feels safe to look at the problems and worries of the inner world. Current stresses all too easily disturb and dysregulate inner thoughts and feelings. So sorting out a nursery place, helping a woman get to a safe house, driving the client to the hospital, or organizing community care are practical ways of lowering stress.

And of course, we all think more clearly and behave more reasonably when we feel less stressed.

> The provision of a reliable, accepting relationship offered within the context of helpful activity, and helpful activity offered within the context of a reliable accepting relationship should not surprise us as an effective combination. (Schofield 1998: 65)
>
> [W]hat the social worker can offer is consistency and predictability. She can ring when she says she will ring, arrive on time for appointments, remain warm and considerate even in the context of having to face up to the possibility of difficult decisions… (Schofield 1998: 67)

And running with similar thoughts, Wilson and colleagues write:

> The central characteristic of relationship-based practice is the emphasis it places on the professional relationship as the medium through which the practitioner can engage with and intervene in the complexity of an individual's internal and external world. (Wilson et al. 2011: 7)

In the final chapter we shall return to the idea of inner and outer worlds, the scientific explanations of behaviour and the subjective understanding of individual experience, and the importance of the relationship as we begin our definition of the *compleat* social worker. But before then, we need to take our discussion of people as objects to be explained and subjects to be understood into the world of social work research, evidence-based practice, and practice-informed evidence.

7

Qualitative and Quantitative

Social Work's Research and Evidence Base

Introduction

As we noted in chapter 4, all professions seek to develop a 'body of knowledge'. This knowledge tells the profession things about the world with which it has to deal. Medicine develops knowledge about the body, disease, illness, and health. It also builds up knowledge about what kind of medical interventions are likely to be effective in treating illness and disease and which bring about good health. Similar observations can be made about the knowledge base of engineers, clinical psychologists, and nurses.

Although professionals acquire everyday practice wisdom, there is a need to develop knowledge that is more systematic, evidence-based, and applicable. Furthermore, when knowledge is ordered and organized, it can be taught to the next generation of professionals, and in their turn they can add to their profession's knowledge base. Knowledge that is conceptually organized and systematically ordered results from the efforts of academics and researchers. It also arises out of the minds of theoreticians who look for patterns and explanations in what researchers find and what practitioners do.

Research seeks to examine and discover things. It then tests the results and ideas that flow from them. Professional practitioners who apply knowledge then go on to ask a further question. 'What should be done in order to solve practical problem X?' (Gredig et al. 2012: 393).

Social work recognises that as a profession it, too, ought to develop a robust body of knowledge. It is interested in knowing about the nature and extent of personal troubles and social problems. As a personal social service it needs to know about the living conditions and life circumstances of the clients with whom it works. Social work researchers have also had a long and honourable tradition of looking at, and helping us to understand the extent and effects of poverty, marginalization, discrimination, powerlessness, abuse, and social exclusion.

Social workers practice in agencies and organizations, both small and large, so there are also research questions to be asked about how well these agencies and organizations function in terms of putting policies into practice and delivering services, how cost-effective they are, how well do they meet their aims.

And finally, there is the fundamental question of 'what works' in practice (Gredig et al. 2012: 394). What brings about change? Evaluation research is research that attempts to discover whether social workers achieve their intended goals (Forrester 2012).

However, because the nature of its work involves people, their thoughts, feelings, and behaviour as they take place in various social and political contexts, social workers have not found it quite so straightforward as, say medics, to develop a consensual body of knowledge. Nevertheless, like all other human services, social work does have to account for itself. In practice, this accountability exists in two basic forms.

First, we might ask 'Has the organization and its personnel provided a service to all those who sought one, needed one, or were referred for one?' Has the agency carried out its statutory responsibilities? How efficient and cost-effective was the delivery of the service? Did the service delivered achieve its aims? Did the client's behaviour improve? Was the residential care needed actually provided? In broad terms, the answer to these questions are matters of *quantity*. The number of clients receiving the service can be counted and matched against departmental targets. The client's problematic behaviours can be rated and measured before and after the social worker's intervention.

Second, we might ask 'What did those on the receiving end of the social worker's input feel about the service provided?' What were their feelings and experiences before and after the involvement? What does it feel like to be them? In broad, terms these are questions of *quality*. Clients can be asked about their experiences. Subjective accounts of their lives and their relationships are of interest. Personal descriptions of subjective wellbeing can be explored.

For the *quantitative* researcher, 'truth' is found in the careful examination of the objects under study. Those with a more *qualitative* approach find 'truths' in the minds and experiences of people as subjects.

Knowledge about social workers and what they do has therefore been generated using both quantitative and qualitative methods. Social work research is an increasingly sophisticated activity and doesn't fall neatly into simple boxes (Gredig et al. 2012), but for the purposes of this chapter we'll divide our enquiries into research which is quantitative in nature and research which is qualitative in character. Thus, *how* things are known (quantitative or qualitative) determines *what* is known (objective facts or subjective experiences). What is known is a matter of epistemology, of values, of ideology. Although there is much research which looks at organizations, policy, and services, the two basic sites of research enquiry that we shall look at are the practices of social workers and the experiences of clients.

Quantitative methods

Quantitative methods of investigation and assessment are more likely to turn to the physical, medical, and psychological sciences for inspiration. We explored elements of this in chapter 6 when we thought about people as potential objects of study.

We can know people by observing what they do, how often they do it, and for how long they do it. The 'it' could be taking illegal drugs, drinking to excess, hitting children, not attending school, falling over at home, or not paying the rent. These behaviours can be measured, weighed, and counted. Numbers are important. Statistical analysis of these numbers is crucial. The methods of carrying out these measures include experiments using control groups, randomized trials, surveys, comparison of variables, comparison of different groups, the search for associations, and cost–benefit analyses.

For example, we might ask whether the provision of extra home helps and supports is more effective in keeping older people at home and in the community than, say, an increase in the number of places available in day care. The money available is finite and a decision has to be made to expand one or other of these services. Which is it to be?

We might hypothesize that providing better housing, increasing the number of nursery places, or improving local job opportunities is a more effective way of reducing child neglect than, say, tightening up monitoring and surveillance procedures. Thinking quantitatively is the best way to test this hypothesis.

A lot of quantitative research adopts a 'cause-and-effect' way of thinking. For example, it might be tested that when her parents argue violently, the teenage daughter self-harms, or when community home support hours are reduced, more elderly people enter residential care.

When researchers examine the effectiveness of social work interventions, they generally adopt the evidence-based approach favoured by the medical sciences. Evidence-based research focuses on solving problems and generating solutions rather than simply creating knowledge for its own sake.

Professional effectiveness is determined by whether or not the worker's stated aims are achieved. Does the young person stop offending? Does the client with a learning disability manage to buy food and cook it themselves?

The researcher is interested in observing exactly what the social worker does and then seeing how it affects the client. It isn't good enough to ask global questions such as 'Is social work effective?' This lacks specificity. Research designs must be tight if the link between what social workers do and its effect on those with whom they do it is to be unambiguously established. 'Who did what to whom, where, when, for how long, and with what outcome?' might be the kind of the questions asked of a particular social work intervention. The problem being treated, the need being addressed, and the outcome intended must be spelt out in concrete, measurable detail.

There are a variety of quantitative methods available, including social surveys, experiments, and official statistics. However, one of the most robust quantitative research methods is the randomized control trial (RCT). Here, the social work cases which receive the intervention under study are compared with cases in which there is no intervention or with those which receive just the usual services. Clients who receive the specified social work intervention are known as the 'experimental group'. People who don't receive the intervention or simply get the usual services are termed the 'control group' or 'comparison group'.

Both the problem being tackled and the interventions being evaluated must be defined in very specific, measurable terms. Input and output, before and after measures are stated clearly and quantifiably. These measurements are destined to become the variables which will allow statistical tests to be carried out to see if the intervention achieved its stated goals or not. At the end of the trial, the researchers should be able to say whether the experimental intervention achieved its aims or not.

Research designs of this kind are not too common in social work but they do exist. It has been shown, for example, that regular, low-tech, community-based social support given to at-risk families reduces the risk of children being admitted into public care (Jones 1985). Intense antenatal and postnatal support, guidance, and educational advice about babies' development and behaviour offered to mothers in at-risk populations reduces the long-term risks of the children of those mothers developing problem behaviours, high levels of school non-attendance, early pregnancies, poor mental health, and criminal records (Olds et al. 2007). Devolving budgets and control to front-line practitioners reduces the number of frail and elderly people admitted to residential care (Challis and Davies 1986). Educating staff, modifying the environment, and implementing exercise programmes has been found to reduce the number of falls and injuries in a Swedish residential care home for older people (Jensen et al. 2002 cited in Taylor 2012: 429). The use of cognitive therapy to treat people in Northern Ireland who have suffered post-traumatic stress disorder related to terrorism and civil conflict has been found to be effective (Duffy et al. 2007).

And when a decent number of these robust RCTs have been conducted in a particular problem area or field of need, it is possible to look at them all together and carry out a systematic review. This boosts numbers, statistical rigour and the strength of the evidence. Systematic reviews of RCTs represent the most powerful of all evidences. Where they exist, there is really no excuse for ignoring them.

Qualitative methods

The assumption of the qualitative researcher is that people are better understood in terms of their own subjective experiences. The research task is to discover what meaning clients, or indeed social workers give to their experience and how this affects their thoughts, feelings, and behaviour. This type of knowledge cannot be gained by studying people as if they were objects. It requires the researcher to understand clients or social workers from their own subjective point of view.

The researcher has to occupy the 'frame of reference' of the client or worker in order to understand it. This can be achieved by interview, conversation, listening to people talk, establishing an empathic relationship, observation, or joining the group in the manner of an anthropologist or participant-observer. People are encouraged to tell their story in their own words. Researchers talk formally and informally to clients and social workers. They accompany practitioners on home visits. They take part in the life of the group.

Clients and practitioners are viewed as experts on their own experience. They can report 'what works' for them. The researcher explores with people the ways in which they create their world, interpret it, and give it meaning. How does what clients think, feel and do make sense to them? The interest is in clients', or indeed social workers' hopes and plans, intentions and beliefs, feelings and fears. The researcher relates to the client or social worker as one subject to another and not, as quantitative researchers do, as a scientist looking at an object, albeit a human one.

For example, rather than describe and count offending behaviours, deeper insights into the nature of criminal acts might be gained by trying to understand the offender and seeing how the world looks from his point of view. Understanding, and not information gathering is the aim.

Children's experiences of attending child protection case conferences and going to court certainly seem worth knowing (Schofield and Thoburn 1996). After all, the whole apparatus of child care social work is geared up to protect them and their wellbeing. Children say they value a trusting relationship with a dependable adult in situations that can all too easily be experienced as intimidating. So we learn that a long-term relationship with a supportive, familiar social worker or independent advocate gives children the confidence to participate and have their voice heard (Gallagher 2010).

One of the earliest, classic qualitative studies was published in 1970 by John Mayer and Noel Timms. The title of their book, *The Client Speaks: Working Class Impressions of Casework*, lets us know what kind of research we're about to meet. The authors recognised at the outset that they were 'profoundly ignorant about the ways in which consumers of ... services respond to the social work help the community makes available' (Mayer and Timms 1970: 2).

The researchers interviewed 61 clients of the Family Welfare Association and asked for their views and experiences. As well as appreciating social workers who were practically minded, clients also mentioned the importance of the practitioners' personal qualities, including honesty, straightforwardness, and being friendly. These results anticipated social work's current interest in virtue ethics which we shall be mentioning later in chapter 14.

Mayer and Timms' research also gave the profession an early message that when there was a mismatch between what clients wanted and what social workers were doing, levels of satisfaction were likely to be low. It is easy to see how the idea of collaborative, partnership-based social work conducted by professionals whose personal qualities allowed them to build strong helping alliances with their clients emerged out of these pioneering qualitative enquiries.

At the time, the research approach taken by Mayer and Timms was still comparatively new in social work. Their findings were fresh and revelatory, helping to blaze the trail for the many hundreds of client view and social work experience studies that have appeared in the years since.

Research in the round

These days it is not unusual to find researchers happily following both the quantitative and qualitative traditions. There is a need to know if the intervention is effective, efficient, and economic. But is also worth finding out what those who deliver and receive the service make of the experience. What was life like before and after the social worker's involvement? It is now also usual to seek the views of other people who have a stake in the service, including politicians and managers.

There is no simple fixed point from which to judge a service or intervention. Hence the need to see the world from multiple points of view using 'mixed methods' in which both quantitative and qualitative techniques are used. Because social life has so many dimensions, we cannot begin to understand it unless we are prepared to look at it from many different points of view. This feeds nicely into our idea of what the *compleat* social worker might look like and be like. We shall paint her portrait more fully in the final chapter.

A classic example of mixed methods research in social work was the 1969 study by Reid and Shyne. They decided to see whether 'brief' casework (eight sessions) was more or less effective than 'extended' casework (open-ended involvement). A sample of 120 families were randomly assigned to receive either brief or extended casework. The interventions were audio-recorded, described, and analysed in detail. The clients themselves were also interviewed about what they felt about the casework and the social workers who delivered it. Summarizing the results, Reid and Shyne found that brief, focused interventions delivered by attuned and responsive social workers were more effective than open-ended, more traditional forms of case-work. This landmark study lead to the highly influential book, *Task-Centred Casework* (Reid and Epstein 1972) which continues to have great relevance for today's social workers and their practice.

Perhaps one of the most attractive methods of research for social workers is that of *participatory action research.* It combines not only quantitative and qualitative methods, but also a belief that clients should be active and potent players in the research process and that research should lead to positive change. It is a type of research which aims to solve concrete problems. The research is therefore both cooperative and collaborative in nature. It is also described as 'eman-cipatory', that is, it helps empower those the service is meant to help and support. This is why Reason and Bradbury (2008) have described this kind of research as political (it asserts people's rights and ability to have a say in decisions which affect their lives) and empowering (it enables people to recognise and realise their own strengths and capacities) (Baldwin 2012: 469).

As involved participants, clients actively help the research team develop knowledge and an understanding of their problems and needs. And because it is their world, their experience, and their needs that lie at the heart of the research, clients also play an active part in deciding what works. The underlying drive is the search for practical solutions.

In his excellent review of participatory action research, Baldwin (2012) offers a number of useful examples in which we see explana-tion and experience, observation and involvement, measure and meaning all thrown into the research mix.

Baldwin (1997) reports a piece of participatory action research in which he was involved. The staff of a day care centre for people with learning disabilities were concerned that their clients were being stigmatized and marginalized by the local community. Together with the researcher, the staff and clients embarked on an action-oriented approach to change. They discussed ideas and possible actions. They reflected on their situation. They thought about how changes and improvements could be made.

Throughout this collaborative process, clients slowly began to gain in confidence. Their understanding of themselves and their situation grew. They saw that choices could be made and that they had a right to be assertive and to be heard. And so gradually the clients began to develop a sense of personal control. In fact, one group of clients and staff grew sufficiently confident to start a small business providing light lunches. The success of this enterprise was the result of all participants engaging inclusively, democratically, and creatively in the project.

Most clients as participants in these forms of action-based research find their self-esteem and confidence rising. They no longer see themselves as passive and helpless but rather as active and potent. They recognise that their voices can be heard and that they can make a difference. All of which is highly attractive to social workers.

Baldwin (2012) reminds us that perhaps too much of modern social work is directed and controlled by managers. This results in practices that are authoritarian, denying clients much say about their fate. He ends his review of participatory action research with a rousing reminder of the profession's core values:

A profession driven by the values of social justice and human rights is completely at odds with an ideology which favours markets and the pursuit of financial gain for the few. Social workers habitually work with people who are marginalised, oppressed and poor. [Participatory action research] is illustrative in its intentions and in its practice of a different way of understanding and instigating social change. Although it may be difficult in such organisations to offer resistance, [participatory action research] does provide a positive and pragmatic call to action. (Baldwin 2012: 479).

It is here that we find a nice fit between researchers who operate in the round and the notion of the *compleat* social worker as someone whose practice is not only effective but also ethically sound, emotionally attuned, and ideologically defensible.

8
Thought and Feeling
How Social Workers Can Best Respond

Introduction

Over the years, the classic divide between thought and feeling has been reflected not only in social work but also in counselling and psychotherapy. Casework based on psychodynamic principles and relationship-based approaches has a keen sense of the part that emotions play in our thoughts, behaviour, and development. Strong feelings crop up whenever we are threatened or confused, under stress or not in control, unloved or abandoned, accepted or rejected. Social workers therefore need to recognise and understand the part that emotions play in relationships. Helping clients recognise and manage their feelings brings about insight and control.

However, structured and ordered thought is also a good thing to bring to professional practice. It is good that social workers have a knowledge base upon which they can think and plan intelligently. Clients feel better if they believe that the practitioner understands what is going on and what should be done. Clients begin to feel less stressed if they, too, can learn to think rationally and more clearly. The ability to think in a relatively calm, controlled and orderly manner in difficult circumstances increases confidence.

Many social work methods emphasize the value of clear, purposeful, undistorted thinking. 'Social work is about helping people in society,' write Evans and Hardy (2010) and to 'be helpful in any situation you need to work out what is going on and what you can do about it' (p. 1). Cognitive behavioural therapies, task-centred practices, and solution-based approaches are good examples of methods which value working clearly and purposefully.

Although different practices might lean more heavily towards either a thought- or a feelings-based approach, in practice the two are not easily separated. The reality is that many clients have thoughts that are confused and feelings that are running high. Whether unruly thoughts are better tamed by emotional insight or whether unregulated feelings might be calmed by gaining cognitive control might be a matter of theoretical preference. But true to the spirit of this book, after we have rehearsed what we understand by thought and feeling in social work, we shall look for a more integrated approach as we construct our idea of the *compleat* social worker.

This position reflects modern thinking about our mental make-up, one in which there is no clear boundary in our heads between thought and feeling. Thoughts affect feeling every bit as much as feelings affect thought.

Thought

Strictly speaking, *thinking* is just one component of our cognitive make-up. Rather oddly, though, much of the first half of twentieth-century psychology ignored thinking. There was an emphasis on behaviour. Because the natural sciences had developed a formidable body of knowledge by observing the way things behaved, it seemed logical that if psychology was to achieve scientific respect, then it, too, would get smart by observing human behaviour. The mind and what went on inside it couldn't be observed, so it was ignored. But clearly that led psychology to find itself in a very odd position – knowing a lot about behaviour but nothing about the mental goings-on that brought it about.

Quietly at first, but with increasing noise and confidence, the 1950s and 60s began to witness the rise of a new branch of psychology which became known as *cognitive psychology* (Neisser 1967). This period is now referred to as the cognitive revolution.

Cognitive psychology is interested in all those mental processes in which information from the outside world, entering the brain via the senses, is processed, stored, recovered, and used. It is a field of study which is interested in how we perceive, learn, pay attention, remember, forget, decide, solve problems, reason, and use language. There is much crossover between these mental facilities.

Individuals vary a great deal in the speed and skill with which they use these mental processes. Individual variation can be affected by nature (genes) and nurture (environment) – topics that will be the subject matter of chapter 10. Past and present situations can influence our ability to learn or attend, remember or decide. What we see and perceive, take note of, or ignore are all subjects of interest to the cognitive psychologist.

Given this range of interests, it is perhaps surprising that social work hasn't taken more notice of the discipline. Of course, cognitive behavioural therapies (CBT) continue to be an important presence in social work's pantheon of interventions. Nevertheless, great swathes of cognitive psychology still appear only on the margins of social work. But we could turn to cognitive psychology with some profit, for example, to ask: how does stress affect what we see and remember? How do early experiences influence the way we perceive and interpret current events? Why do people who feel depressed see so many things negatively in a process that psychologists refer to as 'cognitive distortion'?

In a surprising number of situations, our views, judgements, and decisions are subject to a wide variety of cognitive biases (Tversky and Kahneman 1974). Left to its own devices, human reason is subject to a variety of errors and fallacies (Kahneman 2012). At one level, having a cognitive bias helps speed up our decision-making. Such biases provide us with mental short-cuts in complex, particularly ambiguous situations. However, they also run the risk of drawing us to wrong conclusions and causing us to make bad decisions. For example, if we have worked with individuals with learning disabilities who have enjoyed working outdoors in the plant nursery, we might assume, without any real evidence, that Louis, who has a learning disability and would like to be employed, would also enjoy working in the gardens.

Or we might recall a research statistic that said many men who sexually abuse children have themselves suffered sexual abuse as children, and that Mr Redcrane, who was sexually abused as a boy and who has young children who have been showing sexualized behaviour at school, must therefore be sexually abusing his children. Research statistics, although interesting and useful, can often be used in unconsciously subtle ways to bias lines of investigation, judgements and decision-making.

We might also hold biases and make assumptions at a group or societal level about people who are not of our group or hail from a different country. These unchallenged prejudices and biases can operate between men and women, Black people and White people, Christians and Muslims, the employed and the unemployed, the young and old.

The study of these cognitive attributions is a big and busy field, often referred to as 'heuristics and biases'. Most of us come to most situations with a number of inbuilt assumptions that all too often lead us down the wrong road where we make unfair judgements, faulty assessments, and poor decisions. Any profession involved in gathering information, seeking explanations, forming judgement, making decisions, and encouraging anti-oppressive practices needs to be aware of this burgeoning field of research. In social work, critically reflective practitioners have been early adopters of the kind of insights that heuristics and the study of cognitive biases can provide (Webb 2006).

Professionals like to believe that they think rationally. Rational thinking has certainly helped the professions to develop impressive bodies of knowledge which can be passed on to each new generation. Clear and logical thinking drives research and theory building. Theories help us to make sense of the buzz of experience and the tumult of behaviour. Theories create patterns and order. They help us to understand what's going on, why it's going on, and what might be done about it. To that extent, good theories, as has often been remarked, are extremely practical things to have.

However, this doesn't mean that a particular theory is tapping into some fundamental truth. Even so, if it is a good theory and a useful theory, it will help us make some kind of sense and give us some practical ideas about what it is best to do. Theories provide working and workable definitions of the world in which we find ourselves. They help build realities.

Theories are therefore practical because they find order in what otherwise might look like chaos. They help make the world intelligible. 'The flux of experience is continuous,' wrote Cupitt (1985: 20), 'and has no structure of its own. It is we who impose shape upon it to make of it a world to live in.' And indeed, it is the presence of *structure* in social work practice which turns out to be one of those things that predicts the likelihood of a more positive outcome. Clear structures are good for social work practice and clients like them. They give everyone a feeling of place and a sense of direction. 'We know where we are and together we can work out where we want to go.'

Clear structures, guided by theory, help realize the social work process. Social workers who explain the nature and purpose of the intervention at the beginning and periodically throughout the relationship help clients feel grounded and focussed. Clients respond well to social workers who begin meetings by reviewing where things have been, where they are at now, where they might go next, and how, working together, they might get there. Most thoughtful social workers are also good at answering each of the following five questions, whether asked of themselves, by their clients, or by their supervisors (Howe 1987):

1. What is the matter? (recognition of needs, identification of problems).
2. What is going on? (assessments, explanations, interpretations, diagnoses, formulations).
3. What is to be done? (objectives, goals, plans, intentions, planned outcomes).
4. How is to be done? (methods of intervention).
5. Has it been done? (evaluation of outcomes).

Different theories will give different answers to these questions, and research evidence will support some approaches more than others. Nevertheless, social workers who practice in an orderly, structured and collaborative way tend to have better outcomes and more satisfied clients.

Structure, in the sense being used here, is not necessarily specific to any theory or type of intervention. It can underpin and organize any approach, although some interventions do demand more explicitly structured ways of working than others. The presence of clear structures in practice is therefore described as a *non-specific* factor, that is, it is not specific to any theory or technique. Ideally, clearly structured interventions should be a feature of all good practice independent of the theory held and they certainly form a key part of any practice conducted by the *compleat* social worker as we shall see in the final chapter.

Feeling

Emotions steer us towards certain kinds of response when we find ourselves in difficult circumstances. Emotions arise whenever we feel uncertain about what to do. Most of our basic emotions sponsor particular behavioural responses:

> …one prompts continuation with current activity when things are going well (happiness), another prompts giving up and back-tracking when there has been loss (sadness), another prompts aggression when a goal is blocked (anger), another prompts freezing and paying attention to dangers in the environment when a threat occurs (fear). (Oatley 1998: 287)

Particular emotions therefore tend to lead to certain actions, which may or may not be appropriate or adaptive. Nevertheless, strong feelings are powerful things. They easily override whatever we happen to be thinking at the time. It is hard to concentrate on work when we have suffered the loss of a loved friend. Anger makes most of us impetuous and unreasonable.

Fear is the most powerful of all the emotions. It is a fast-acting response to perceived danger. It is to do with survival. Fear is the most dysregulating of the emotions. Thinking straight while feeling frightened is very difficult. This applies to social workers every bit as much as clients. This is why an understanding of anxiety and stress and what brings them about is so important for social workers if they are to practise with wisdom and sensitivity.

Emotionally intelligent social workers, therefore, pay great attention to their own as well as their clients' feelings (Howe 2008). Emotions can be gauged by how our bodies feel (hot and bothered, shivering with fear, aching with grief, tense with anxiety). We express emotions on our faces and in our body language. We feel emotions in the mind where we experience them subjectively.

When our feelings are running high, we can make threats, withdraw, run away, become tearful, suffer guilt, belittle, lash out. Our feelings can also be mixed or in conflict. Mixed emotions are the ones that typically confuse us and make us restless and ill at ease. A client might express fear *and* anger towards her partner and yet resist all attempts by others to help her leave him as her anxious need to be loved wins out. Both anxiety and sadness might be felt by an old person living on her own.

Given that social workers deal with people who have problems and people who are problems, it is not surprising that strong emotional agendas run through much of what they do. Emotions can be described as dysregulated or disordered, consuming or confused.

Anger, fear, and helplessness typically overwhelm parents who abuse or neglect their children. Their children, in turn, have to cope with strong feelings of fear and rejection, anger, and abandonment. Many mental health problems are presented in terms of emotions being too extreme, too pervasive, too dominant. Social workers meet clients who feel depressed, anxious, aggressive, phobic, agitated, ashamed, helpless.

To be effective, practitioners have to tune in to people's emotional distresses, emotional conflicts, and behavioural contradictions. Tuning into other people's feelings helps us to understand them, which in turn promotes empathy, which is a known good in most worker–client relationships.

However, before they can tune into other people's feelings, social workers first have to tune into, recognise, understand, and regulate their own emotions. Clients can easily make workers feel helpless or angry, loved or hated, anxious or sad. Being in touch with these feelings, making sense of them, and recognising what has caused them is a core social skill. Feelings give us clues about our own mental condition as well as the emotional state of the other. Clients who feel emotionally recognised and understood by practitioners see this as an important first step, not just in establishing the worker–client relationship, but on the road to recovery and change.

One of the key skills of social work, therefore, is to help clients stay with difficult feelings. Not until clients have acknowledged, recognised, and explored their feelings of stress, anger, anxiety, or shame can they begin to regain control. Managing feelings goes hand in hand with the ability to regulate stress, and stress regulation is a key component of the resilient, coping self.

From its inception, social work has recognised the important part that emotions play in working with and understanding other people. Emotional intelligence is basic to psychodynamically based practices. Attachment theory is sometimes referred to as a theory of affect regulation in the context of close relationships. All relationship-based approaches require practitioners to be emotionally intelligent. Cognitively inspired interventions routinely deal with clients whose ability to regulate their arousal and manage their feelings is out of their control. Social workers therefore need to be experts in both thinking about feeling and feeling about thinking.

Thinking and feeling

People who doggedly appeal to logic and reason in their dealings with others are unlikely to score well on the social skills front. They lack warmth and are often dismissed as too cerebral. Their logic might be impeccable but something appears to be missing when there is a failure to connect with people's emotions. Purely rational individuals are likely to get impatient with those who dither or behave erratically. For example, the more disorganized and mired in feelings a client appears to be, the more the rigidly rational practitioner is liable to instruct, advise, and direct. Concentrating solely on thinking rationally about planned outcomes and how they are to be achieved leads to practices that are mechanical, brief, and far too business-like. It puts people off.

Equally problematic are professionals who get caught up in their own and other people's emotions. They may be friendly. They may pick up your feelings and be emotionally affected. However, they lack direction and purpose. Clients get frustrated. It's all very well being emotionally affected but helpers need to help, and for that reflection and thought are required.

To be effective, social workers need to understand how feelings affect thought and how thoughts trigger feelings. In fact for Tompkins (1962: 112), 'reason without affect would be impotent, affect without reason would be blind'. Over recent years there has been a lot of research by cognitive psychologists looking at how emotional states affect mental processes. There is constant interaction between cognition and emotion in our everyday lives. Our moods affect what we see and remember. Strong feelings influence the type of decision we are liable to make. Emotions colour how we judge people.

It is also true that the way we cognitively weigh up situations triggers emotional responses (Lazarus 1982). The thought of giving a speech in public induces feelings of panic. Attending a case conference in which parents think everyone assumes they have neglected their children causes feelings of shame. A loss of home support services creates worry as well as anger. The installation of a stair lift is greeted with pleasure and relief. The way we appraise a situation invariably involves an emotional response. And the appraisal we make is governed by a whole host of factors including our personality, upbringing, experiences, beliefs, hopes, plans and circumstances.

Those who cannot regulate their emotions, said Salovey and Mayer (1990: 201), become slaves to them. The ability to understand and manage our own and other people's feelings not only defines good mental health but also whether or not we are likely to be socially competent and skilled in relationships.

Social work therefore requires practitioners to understand their own and other people's emotions. The ability to think about and manage feeling states, both in the self and others, defines the *emotionally intelligent* social worker (Howe 2008; Ingram 2013). It also becomes the goal of many types of social work intervention. Helping clients recognise, understand, and manage their feelings becomes an important aim of practice. Bateman and Fonagy (2011) call this capacity to think about and regulate one's own and other people's emotional and psychological states *mentalizing*, and they have gone on to develop a whole evidence-based intervention programme based on it which they call mentalized-based treatment or MBT (Allen et al. 2008; Bateman and Fonagy 2006).

Emotions and their regulation therefore underpin much of what clients want and what social workers do. The inability to manage and regulate strong feeling states is stressful, and few of us cope well under stress. If we are to help clients cope, then we have to support them as they seek to recognise, think about, and control their own and other people's feelings, particularly in the context of close relationships.

The aggressive partner tries to manage his anger. The neglectful mother hopes to rise above her depression and think more positively about herself and her children. A recently unemployed physically disabled man looks for support as he grieves the loss of the job he has held for the last 14 years. A depressed man is taught to recognise, monitor, and then challenge his tendency to slip into 'automatic negative thinking' whenever he contemplates a new situation, the idea of changing, or imagining a better future (Beck et al. 1987).

We are beings who think *and* feel and it's not possible to divorce the two. The intelligent worker seeks the wisdom that thinking about feelings gives us. The *compleat* social worker is an effective practitioner who can build a therapeutic alliance as well as be clear about structure. Her practice is one in which empathy runs alongside purpose and intent. And her emotional intelligence gives her the key to unlock the power of evidence-based interventions.

9
The Past and the Future

What Should Be the Focus of Social Work?

Introduction

Social work has had an on–off relationship with the past. There is a good case to be made that the best way clients can sort out problems in the present is for them to revisit and resolve problems in the past. If they can get past hurts and pains sorted, these old feelings no longer have the power to disturb the present.

For example, we might argue that before a parent can improve the care of his own children, he has to recognise and resolve the painful memories associated with his own abusive childhood. Or the mental health client incapacitated by anxiety might need to explore her own troubled history if she is to get to the bottom of her current worries and distress.

However, there are equally persuasive arguments that dwelling on the past isn't really helpful. Problems are best solved by seeing what changes can be made in the present in order to bring about improvements in the future. We are where we are and there's no point in dwelling on the past. Time to move on.

For example, the overprotective father of an increasingly anxious little girl is helped to curb his tendency to see danger and threat every time his daughter attempts to be independent. As he manages to contain and not give voice to his worries, so her anxiety decreases. The reasons for his over-protectiveness are of no practical interest. Or the woman suffering social phobia is encouraged gradually, step by step, to journey further and further from the house until she can visit the local shops on her own. She is taught relaxation exercises which she must use every time she feels her level of anxiety rising above zero. Thus, a focus on the future motivates people to make changes in the present.

The past

Certainly for those who work with parents, children, violent offenders, and clients with mental health problems, it comes as no surprise when they hear that their clients suffered abuse and neglect or loss and rejection in their childhoods. It can also be the case that the willingness of adult children to help care for their elderly and frail parents can sometimes depend on how they were cared for and loved when they were growing up.

There is a long tradition of philosophers, psychologists, and novelists believing that the past remains active in the present. Our memories colour our feelings; our feelings affect our behaviour.

A character in one of Anita Brookner's novels reflects that 'once a thing is known it can never be unknown. It can only be forgotten' (Brookner 1982: 84). And as forgotten memories haven't really gone away, we are also told that 'Those who cannot remember the past are condemned to repeat it' (Santayana 1905: 284). Past traumas get re-enacted. In one of her books, Iris Murdoch, a novelist and philosopher, writes 'We are human beings... We can't just live in the present' (Murdoch 1968: 82). One 'must do something about the past. It doesn't just cease to be. It goes on existing and affecting the present, and in new and different ways...' (Murdoch 1968: 125).

Connecting with the past also gives a narrative sense of self, a self that continues over time and through time. In her 'not quite' memoir, the 80-year-old novelist Penelope Lively writes that 'if you have no sense of the past, no access to the historical narrative, you are afloat, untethered; you cannot see yourself as a part of the narrative, you cannot place yourself within a context' (Lively 2013: 137). Those who have gaps in their story often say they feel incomplete or troubled. Adults adopted as toddlers wonder about their lives prior to placement. Women who suffered the trauma of sexual abuse as children often find it difficult to remember vast tracts of their unhappy childhoods.

Psychoanalysts explore how the external world of people and relationships help shape our internal world of feelings and thought. And it is in that internal world that past experiences remain, for good or ill, conscious or unconscious, understood or unrecognised, blocked or denied. Fragments of powerful past traumas – of sexual abuse, severe neglect, danger from parents, feeling unloved and unlovable, loss – can break unbidden into present relationships where they wreak havoc. Feelings of aggression, fear, sadness, and dissociation can suddenly explode into the present as unconscious reminders trigger old memories. Clients are generally unaware where these strong, disruptive feelings are coming from, and so they remain unprocessed beneath the surface, liable to crash destructively into any present relationship.

When past experiences distort current experiences they lead to what, on the face of it, looks like irrational, often self-defeating behaviour. How else can you explain a man's violent and abusive attitude to every woman he meets, whether partner or practitioner? And why does a client escape from one relationship with a needy, alcoholic, aggressive man only to end up in another relationship with an equally needy, substance-abusing violent partner?

> Although emotional disturbance and the power of the unconscious internal world have been pushed to the edges of social work training, they are central aspects of our clients' lives and make their presence powerfully felt in the relationships between clients and workers. (Bower 2005: 3)

The therapeutic task in such cases is to bring buried, often unconscious feelings out into the open so that they can be recognised, reworked, and understood. Only when the unresolved past becomes the resolved present do symptoms disappear. Gaining insight into what goes on in our minds is liberating. It helps us recover control over the meaning we give to our own experiences, and thus frees us from the shackles of the past.

However, for most of us this is easier said than done. We tend to resist dealing with difficult memories in which either unpleasant things happened to us or we did unpleasant things to other people. Whenever these difficult, often painful memories threaten to invade the present, we are liable to get *defensive*; we become angry, get niggled, grow distant, feel anxious, or fall ill.

Freud was one of the first to recognise that patients often relate with their therapists in ways which were similar to the way they related to people who were important to them in their past, especially parents. What we see is clients *transferring* aspects of these early relationships onto the worker (or indeed, workers transferring aspects of their early relationships onto the client). Bits of the forgotten past are inappropriately and unconsciously repeated in present relationships (Britton 2005). The self-aware, reflective worker is alert to these processes. She picks up clues about how the client's relationship past continues to distort their relationship present.

Workers who can *contain* their client's raw emotions allow clients a glimpse of a safer world, one in which painful memories and hurtful feelings can be looked at, recognised, named, thought about, processed, and tamed (Bion 1963). Many clients have never experienced a relationship with someone who cares for and protects them, someone who helps them contain and manage powerful feelings of sadness, anger, and fear.

It is within the safety of a secure relationship with the worker that clients can slowly begin to manage their difficult feelings. The unconscious is made conscious. Getting this unprocessed material out into the open and helping clients gain insight helps them work through and make realistic sense of difficult, often painful memories so that they no longer have the power to distort and disfigures relationships in the present. Freud (1914) described the process as remembering, repeating and 'working through'. The previously intolerable becomes tolerable. Rather than be at the mercy of unruly emotions, clients learn to self-regulate. Control returns and stress disappears.

A father begins to remember and acknowledge that his mother didn't love him or protect him as a boy. She laughed when his stepfather beat him and belittled him. At some deep, previously unconscious level he had learnt to defend himself against his feelings of vulnerability and the fear and pain inflicted by his stepfather, and the humiliation felt in relationship with his mother. No woman was ever going to hurt or humiliate him again. No woman would be allowed to get emotionally close. Intimacy and trust were dangerous then, and so foolish now. The best form of defence is therefore attack and so now he belittles, intimidates, and abuses any woman who he feels might be getting emotionally close to him – by loving him, being like a mother, being strong and protective, being interested. This includes women who are lovers, social workers, health workers, and teachers. The only way to keep them at emotional bay, and so not get hurt, was to verbally, emotionally, and even physically attack them and dismiss them. Only when these ancient, unresolved, hurtful memories become recognised and understood do they lose their power to trouble the present.

Attachment theory also takes a particular interest in the relationship history of clients. The belief is that to make sense of current relationship styles and approaches, we need to look at how people experienced and adapted to previously emotionally significant relationships, particularly when they were children. Most people will have enjoyed 'good enough' parenting. This allows their 'natural' personality and temperament, based on their genetic make-up, to be fully and roundedly expressed (Howe 2011).

But children who receive 'suboptimal' parenting, parenting which is rejecting, neglectful, unloving, or abusive, have to adopt a variety of adaptive strategies to survive and try and stay on the right side of otherwise dangerous carers. Unless their caregiving experiences improve, these children are likely to take forward the defensive strategies and distortions which became necessary to help them survive the relational trauma of their childhoods into all future relationships, including those with their partners, children, and professional workers with whom they have to deal (Howe 2005, 2011).

The feelings of helplessness, anger, and distress which many abusive and neglectful adults feel when caring for their own children only make sense when we consider their own difficult and traumatic childhoods. The parents' emotional past distorts and disfigures their emotional present. If social workers are to understand and work with these parents, they need to take a great interest in the parents' social and relationship histories. Only by making sense of the parents themselves can social workers make sense of, and stay with the turbulent, chaotic, and dangerous environments that these mothers and fathers generate. The ability to make sense of, and emotionally contain these very damaged people offers them the chance of psychological change and a glimpse of a safer kind of parenting.

It is in relationship with an emotionally attuned, psychologically mind-minded worker that parents can begin to think about difficult feelings. The past is remembered, and only then can it be processed, reworked and its power to disturb curbed. There are many preliminary techniques that can aid this kind of work including genograms, ecomaps, social histories, and life road maps (Parker 2013). These aids help people locate themselves in their own story. They help fill in the narrative. They give clients a context in which they can begin to understand themselves. Making sense of who you, where you are, and where you have come from is often one of the first steps clients take in their attempts to regain control of the meaning of their own experience.

Of course, not all memories are bad. Happy memories and vivid memories can evoke the past in ways that give continuity to our sense of self. *Reminiscence therapy*, particularly with older people and patients with dementia, takes advantage of our ability to recall important and meaningful experiences. Life events are recalled and explored (Webster 2002; Gibson 2011). Reflection on what is being remembered is a key component of the therapy.

Memories can be evoked by film and photographs, songs and everyday objects, people and places. Sharing memories in a group can be particularly powerful as people recall feelings and events. Reconnecting one's present self with one's past self can bring peace of mind as well as a more solid sense of who one is. When used well, reminiscence therapy helps people age happily and with success.

And life-story work and the making of life-story books with children in foster care or who have been adopted is standard practice (Ryan and Walker 2007). The work has several purposes. It can be a simple record of the child's history, family, and current life journey. It can also help children make sense of and process past events and the feelings associated with them. By understanding their past children can be helped to live more fully in the present and so approach the future with a greater sense of completeness and confidence (Rees 2009).

The future

We are where we are. To change the future we have to make changes in the present. We need to be forward-looking rather than dwell on the past. We need to take an honest look at what we are doing now and if it looks unhelpful or is part of the problem, then we must make a determined effort to change our current behaviour, mindset, or situation.

Behaviourists set about helping people change their current behaviour to solve their present problems. And insofar as thinking affects behaviour, *cognitively oriented* practitioners seek to change what people are thinking now in order to change their future behaviour.

Ecologically minded professionals try to solve problems by changing people's relationship with their environment. The environment might include other people's behaviour, services, income, housing, policy, or attitudes.

A strong emphasis on dealing with the here and now has risen up the social work agenda over the last few decades. It chimes with the political times. There has been an ideological shift from seeing people as passive victims of their past (unhappy childhoods, broken homes, poor schooling) to believing they can be active architects of their own future. Positivity replaces pathology. Clients must not think of themselves as victims but rather as agents of their own destiny. A change in behaviour and a positive attitude can work wonders. Can you do it? Yes you can!

Early adopters of viewing the future from the perspective of the present were practitioners who used behavioural modification techniques. The argument is that much of our current behaviour is shaped by the way the environment, particularly the environment of other people, responds to what we do. Change the environment, either before or after the display of a given behaviour, and it is possible to either increase or decrease that behaviour.

If a residential worker is repeatedly critical of a client who has a learning disability because the client finds it hard to work out the right money for his bus fare, that client will either stop wanting to travel into the city, avoid that worker, or both. If the client is to recover his confidence and once again catch a bus on his own into the city, the new worker will have to teach the client money-counting skills, praise and reinforce every success in counting the money correctly, and gradually build up the client's confidence as he practices each step of the process, from gathering the money, to walking to the bus stop, and, finally, catching the bus. By changing the way the environment responds, in this case the introduction of encouraging responses by the worker, so the behaviour of the client changes. The client's behaviour is modified by rewarding, that is reinforcing, every behaviour that helps him recover the skills involved, in this case travelling on his own into the town centre.

Two of the sharpest examples of these forward-looking, positive approaches to helping clients meet future needs and solve present problems are solution-focussed brief therapies and strengths-based approaches.

Strengths and resilience-based approaches recognise that individuals and families do survive and overcome setbacks, major as well as minor. These approaches tap into people's innate abilities to cope and carry on, in spite of what life has thrown at them. Given the stresses and strains under which many clients live, rather than see their lives as ones of incompetence and failure, practitioners might be impressed with their ability to survive and get by. It takes some skill and resourcefulness to manage with little money in poor housing with four children. It demands a lot of effort and determination to negotiate everyday life if you have a severe mental illness.

The job of the social worker is to recognise, support, and promote the client's strengths, skills, and resources. In helping clients acknowledge their strengths, social workers encourage people to see themselves in a more positive light, as people who have succeeded, often against the odds, and therefore as people who can succeed again. The focus is on what has gone right and not on what has gone wrong. Thus, a social worker might say:

> Three days this week you managed to get the children to school on time *and* not spend any money on alcohol. That's fantastic. So tell me, what made the difference? Take me through what happened, what you did and how you felt on those days that made you so successful. You've clearly got it in you to make it work, so let's stop and see what strengths you were drawing on that helped you get your act together. I bet the kids know! What do you think they'd say if I asked them what made the difference?

Out of such exchanges, a shared assessment emerges. And based on the agreed recognition and understanding of the client's strengths, behaviourally concrete goals can be set, and plans made.

By marrying the hopes of clients with their revealed strengths, workers boost people's belief in themselves, that they can make a difference. The strengths-based approach helps clients face the future by exploring *possibilities*. Having survived adversity means that clients do have the strength and resources to cope with current problems. By helping them recognise what they did that worked before, clients can begin to see themselves as survivors, as copers, as resilient. The approach is collaborative. It encourages personal responsibility. And it celebrates an optimistic, 'can do' attitude that can inspire and motivate not only individuals but also families and whole communities (Saleeby 2008; Sullivan 2012).

Past, present, and future

In practice, most social workers slip naturally in their interests between past, present, and future. Certainly when working with children and families, it is difficult to make sense of many current difficulties without having some idea of people's troubled histories. There is also a good deal of evidence that many adults with mental health problems, including borderline personality disorders and anxiety disorders, suffered abuse, neglect, and trauma during key phases of their childhood (Cicchetti 2015). And many older people diagnosed with depression or dementia are helped when they revisit past happy memories.

But social workers are faced with doing something about problems in the present by people who want things to be better in the future. It is often the case that although an intervention itself is solution-focussed and forward-looking, and as such takes no cognisance of the past, the relationship that must be established with the client in order for the intervention to work requires an interest to be taken in the person's story to date. Before clients can engage in collaboratively based, behaviourally-targeted treatments, they need to feel understood and accepted. The message is: to work with me, you must first know me, and to know me you must be interested in me and how I got to be where I am today.

There are interventions which deliberately explore the links between past experiences, present problems, and future behaviours. For example, interventions that promote positive parenting seek to resolve relationship issues based in the past, improve parenting behaviours in the present, and increase children's feelings of security in the future.

These attachment and evidence-based interventions recognise that children need their parents to be a haven of safety at times of need, and also a secure base from which they can explore and engage with the wider world of people and things (also see chapter 12). In order for parents to be experienced as safe havens and secure bases, they need to be able to tune into their children's minds and see and feel the world from their children's point of view. Parents who are good at this are described as sensitive, attuned, mind-minded, and empathic. They are people who understand the intimate links between what we do and how we feel, how we behave and what we think. In other words, their skills as social players are the result of their ability to see the world of behaviour from a psychological point of view. To make sense of people we have to be interested in what goes on in their heads.

Good enough parents tune into their children at this mind-to-mind level. They find their children psychologically both meaningful and fascinating. And children who have been on the receiving end of empathic, *mentalizing* parenting become, in turn, empathic, mentalizing people, skilled at relationships and likely to enjoy good mental health. From the word go, children of mentalizing caregivers become very active partners in the parent–child relationship.

However, some parents do not interact with their children at this 'mental state' level. Because of their own troubled childhoods, they lack the capacity to see their children as burgeoning psychological little beings in their own right. As a result, these parents find it difficult to make sense of, or even be interested in their children's behaviour, their wants, intentions, hopes, fears, frustrations, and joys.

Not being able to understand or reflect on their own or their children's emotions, parents quickly feel either helpless or hostile and so become either neglectful or abusive. And if your parents find it difficult to make psychological sense of you, you will find it difficult to make psychological sense of yourself and other people. Thus, children who suffer neglect and abuse are at increased risk of a range of behavioural and mental health problems.

The Promoting Positive Parenting programme works with parents who appear to be neglecting their young children at this level of attuned, mind-to-mind, reflective caregiving. The programme addresses issues from the parents' past. But it also aims to improve their parenting skills in the future (Juffer et al. 2008). Workers therefore talk about helping parents make changes at the psychological and *representational* level (that is, help them make sense of their past), and also support them to make *behavioural* changes in the present.

In some versions of these home-based programmes, parents are helped to think about and reflect on their own childhood experiences and how they were parented. For many parents, it soon becomes apparent that they appear to be parenting their children the way they were parented when they were young. As they begin to recognise and explore their own feelings and relationship history, they begin to recognise that if they are to parent their own children with skill, sensitivity, insight, joy, and pleasure, they will have to reflect on and re-process many of the distressed thoughts and feelings associated with their own childhoods that have been triggered by becoming parents themselves.

However, the programme also aims to improve parents' sensitivity and attunement by recognising, celebrating, enjoying, praising, and reinforcing any current glimmers of empathy and attunement between parent and child. First, the intervention video-records inter-actions between parents and their children. It is during the playback sessions of these videos that workers help parents see and enjoy those moments when there *was* a 'mental' connection between them and their babies, however fleeting. In effect, the workers are *behaviourally reinforcing* each and every display of parental sensitivity and attune-ment. The research evidence shows that such feedback sessions are good at improving parental sensitivity, and as a result children's sense of security and social skills increase.

Social workers are time travellers who should feel comfortable exploring the past, assessing the present, and planning the future. These temporal skills apply equally well when working with individ-uals and families as well as with groups and communities. To the extent that we are products of our past, changing our thoughts, feel-ings, and behaviour in the present are good ways of creating, and recreating better futures.

10
Nature and Nurture
How to Make Sense of Human Behaviour

Introduction

Are we born the way we are? Or is it experience that shapes us?

Those who believe that our personalities and behaviours are in-born argue that biology determines who we are and what we do. It is our genetic make-up that drives our physical, medical, and psychological destiny. Nature rules.

In contrast, there are those who think that life as lived has the biggest influence on our personality and behaviour. We are shaped by our experiences. The world, especially the world of other people, supports and sponsors our development from the day we are born. Nurture rules.

For many centuries, people were inclined to take one side or the other. The nature–nurture debate divided scientists and philosophers, educationalists and politicians into those who believed that biology is destiny and those who didn't. And as the underlying sciences informing these debates began to change, so the language of the debates also changed. People began to talk of not only of nature and nurture, but also genes and environment, the biological and the social.

At first glance, it might seem inevitable that social workers would find themselves on the side of nurture. Their brief is to change the social world in order to improve people's lot and make their lives better. Improving the childrearing skills of distressed parents helps keep children safe and promotes young people's emotional development. Ignoring someone's bad behaviour and rewarding their good behaviour is an effective way to change their antisocial ways. Improving the quality of a client's accommodation reduces their feelings of stress.

By reshaping the way the social environment responds, you reshape the behaviour of those with whom you work. In this sense, social workers are social engineers, working to change people's behaviour by changing their social and physical environments. The professional world, here, is one of cure and change.

However, on second glance, it is also true that much of what social workers do is support those whose needs are simply the result of a biological given. Nature has dealt certain individuals a particular hand. For example, as a result of some neurodevelopmental disorder, a child has a severe learning disability. Or a genetic condition is the cause of someone's physical disability or mental illness.

To help some people cope well and function in the world in which they find themselves, social workers become service providers. The services they provide are typically tangible. A package of supportive care for the parents of a boy diagnosed with autism. House adaptations for the woman with a physical disability. Or even a brief episode of compulsory treatment in a psychiatric hospital for a young man with schizophrenia whose behaviour is becoming a danger both to himself and others.

However, current thinking about nature and nurture paints a much more dynamic picture, one in which social workers can and do play a very active part.

Nature

A biological view of the way we develop suggests that it has already been mapped out in our genetic blueprint. We are pre-programmed to be a certain height, to have a particular temperament, to possess certain talents. This is a form of rationalism. We contain within our make-up the rules for our own organization and progress. When these are worked out, the end product is a logical deduction from the initial premises. Our appearance, talents, and traits are a priori. They appear without being derived from experience. We are born with the principles of our development built into our genetic blueprint. As we grow and develop, we see an unfolding of these inherent properties.

This being the case, we define our own experience, rather than experience defining us. We make sense of the world using structures and capacities that are innate, that are a property of our essential biological make-up.

'One of the most dramatic developments in the behavioural sciences during the last few decades,' write Plomin et al. (2013), 'is the increasing recognition and appreciation of the important contribution of genetic factors to behavior' (p. xvii). It is biology that makes us different. It is our genetic inheritance that determines whether we are musical, sporty, cautious, or short-tempered. It is genes that govern much of our educational success.

This is why identical twins, who share 100 per cent of their genes, are much more similar – physically, cognitively, verbally, academically – than non-identical twins who only share 50 per cent of their genes (Bartels 2007).

It also the case that many mental health disorders carry a heavy genetic load. Although the world will react to whatever natural characteristics we have, these characteristics are present from birth. The most straightforward examples of biology determining development are the single-gene disorders, including Huntington's disease. Here, the disorder clearly runs in families suggesting a high level of heritability.

However, in most other cases in which behavioural development is thought to be influenced by biology, multiple genes are involved, interacting in complex ways. In most cases, no single gene on its own predicts a particular behavioural or mental health trait or outcome.

For example, the lifetime risk of developing schizophrenia for the general population is about 1 per cent. However, the risk of developing schizophrenia is certainly higher, possibly up to 10 per cent, if one or both parents have been diagnosed with the illness but still, most children of schizophrenic parents don't in fact develop the condition (Heston 1966; Stefansson et al. 2009). This suggests that a genetic risk needs to be present in order to develop schizophrenia, but it is only when certain combinations of these risk-increasing genes are present that the chances of developing the disease increase.

Biology explains why siblings, raised by the same parents in the same family, can be so different in terms of their personalities, interests, and aptitudes. And conversely, an identical genetic make-up explains why identical twins raised apart so often look alike, dress alike, behave alike, and achieve alike (Asbury and Plomin 2013; Plomin et al. 2013).

Those impressed by nature really can't understand the antipathy shown by died-in-the-wool nurturists to the part that genes play in shaping who we are and how we are. If genes determine eye colour, height, and skin tone, why not personality, temperament, and aptitude?

Nurture

In contrast, theories based on nurture emphasize the part that *experience* plays in shaping behaviour and development. There are no genetically inherited principles that guide development. It is the accumulation of experience that builds up our behavioural repertoire. The individual infant arrives in the world as a *tabula rasa* – a blank slate upon which life writes the developmental script. Our relationship with the environment is therefore entirely *empirical*. Experiences, entering the brain through the senses, build up our knowledge of the world creating our particular characteristics. The organizing principles that inform how we make sense of the world are inherent in the properties of the world. They are not *a priori*; they are not initially present in our cognitive structures.

The social and psychological sciences have had a long tradition of exploring how the environment affects people's lives, for good or ill. Psychologists have helped us to understand how other people's reactions shape our behaviour, both as children and adults. Praising and encouraging a behaviour is likely to increase the likelihood of us displaying and developing that behaviour in the future. Loving and interested parents build up their children's self-esteem. Involved and emotionally reflective carers increase young people's social skills and understanding.

Even though we are nervous when we stand and give a formal speech to our colleagues, if the audience smiles and claps enthusiastically we are likely to feel encouraged and so gain in confidence. But if people look bored, are not listening, and are busy sending text messages, mock or belittle our efforts, our confidence will plummet and we are unlikely to want to repeat the experience again.

We see dozens of examples every day in which people shape other people's behaviour by the way they react and respond. Parents may or may not react with interest to whatever their children are doing. A father might ridicule and humiliate his son as he tries but fails to kick a ball with skill or when the boy says that he would like to have ballet lessons.

On a bigger scale, we see the stress suffered as families struggle on low wages living in substandard housing, and how stress can increase the risk of depression, substance abuse, and aggression. Or we recognise the deep and damaging effects of discrimination based on sex, race, religion, age, and physical ability.

Many of social work's most influential theories are nurture-based or environmentally inspired. The list is long and includes social learning theory, attachment theory, ecological approaches, and radical models of social injustice and economic inequality.

Nature and nurture

Current thinking sees nature and nurture *interacting*. It is not a matter of so much nature and so much nurture; it is not a simple a mixture of the two. Rather, we see a complex, interesting, much more dynamic *interplay* between nature and nurture, between our genes and our experience of the environment.

Ridley (2003) talks of 'nature *via* nurture.' He observes that 'Genes are designed to take their cues from nurture... nature is designed for nurture' (Ridley 2003: 4). Simple determinism (the idea that all characteristics of the person are 'hard-wired' by the genome) and simple reductionism (the view that all we need is complete knowledge of the human genome sequence) should both be avoided.

The whole process of being, becoming and behaving is dynamic. There are continuous interactions, or more exactly *transactions*, between the individual and his or her environment. The environment affects the individual who affects the environment, and so on in a never-ending series of dynamic transactions.

> The problem of development is the problem of the development of new structures and activity patterns from the resolution of the interaction of existing ones, within the organism and its internal environment, and between the organism and its outer environment. At any stage of development, the new features emerge from the interactions within the current stage and the environment. The interaction out of which the organism develops is not one, as is often said, between heredity and environment. It is between organism and environment! And the organism is different at each stage of its development. (Lehrman 1970 cited in Bateson and Martin 2000: 89).

Developmental scientists now see our individual selves forming as we relate and engage with the world in which we find ourselves, especially the world of other people. Indeed, the discipline of *behavioural genetics* is as much interested in the environment as it is in genes. Genes influence behaviour but they do not simply pre-programme it. Things at both the genetic and environmental levels are certainly much more complicated. And as a result, they are also much more interesting.

For example, genes influence things such as temperament, interests, and aptitude. But an individual's temperament, interests, and aptitude also influence their environment.

If a child has a musical aptitude, the chances are that her parents will spot this and react by providing the child with opportunities to develop her talent. They might buy her an instrument and send her for music lessons. As a result of the parents' response to their child's interests, the environment changes and it will begin to have its own effect on the girl's abilities and development. This as an example of gene–environment interaction, in this case one in which the individual *evokes* an environmental response, a response that augments the child's genetic character (Plomin et al. 1977; Rutter 2005).

However, it might be the case that the child's parents fail to pick up on her musical interests, in which case we might see the young girl begin actively to seek out her own environment. She might be determined to join the school orchestra, save up her pocket money and buy her own flute, or become friends with someone who just happens to have a piano on which she is allowed to play. Plomin et al. (1977) and Rutter (2005) call this *active gene–environment correlation* in which the individual actively seeks out and creates their own environment. We see examples of this all the time as children become actively interested in a particular sport, hobby, skill, academic subject, or group of friends. As individuals we therefore play an active role in selecting, modifying, and creating our own environments.

In this sense, Rutter (2005) suggests that genes actually cause environments. And as we get older and have more freedom and opportunities to seek out our own worlds, so genes begin to influence more of our behaviour. This might sound counterintuitive. But on reflection, it makes sense. When we are very young, we have little choice over the environments our parents create for us. But as we get older, we begin to choose our own friends, pursue our own interests, read our own books. Thus, genes influence our environment, and in turn the environment begins to shape the kind of person we are.

In fact, behavioural geneticists recognise two types of environment: *shared* and *non-shared*. One way of thinking about the difference between these two environments is to ask 'Why are siblings different?' (Plomin et al. 2001). On the face of it, you might imagine that because siblings share 50 per cent of their genes, are raised by the same parents, eat similar food, go on family holidays together, and probably attend the same school, they ought to be much more alike than they are. But it turns out that most of the environment that siblings experience is non-shared.

For example, children with an easy temperament are less challenging to parents than children who have a difficult temperament (Kagan 1994). To some extent then, we might say that children provoke particular parenting styles. The same parents are therefore likely to interact with each of their children slightly differently. Parents and their parenting skills change over time, and so where you are in the birth order makes an environmental difference. As you get older you develop different interests, friendship groups, and school experiences. Parents, siblings, and others begin to react to your particular temperament and character. Thus, as you grow older, the non-shared environment becomes more and more significant in its influence. This goes some way to explain why siblings are different.

So, whether its gene–environment correlations or non-shared environments, we see highly complex and fascinating interactions between genes and their environment. This insight is being used to make sense of a wide range of human behaviours and conditions.

For example, although certain types of gene have been linked to the increased risk of depression, individuals carrying these forms of the gene also need to experience one, and often more environmental life stressors (Caspi et al. 2003). People who do not carry these forms of the gene, even if they meet major life stressors, are unlikely to get depressed. However, individuals who inherit two short forms of this particular gene allele and who do experience serious stress find themselves at much higher risk of becoming clinically depressed.

Many life stressors coupled with the risky gene have been identified, including early loss of a mother along with the relative absence of good-quality care subsequent to that loss, poor-quality and unsupportive emotional relationships in adulthood, loss of a job, being married to someone who criticizes and belittles you, and the loss of home and country (Brown and Harris 1978; Brown 1998). Underlying many of these stressors are feelings of powerlessness, entrapment, humiliation, loss of a loved one, and a lack of control over one's life.

Similar gene–environment interactions have been looked at to help make sense of a variety of conditions, including substance abuse, lifestyle choices, obesity, Obsessive Compulsive Disorders, and anxiety disorders (Plomin et al. 2013). It seems that in order to make sense of most behaviours, we need to recognise the dynamic relationship between nature and nurture, genes and environment. We are born into a particular world with our own unique genetic make-up. We react to that particular world which in turn reacts to us, and so we are propelled through life along our own unique pathway. In this analysis, the quality and character of the environment, particularly the social environment, is as important, if not more so, than the cards that biology has dealt us. Thus, social workers, who are experts in bringing about changes in the social environment, find themselves playing a key role in helping people find and follow the best life courses possible.

Developmentalists have also turned to the relatively new science of *epigenetics*. This science recognises that genes have to interact with their environment before they can be 'expressed', and before they can be either switched on or switched off (Allis et al. 2007; Tollefsbol 2011). It is the quality and character of the environment that determines how genes get expressed, and whether or not they get switched on. In good-quality environments, children will therefore achieve their genetic potential and fully realize whatever strengths and talents nature has given them.

The science of epigenetics has particular relevance for social workers. The environment continues to have a profound bearing on how genes are expressed as we develop over the lifecourse. Life events have the capacity to alter the behaviour of our genes by affecting the behaviour of chemicals in our bodies. These chemicals are part of the 'methyl' group of molecules which can attach themselves to our DNA in a process described as *DNA methylation*. Thus, gene expression and methylation are sensitive to the environment.

When methyl does become attached to DNA molecules it can inhibit, turn down, or block the production of a whole range of key

proteins, many of which are involved in dealing with disease, distur-
bance, and general wear and tear. In effect, the methyl molecule
silences the gene's expression. Conversely, when a gene is not methy-
lated, the gene can 'turn on' and express itself (Plomin et al. 2013: 147).

The quality of our *physical* environment therefore affects the way
our genes get switched either on or off. Diet and pollution, smoking
and alcohol, drugs and medicine, for example, can have a deep, long-
term effect on our biology and DNA, influencing how tall we grow or
how susceptible we might be to a whole range of diseases, including
cancer, diabetes, and heart problems (Spector 2012).

Perhaps even more interesting is that the quality of our *social*,
psychological, and *emotional* environment can also affect the way our
genes get expressed. There is growing evidence that early life experiences of stress, emotional neglect, rejection, and trauma increase the
long-term risks of adults developing not only mental health problems but also one or more of a range of serious health conditions
including heart disease, diabetes, and cancer, even when controlling
for such things as an unhealthy lifestyle. For any two given populations sharing exactly the same risky lifestyle, such as smoking, those
with early histories of emotional neglect and trauma are even more
likely than their non-neglected counterparts to suffer serious physical ill-health in adulthood. It appears that emotional stress affects
certain genes and their expression, which, in turn, affects the
immune and stress response systems. When these systems are
compromised, the body deals less effectively with everyday risks such
as being infected by a virus, drinking too much alcohol, eating a poor
diet, suffering a relationship breakdown, being in a violent partner-
ship, or dealing with worry.

The related science of psychoneuroimmunology (PNI or the study
of how psychology, the brain, the nervous system, and the immune
system all interconnect) also links early caregiving experiences,
emotional states and their regulation with the immune system and its
functioning, and ultimately people's physical health. In short,
emotional stress, particularly if experienced chronically, adversely
affects our immune system. Children and adults who suffer major
trauma and chronic stress are therefore at increased risk of disease
and illness (Sapolsky 1996).

Of course, it also the case that people who experience anxiety,
stress, anger, and depression as a result of poor-quality caregiving or

severe poverty and deprivation in early life are more likely to develop risky lifestyle habits. These lifestyle choices can represent inappropriate attempts to deal with feelings of hurt, pain, and confusion. These are people who are more likely to drink excessively, take drugs, and self-harm in their attempts to deal with painful memories and unmanageable feelings. But these are the same people who have compromised stress and immune systems as a result of epigenetic changes to their DNA. Thus, the least robust people, biologically speaking, face the biggest risks, environmentally speaking.

The richer and more nurturing the environment, the more we can help people achieve their genetic potential. Genes plus protective, optimal environments, particularly high-quality social environments, promote good mental health and help build resilience.

The more deprived, damaging, and dangerous the environment, the less chance people have of realizing their strengths, talents, and aptitudes. Extreme suboptimal environments increase the risk of people suffering poor mental health and becoming more vulnerable as they face risks of one kind or another.

It is the job of social workers to help clients improve their environments (more money, better housing, good diet, decent nurseries, supportive aids and adaptations), reduce stress (better relationships, less danger, more safety), increase their strengths, and cope better. Although the genes inherited are as they are, the world in which they express themselves can be made better. By attending to nurture, social workers optimize nature. By tackling the environment, including the social environment, social workers help clients realize their genetic best.

The social brain

The brain's development is also a product of the interaction between nature and nurture. The brain mediates the relationship between the world outside (physical and social) and our world inside (biological and psychological).

The brain is a complex mass of nearly 100 billion highly interconnected cells known as neurons, vast numbers of which are genetically programmed to 'make sense' of the world in which the brain finds itself. This world includes the physical, interpersonal, and cultural. The human infant has to make sense of this world if he or she is going to survive and function well. There is an evolutionary advantage in understanding how one's self and the world in which one finds oneself works.

We are therefore genetically precoded to engage with our environment, but that coding does not, a priori, tell us how to make sense of experience. What, however, is deeply significant is that although the brain is programmed to make sense of experience, it needs to be exposed to the experiences of which it needs to make sense before it can make of those experiences. At birth, particular neurons are sitting there waiting to be stimulated by particular environmental experiences. These experiences include all that life can throw at us – speech and language, visual stimulation, movements of objects in space, numbers.

For example, as those bits of the left-hand side of the brain genetically programmed to make sense of language are stimulated by the child hearing sounds and words, the neurons in that part of the brain begin to make connections with the thousands of other neurons that surround it. The vast number of connections that each neuron makes with other neurons leads to the development of neural networks. In the case of those stimulated by language, we see the growth of networks that become more and more adept at processing language. And lo, the child begins to understand talk as well as becoming an active member of the speech community.

As Donald Hebb famously said, neurons that fire together wire together. The corollary is that if the 'expectant' neurons are not stimulated at the right time, there is the danger that they will disappear or be 'pruned'. This prompted Hebb to add that in terms of development, as far as any one neuron is concerned 'use it or lose it'. This is yet another reminder that children need rich, stimulating environments if they are to enjoy optimal neurological development.

In summary, environments first have to be experienced in order to stimulate the brain to develop structures capable of perceiving and interpreting those same environments. The brain is therefore often described as a self-organizing developmental structure.

One of the most important lessons from a social work point of view is to recognise the importance of early environments for brain growth and development. Some of the key experiences of which the brain needs to make sense are emotional, psychological, and social. The brain (and therefore the child) can't process and make sense of emotional, psychological, and social experiences until it has been on the receiving end of caregiving relationships which have been 'good enough' in terms of perceiving, recognising, managing, and regulating these experiences.

Children learn to make sense of, and regulate, their emotions and social behaviour because they have been in relationship with parents and others who themselves are skilled at making sense of, and regulating, their own and other people's emotional states. Children become emotionally literate if they engage with people who are themselves emotionally literate. Children develop complex, competent psychological selves because they have been thought of and treated as if they are indeed complex, interesting little psychological selves.

Children in relationship with carers who are stressed, who lack emotional intelligence, and who can't reflect on and regulate their own emotions and social conduct, are less likely to develop a good understanding of their own and other people's mental states. Poor social cognition puts children at risk of failing to develop emotional intelligence, the ability to self-regulate, and the skills needed to set about social life with fluency and competence. Children, and indeed adults, who lack these psychological skills and competences find social life difficult and therefore stressful. As a result, they are at risk of either being a problem for society or finding that society is a problem for them.

This is why much of social work should concentrate on early support and intervention, particularly with families where children are suffering abuse and neglect. If parents can be helped to see, feel, and understand the world from their child's point of view, their parenting will become more attuned and sensitive. It is in such relationships that young brains develop the ability to make sense of and regulate complex emotional states. Children whose brains can do this are destined to become socially skilled and competent, robust and resilient.

The brain is often described as 'plastic'. That is, although much of the basic architecture of the brain is laid down and shaped in the early years, neurons and the connections they make continue to be stimulated by the environment. These days, neuroscientists are increasingly interested in taking a lifecourse view of the brain and its organization, recognising that it is never too late for the brain to benefit from a rich, stimulating, safe environment. From infancy to old age, active and engaged brains tend to be the most flexible, adaptive, and busy brains. Insights of this kind continue to inspire much of the creative work we see with babies, toddlers, teenagers, and the frail elderly.

So whether the science is genetics, epigenetics, or neurodevelopment, our long-term physical and mental health depends on good experiences of parenting, family life, and social relationships. Ensuring that experiences are good ones should encourage more family support and attempts to reduce parental stress. Social workers need to promote the belief that it is never too late for people to change and learn how to love, work, and play (see chapter 12 for more on this).

Interventions to bring about improvements in family life and personal wellbeing cover the full range of social work's repertoire. To these ends, we might therefore see social workers attempting to reduce poverty, make better housing available, tackle domestic violence, increase nursery provision, beef up mental health services, support individuals in the community, boost people's strengths, help them solve problems, and enhance their emotional intelligence and relationship skills. Social workers who nurture help brains to grow and nature to flourish.

11

Art and Science

The Craft of Social Work

Introduction

Social work has long aspired to be an applied science. As we have seen in earlier chapters, envying the professional status of medics and clinical psychologists, like them, there has been a determination by many that its practices should be evidence-based. There is a strong argument that social workers should try to do what has been shown to work. Ideally, only those interventions which have proven to be effective should be chosen. After all, if medical patients expect their treatments to be based on the best medical evidence, then shouldn't clients expect similar evidence-based findings to underpin what social workers do?

As a science, medicine is committed to following the scientific method in all that it does. Experimenting and observing, hypothesizing and testing are part of the everyday make-up of medical research, theory, and practice. And so if there is a conviction that social work should also be research-driven and evidence-based, then it, too, should adopt a scientific attitude.

However, this begs the question 'What is the science that social work seeks to apply?' If medicine is the application of the medical sciences and clinical psychology is the application of the psychological sciences, then what kind of social science is it that social work should apply? And this is where the idea that social work should based on the social sciences gets a little blurry.

There is agreement that medicine is a subdivision of the biological and life sciences. However, it is not so easy to establish social work as an applied science if the science which is to be applied is 'social'. There are certainly strong strands of a scientific tradition running through sociology and anthropology. Most of social psychology and developmental psychology are science-based. And as many branches of social work feed off these primary disciplines, it would seem to follow that social work should also see itself as an applied science. Many social workers who engage with children, families, and clients who have a mental illness are happy to be seen as applied social scientists.

But there are other debates going on in sociology, moral philosophy, the political sciences, and law that also impact on social work and what it does. Issues of discrimination; when to intervene in family life and override values of freedom and privacy; the nature of care and compassion; definitions of deviant and non-deviant, functional, and dysfunctional behaviours – all of these sweep social workers into the swirling waters of politics and philosophy, roles and relationships, psychological selves and social reality, values and judgement, the personal and political. Negotiating these waters is more of an art than a science, a task for the humanities rather than the more technologically-based disciplines.

There has been a long-held suspicion that these two worlds – the sciences and humanities – don't speak to each other very much. This is a shame. It impoverishes our outlook on the human condition. If social work, by its nature, does straddle these two worlds, then it would be particularly important for it to embrace the idea of itself as both an art and a science.

It was C. P. Snow, an academic scientist as well a novelist, who famously raised the problem of a world divided between the arts and the sciences in his 1959 lecture *The Two Cultures*. He feared that the intellectual life of the time was splitting into two polar groups, to the detriment of both. He felt 'a gulf of mutual incomprehension', even dislike, was opening up between the two worlds (Snow 1959/1964). Those raised in the humanities, even today, confess cheerfully, almost as if it was a badge of honour, that they're no good with numbers, they're innumerate, and certainly wouldn't have a clue what the Second Law of Thermodynamics was about. But there are also scientists who have little truck with the woolly thinking that they believe clouds the minds of literary intellectuals as they speak of a universe full of feeling and beauty, words and relationships, stories and sentiment.

Yet for Snow, humanity's most creative moments come when these two cultures meet, engage, even clash. And so it is for social work. It is a people-oriented profession. People can be studied scientifically. But they can also be thought about existentially, socially, relationally, poetically, aesthetically, narratively, spiritually, and creatively.

Social work as science

As we have seen in several of the earlier chapters, there have been steady and repeated calls over the decades for social work to be more rigorous in its thinking and practice. If social work is to play its part in remedying social ills, it should approach matters with the same rigour and discipline that the sciences use when they seek to explore and explain natural phenomena. Like medicine and clinical psychology, social work should adopt the scientific method to build a body of knowledge that is valid, reliable, and testable. Science provides the key with which social work can unlock its own body of knowledge. There should be evidence to support and guide what social workers do whenever they are asked to help clients who are no longer able to cope, whose behaviour is deemed socially unacceptable, or whose circumstances are of growing concern.

Practising scientifically requires social workers to think about their interventions in ways that are measurable, for how else will you know whether you have brought about the changes you planned? Close empirical observations provide the information upon which the worker can make an assessment before coming up with a clear formulation of the problem or definition of the need (see chapter 7). Using the best research evidence available, the worker then proposes an intervention (a treatment, a support, a plan of action). The planned, or hypothesized outcome is then stated in terms which can be observed and measured.

For example, the problem behaviour presented is one of poor school attendance by a seven-year-old caused by his mother's social anxiety and isolation. Her anxiety is so severe that she finds it difficult to leave the house and take her son to school. After a careful assessment and with the mother's agreement, the plan is to overcome her social phobia using an exposure treatment (systematic desensitization). This is a type of behavioural therapy in which the patient is exposed to the feared thing in very carefully, graduated stages, each stage accompanied by support, relaxation, and encouragement. The behavioural aim is to get the mother to accompany her son from home to the school gate by helping her overcome her social phobia. This has the knock-on effect of improving the boy's school attendance. This planned behavioural outcome can be observed, measured, and evaluated. There can be no objective doubt whether or not the intervention has been successful. The boy either attends school or he doesn't.

Two of the most tireless advocates of social work adopting a scientific, evidence-based approach are Brian Sheldon and Geraldine Macdonald (2009). Their writing is elegant and often witty as they mount a compelling case for social work to see itself as an applied social science. They don't hide their frustration as they despair of much of social work's continued failure to think rationally and practice scientifically. If social work is to build a respected knowledge base it must progress as the sciences progress. 'If some theories prove more valid and reliable than others that are less testable, then,' say Sheldon and Macdonald (2009), 'the latter must be relegated' (p. 54).

> Knowledge of 'what works, for whom, at what cost, in what circumstances, over what time scale, against which outcome indicators, how and why?' should surely be the main preoccupation of training courses for social workers. All other values and ethical considerations, however exciting in debate, are marginal unless such concerns predominate. (Sheldon and Macdonald 2009: 89)

For example, we know from many evidence-based studies that prevention is better than cure (e.g. Olds et al. 2007). We know that the provision of help and support before there is a crisis, whether it is given to those who care for their dependent elderly relatives or those who look after foster children, is, in the long run, cheaper and more effective (Macdonald and Kakavelakis 2004).

But in spite of the strengths of the evidence, prevailing policies and practices are still heavily biased towards working with hard-end cases which breach some high-level threshold or other, and in which crises are constant and outcomes disappointing. It is easy to sympathize with evidence-based practitioners who despair of both politicians and professionals who perversely continue to ignore the messages of 'what works'.

And it remains something of a puzzle, too, not to say outrage for many scientifically-grounded, evidence-based social workers that one of the most proven interventions – cognitive behavioural therapy (CBT) – is often not taught or used that much in practice:

> The results of systematic reviews and experiments show that in juvenile justice and probation, in cases of depression, in relapse prevention, in schizophrenia, in the field of child behavioural problems, in helping families cope with an autistic child, and so forth, cognitive-behavioural approaches never come second to anything. It should therefore be the preferred therapeutic option. Perversely, and unethically, it is probably the approach least likely to be taught on qualifying courses... (Sheldon and Macdonald 2009: 64)

CBT recognises that thoughts affect feelings and behaviour (Sheldon 2011). When our thoughts are negative, that is we have 'thinking errors', we can be plunged into anxiety, fear, or anger. Cognitive behavioural therapists help clients challenge and modify their thinking errors. It is often the way we interpret things, rather than the things themselves, that's the source of our worries and concerns. Although you might not be able to change the facts of the situation, you might be able to change your assumptions and beliefs about those facts.

Clients, or indeed social workers themselves, need to ask 'Why am I feeling this way? What's causing me to think, and therefore feel this way? How realistic is this negative thought, this worry?' People with a negative cognitive bias see the glass as half-empty rather than half-full. The positives are ignored and the negatives exaggerated. So, someone might believe that there is no point in putting in a job application because they're bound to be rejected, or they don't persist in trying to solve a problem because they've failed before and so will fail again.

Cognitive therapists aim to change the client's pessimistic beliefs and outlook so that the world is viewed more realistically. By helping clients recognise this tendency to see everything in a negative light and then challenging the accuracy of this despairing belief system, therapists see a change in cognitive outlook from negative to positive. When the errors are corrected, so the troubled feelings and behaviours disappear. People, events, and situations are 'read' more appropriately, accurately, and realistically (Hofman et al. 2012). CBT helps people recover a sense of control.

The scientific method and the scientific mind have clearly worked for medicine. They are working for clinical psychology. Nursing is keen to follow the same professional path. And perhaps, just perhaps, there are glimmers of hope in the minds of evidence-based advocates that the number of social workers convinced that social work, if it is ever to be taken seriously, has no choice but to go down the same scientific road, is growing. However, others beg to differ.

Social work as art

Human experience, say artists and philosophers, is always more, much more than the world counted and weighed, tested and explained. Life as lived can never fully be captured by measurement and mathematics. The arts explore experience and ambiguity. Only the arts are free to examine life as experienced. Only the arts can feel the whole texture (Williams 1965).

It is because social work finds itself deeply immersed in life as lived that its appeal to the sciences for all its answers is bound to disappoint. For Jordan (1978), 'literature and poetry afford far more penetrating and meaningful insight into the human heart than psychological texts' (p. 25). The problems presented by social work's clients are just too complex and involved, shifting and blurred to be resolved by simple formulae. As we saw in chapter 5, uncertainty and unpredictability are what social workers face every day. There is no precision. The boundaries are loose and permeable. Indeed, say Timms and Timms (1977), this looseness, imprecision, and uncertainty in the lives of our clients is, in fact, one of the profession's glories.

It is therefore 'in the nature of the social worker's task that he will encounter diversity greater than that for which he can be specifically prepared, not least because each situation will be specifically distinct' (England 1986: 35). This is, in part, why social work has never been able to identify a well-defined knowledge base or itself be tightly defined. What it does, who it does it with, and how it does it, is just too varied and lifelike to succumb to simple rules and procedures. Social workers must adopt multiple perspectives if they are to make sense of situations which are themselves many and diverse (England 1986: 37).

And so to the extent that social workers find themselves trying to help people make sense and cope, what they do is as much art as it is science. Because social workers constantly deal with uncertainty and ambiguity they have to be 'not so much theoretical as practical, concrete and intuitive and incorporate elements of art and craft as well as disciplined reasoning' (Parton 2003: 4).

Moreover, art has the virtue of being able to accommodate ambiguity and uncertainty which the more technically-based approaches often find difficult (Parton and O'Byrne 2000: 32; Goldstein 1992). In similar vein, Adams et al. also recognise social work's artistic overtones:

> We argue that the social work practitioner engages in practice much as a musician performs. Each performance is unique. Practice, therefore, is a creative act of choosing in a planned way between myriad possibilities. (Adams et al. 2009b: 7)

One of the most thorough and eloquent cases made for social work being seen as an art was made by Hugh England in his 1986 book *Social Work as Art*. In it, he repeatedly argues the therapeutic value of people simply being understood. 'Listen to me, know what I mean, and understand me.' To be understood by another anchors us when all around feels stormy and out of control. To be understood makes us feel safe and that we belong.

It is difficult to define what social workers do because they work with so many different people with so many different kinds of problems. They work with children and their families, people with physical and learning disabilities, older people, people whose behaviour is antisocial and criminal, and those who have mental health problems. They work in homes, the community, hospitals, prisons, schools, and residential homes. They work with individuals, families, and groups.

There are few common threads that link all these diverse strands together. However, the concept of *coping* has been suggested by Harriet Bartlett (1970) as a good candidate for a common base for social work practice.

One defining characteristic of social work is its wish to understand people in the context of their environment. Whenever individuals find themselves in environments that are too demanding (lack of money, discriminating, violent) and their personal resources to deal with them are stretched beyond their limits (low thresholds of stress, learning disabilities, physical disabilities, frailty, old age, mental illness), their capacity to cope is lost. When we feel unable to make sense of things or deal with them, we experience stress. *Stress*, and its knack of upsetting our ability to function, is a key concept in social work. For all of us there is a balance between our capacity to cope and what the environment, including other people, sends our way.

Therefore, much of what social workers do is to try and improve people's capacity to cope and help them recover feelings of being in control rather than being at the mercy of events. Social workers can do this by bringing about changes in the environment (more money, better housing, leaving a violent partner, getting aids and adaptations into the house), helping clients improve their cognitive and emotional strengths, and increasing people's social and relationship skills.

It is the concept of coping which England picks up and runs with throughout the rest of his book on social work as art.

> Social workers work not with those people who have problems but with those people who have difficulty coping with their problems... all coping is a function of the interaction between available subjective resources and external resources, both social and material. The relativity of the concept explains the 'selection' of the social worker's clients; social workers do not, for example, help all old or all poor people, but only those who cannot cope. Similarly, social workers may focus upon either the subjective or external resources of their clients, they may offer counselling or material help, according to their judgement of the balance of the 'coping equation.' Social workers constantly make judgements about their clients' coping capacity and how this may best be improved. (England 1986: 13–14)

Making judgements about people's capacity to cope involves weighing up the strengths of their material, social, and psychological resources. Failures to cope occur when any one, or more – and it is usually more – of these resources is judged weak.

For example, someone who has suffered rejection and neglect as a child might find raising their own children stressful, and a stressful state of mind is not one likely to be gifted in planning how to spend a limited income in an economical way. It feels less stressful to send the children off to buy a burger and Coke than to think about what food to buy and cook that is cheap and nourishing. The trouble with buying burgers and Coke is not only are they unhealthy but that they are also relatively expensive. So the rent doesn't always get paid, and the landlord threatens eviction, and the stress mounts on someone who isn't very good at regulating stress, so the children are poorly handled as well as poorly fed, and their behaviour gets difficult, and so they, too, become part of the problem. And so on.

There is no off-the-peg response to this situation. The social worker has to make a judgement about unique circumstances. 'Coping capacity is thus the principal focus of the social worker...' (England 1986: 15). And, more specifically, the capacity to cope is itself a function of the client's perception of their situation, how they experience that situation, the *meaning* they give to that experience, and how they *interpret* that meaning.

In England's thesis, coping, the meaning given to experience, and the way clients interpret that meaning go hand in hand. The social worker is interested in the way people see things, interpret events, and feel about their lives. This is the language of the arts and the approach of the humanities and not the evidence-based sciences.

As so much of the meaning we give to experience is the product of our interaction, talk, and exchanges with other people, it is in the process of talking, exploring, and feeling understood that meanings change. Social workers, just like artists, are therefore merchants in meaning, explorers of experience, communicators of understanding, and experts in empathy.

When social workers meet clients, there are lives to be understood. The search for understanding and meaning in these lives is as much art as science. In fact, the more dense, complex, and distressed the life being lived, the more the approach of the artist makes sense. By working with clients to find understanding and search for meaning, connections are made, meanings established, and control recovered. No science can tidy up human experience (Rickman 1967); no evidence-based practice can capture the client's reality. Only the arts and humanities can grapple with the subjective experience of individuals and their social environments.

When lives are messy and values clash, when emotions are high and thoughts confused, we turn to the novelist or the poet or the playwright for understanding and empathy (Goldstein 1992; Irvine 1974; Turner 2013;Valk 1979). Poems and good fiction explore life. 'We go to fiction to extend experience, to go beyond our own' (Lively 2013: 179). We learn to understand ourselves as we begin to make sense of others. In his biographical film *Shadowlands,* the playwright William Nicholson has C. S. Lewis say 'We read to know we're not alone' (Nicholson 1993).

Both art and social work involve the shared exploration of subjective experience and the communication of meaning (Rapoport 1968). More particularly, social work is an activity which depends on the process of understanding other people, and the conversations and communications which then take place based on that understanding (England 1986: 101). So whether artist, social worker, or client:

> It is, in the first instance, to every man, a matter of urgent personal importance to 'describe' his experience, because this is literally a remaking of himself, a creative change in his personal organization, to include and control his experience. This struggle to remake ourselves – to change our personal organization so that we may live in a proper relation to our environment is in fact often painful…the impulse to communicate is a learned human response to disturbance of any kind. For the individual, of course, the struggle is to communicate successfully by describing adequately…For unless the description is adequate, there can be no relevant communication…Genuine communication depends on this absorbed attention to precise description… (Williams 1965: 42–3)

We therefore communicate, in part, to make sense of both ourselves and others. In many cases, the simple act of communication can be good in itself. This is why we value talking with family and friends. In conversation we constantly reflect, refine and re-form. 'We have invented language,' wrote Hugh Trevor-Roper, 'refined it so that it can express even the subtlest thought, even the obscurest sensations; why then should we not use it, and dissolve difficulties by articulating them' (quoted in Davenport-Hines and Sisman 2013: 74).

Thus, if language is the medium in which individual selves form, clients who wish to re-form and re-organize their psychological selves have to immerse themselves in talk – to connect, to communicate, to explore, to find meaning, to be understood, to understand. This is what clients will do if they engage with an empathic, emotionally intelligent social worker (Howe 2008, 2012). They will talk and tell their story and slowly find their way back.

> In every encounter, client and social worker share in performing, narrating, composing and interpreting experiences, transforming them into complex creations... The intimate relationship of the social worker to the client is the medium through which the artistic is expressed in practice… [the social worker] is not an artist who imposes order and creates beauty through a process of domination and subjugation of raw materials or symbols, but a co-creator of harmony… The artistry of the social worker is fully dependent on the imaginative freedom of the client to change pain into gain, powerlessness into strength, or weakness into resolution. (Martinez-Brawley and Zorita 1998: 205–7)

Social workers have to make the incoherent coherent. Clients want to understand and be understood. Control of the meaning of experience has to be wrested and shared. And so, slowly, the capacity to cope recovers. Then, and only then will calm return.

Although England's book received good reviews at the time and has continued to be well regarded, the idea of social work as art has never fully taken off. If anything, since the book's publication the tide of ideas has run in the opposite direction. Empirically-minded and evidence-based approaches have repeatedly claimed the right to define the social work agenda. The fact that these approaches have had only partial success hasn't necessarily led practitioners back to the artistic life, at least in the sense in which England presents it. Nevertheless, social work's limited ability fully to receive the sciences continues to see it taking curious looks at the arts for alternative ways of being (Goldstein 1992, 1999), as some more recent writings reveal.

Exploring the idea that social work might be seen as a kind of artistic endeavour has been the subject of some particularly serious thinking by Mel Gray, Stephen Webb, and colleagues. Over a series of critical papers, they have toughened up England's cosy, even nostalgic views of the 'intuitive use of self' by arguing that art, as much as anything, is a rebellious business, an activity that provokes us into seeing and thinking about the world in ways that are new, fresh, different. Whereas England is more interested in how clients cope with their problems, the gaze of the critical artist focuses on the nature of the problems themselves.

Art in this more robust sense is political as much as aesthetic. This is 'art in the service of liberation' (Gray and Webb 2008: 184). The social worker as artist is in the business of getting us to see the world more clearly, more truthfully. To the extent that the lives of clients are ones of deprivation and disadvantage, hurt and pain, inequality and injustice, then social workers have to paint pictures and tell stories which can be put 'in the service of those whom we seek to free from oppression' (Gray and Webb 2008: 184).

Somewhere in their thesis is the idea that in the encounters between social workers and clients there must be a striving to see things just as they are, stripped of all political camouflage – to see them as naked oppressions, injustices, inequalities, therapeutic manipulations, state denials, conformity. The art in social work represents an attempt by worker and client to re-write the story, to paint a more direct picture.

This brief review fails to do justice to Gray and Webb's demanding essay on 'art's work in social work'. Suffice it to say, applying Heidegger's (1971) ideas, they attack social work's descent into measurement-minded, technically-based, performance-driven practices. They prefer a notion of art which allows them 'to set this aesthetic conception of social work against the perverse and inauthentic forms of calculative reason that have come to dominate much of social work' (Gray and Webb 2008: 191).

Social work as craft

Undoubtedly, the social sciences have informed and enriched social work in all sorts of ways. They have told us about how early neglect adversely affects children's development. They have taught us about loss and mourning in old age. They have helped us understand the economic and psychological effects of poverty. And with their evidence-based hat on, they have also told us what works and with whom.

However, there is also an artistic thread that weaves its way into practice. It is not only what you do but also the way that you do it. The best social workers, therefore, fuse art and disciplined reasoning (Martinez-Brawley and Zorita 1998: 197). Blending reason and emotion, experience and experiment, the best social workers fit their practice to the subject and not their subjects to the practice. The blend of technique and creativity, science and art define craft and what craftsmen and craftswomen do.

One of the most eloquent and scholarly essays on craft and the craftsman is that written by Richard Sennett (2008). Craftsmanship is the skill of making and doing things well, often for their own sake. Craft is found in the work and character of those who make things, including cabinet makers, goldsmiths, and builders, but also in the work and character of those who do things, including doctors, nurses, and social workers. Craftwork requires skill, commitment, and judgement. It involves an intimate connection between head and hand, thought and concrete action, problem-solving and problem-finding.

It is when these elements become separated, as they so often do in organizations whose outlook is instrumental, that craftwork suffers. When science and art become uncoupled, workers can no longer engage with their materials (whether objects or people) in ways which foster understanding and expression. Mechanization of any kind generally dulls the understanding of its users. Factory workers on production lines have no need to understand or revel in the nature and potential of the things that pass their way. Fast food workers, unlike committed chefs, have no need to become expert in taste and texture. Social workers who look at computer screens and follow guidelines risk losing that deep and particular knowledge of this client, this family, and the warp and woof of human experience.

To become skilled in their craft, craftsmen and craftswomen have to practise. Doing the work well and with fluency takes time. The acquisition of technique and technical understanding also requires imagination. The craftsman and craftswoman have to develop an intimate understanding of their materials and methods. The grain of the wood and the effects of the chisel for the carpenter. The body and patient, the treatment and the response for the doctor. The social and psychological, the personal and political, the role and the relationship for the social worker. The craftsman and craftswoman become engaged with their work, absorbed by it, and committed to it.

Craftsmen and craftswomen have to learn how to deal with ambiguity and resistance in their materials and methods. They have 'to learn from these experiences rather than fight them' (Sennett 2008: 10). By working *with* resistance rather than against it, practitioners develop new understanding and new ways of working. Techniques evolve and artistry flourishes.

The social worker as craftworker is pragmatic. To work well, pragmatists have to be free from means–ends thinking and relationships. He or she is open to new problems and new cases, new knowledge and new solutions as he or she works with each individual case. Bureaucrats are:

> …unwilling to make a move until all the goals, procedures, and desired results for a policy have been mapped in advance. This is a closed knowledge-system. In the history of handcrafts, closed knowledge-systems have tended toward short lifespans. (Sennett 2008: 26)

It is by allowing workers freedom to connect and engage fully with their materials, again whether objects or people, that skills develop, new thoughts arise, and fresh solutions emerge. These are the special talents of the craftsman and craftswoman, talents that can only blossom in open knowledge-systems.

> When practice is organized as a means to a fixed end, then the problems of the closed system reappear; the person in training will meet a fixed target but won't progress further. The open relation between problem solving and problem finding….builds and expands skills… (Sennett 2008: 38)

Open-knowledge systems do not try to pre-configure and box-in how we think about a case or a person. They allow exceptions, resistance, and ambiguity to slip in. They appreciate that there are limits to dealing with human relationships scientifically. Technical solutions must adapt to particular cases. If real people in the real world are to be helped, they need practitioners who are alert, curious, and responsive to the different, the particular, and the shifting. Science helps us to make sense of the general. Art gives us licence to be creative with the particular. Craft blends the two.

Open-knowledge systems also require organizations to be open to challenge and change. In social work organizations, the only people who routinely meet, and therefore know clients in all their varieties and with all their idiosyncracies are social workers. Experienced social workers understand their clients over time and in context rather than as a problem or a category at a point in time. If organizations are going to be responsive as well as effective in what they do, they must be open to the new and the resistant. They must welcome challenge. They must listen and communicate. If social workers are allowed to practise their craft, as opposed to follow the rules, listening and responsive organizations will remain attuned and effective.

Senior managers and front-line workers need patience. Frustration has to be tolerated. Imagination is required. The craftsman and craftswoman learn to improvise and invent. Entrenched needs and problems are re-thought and re-formatted. They learn to work with resistance rather than fight or discipline it. They acknowledge mistakes and repair errors and disruptions.

The good craftsman or craftswoman finds the most forgiving element in a difficult situation. To work well with clients, workers and organizations have to understand them. 'The skills of working well with resistance are in sum, those of reconfiguring the problem into other terms, readjusting one's behaviour if the problem lasts longer than expected, and identifying with the problem's most forgiving element' (Sennett 2008: 222).

It is working in this way that social workers, as craftsmen and craftswomen, learn not only about other people, but also about themselves. Social workers are the instruments of their own practice and, just like the gifted craftsman or craftswoman, through practice and experience they learn to use their selves better and better. In the freedom of doing, we get better at being. Clients too, when they trust and feel safe enough to think and reflect, experience less stress. They, too, can then begin to understand more clearly, cope better, and live well.

Social work craftsmen and craftswomen can be found working with individual cases, families, groups, and communities. Their skills and imagination can also be brought to bear on wider issues and social problems. The social worker and her client, who has severe physical disabilities but a first-class mind, fashion a plan together that gradually takes shape leading to the young woman setting up an interactive website for disabled people in the city where she lives. Her depression lifts and her horizons grow. She now gives talks and can hardly believe how her life has changed.

In chapter 2, we cited examples of practitioners working with domestically violent and coercively controlling men. Rather than ignore them or condemn them, these practitioners worked with the resistance rather than against it. They brought the men together, to talk, reflect, acknowledge, Recognise, and understand themselves and their violent behaviour. The aim was to change their behaviour, make them less coercive, and, if possible, safer partners and better fathers (Stanley et al. 2012; Westmarland and Kelly 2013).

And finally, and more literally, we see a nice example of the marriage of art and science in Teater and Baldwin's (2014) description of a community-arts programme. The programme provides an opportunity for older adults to come together for an hour a week and sing songs from the 1950s, 1960s and 1970s. Prior to the Golden Oldies programme, many participants were experiencing social exclusion and feelings of isolation. We know from existing research and the medical sciences that loneliness, poor mental health, and deteriorating physical health all too often cluster. We also know that singing together has many benefits. Putting the two together led to the Golden Oldies singing project. The researchers found that the activity had positive benefits on health and wellbeing. Participants felt less isolated and more socially involved. Many of the older adults who joined in the group singing reported a new lease of life. This is a nice of example of skill, understanding, engagement, technique, and imagination coming together to create an innovative experience for vulnerable of older adults.

12
Good Relationships and Working Well

How to Practise Empathically and Effectively

Introduction

The claim that mental health lies in getting the balance right between being and doing, relationships and creativity, love and work has been made many times. Among others, credit for this sentiment has been given to Sigmund Freud and Erik Erikson, although Erikson (1950) went on to suggest the fullest, richest lives are those that enjoy a happy balance between love, work, and play. Thus, for Jones (1974), love and work are the cornerstone of our humanity.

In professional practices, love and work translate into establishing a good relationship with your client before going on to solve problems, meet needs, provide services, and address concerns. The recognition that success in social work, counselling and psychotherapy requires the presence of both a good relationship and a plan of action, has been long established. And to the extent that the relationship has a strong emotional tone, and work demands clear thinking and rational action, we shall pick up some of the ideas aired in chapter 8 on the part that both thoughts and feelings play in social work practice.

In practice, maintaining a balance between achieving a good social work relationship and adopting a purposeful stance can be difficult. The soft nature of the relationship is an easy target for scorn and cynicism. It is the side of social work that is dismissed by the press and politicians as gullible, namby-pamby and 'do-gooding'. In the increasingly market-dominated, performance-driven climate of all modern public services, including social work departments, the emphasis is on efficiency, value for money, results achieved, and targets met. Although lip-service might be paid to the value of the caring relationship, compassion and empathy are easily crushed under the weight of heavy caseloads and performance-anxious managers.

And yet professional practices which fail to establish good working relationships with clients run the risk of being not only insensitive but also ineffective. When the client's subjectivity is lost, practice is liable to become hard and impersonal. Techniques, if they are to be effective, need a human touch. So the irony is that in bureaucratic cultures which support only those practices which can be counted and measured, the key but difficult-to-measure ingredient of successful practice – the good relationship – goes missing, and, with it, professional effectiveness and the attainment of goals.

Good relationships

Most of social work's early trailblazers recognised the importance of establishing a good-quality relationship with clients. Without a good working relationship, clients, they felt, would be more wary of engaging with the service. Trust would be lacking. Whether it was helping people to help themselves, offering better housing, educating parents about raising children, or supporting families who were looking after their old and frail relatives, warmth and compassion had to be present. In 1869, Octavia Hill, the 'grandmother' of social work, said:

> Only when face meets face, heart meets heart; only in the settled link with those who are old friends... is there more opportunity... to grow and to shine. (quoted in Woodroofe 1962: 52)

And just over a century later, another of social work's heroes, Florence Hollis, reminded her readers that: 'Basic to all casework treatment is the relationship between worker and client' (Hollis 1972: 228).

Emotions and their regulation lie at the heart of much social work. It is in our unconscious attempts to protect ourselves from emotional distress and anxiety that our defence mechanisms come into play. However, because they also involve blocking out and distorting some aspects of reality, they are not the healthiest way with which to deal with stress, anxiety and challenge. As we saw in chapter 8, the defences represent attempts to keep anxiety at bay.

For example, *denying* that you are bothered by your partner's fleeting affair is a way to keep the pain and hurt out of mind. But the pain and hurt haven't really gone away. They show themselves in other ways. You get angry very quickly. You pick fights over the smallest things. Your body is tense and tears are never very far away. Or a recently disabled man who *projects* a great deal of anger at his social worker, blaming her for the delay in getting a new wheelchair and the uselessness of the aids the occupational therapist has supplied, is still finding it difficult to accept that his life has changed in so many ways.

The emotionally intelligent social worker recognises and understands that when we feel hurt and alone, anxious and frightened, we often react in ways that are unreasonable, counterproductive, and destructive (Howe 2008). Social workers who recognise, acknowledge, accept, understand, and stay with clients and their distressed feelings are likely to engender trust. Trust and acceptance lay down the first steps in the practitioner–client relationship. They mark the beginnings of the working alliance. But all of this takes time.

Many clients have learned not to trust. Their anxieties have gone unrecognised. Their anger misconstrued. Their strong feelings have merely fuelled more criticism and rejection, punishment and finger-wagging. So some clients keep people at bay. Letting people get close, emotionally and professionally, has only led to judgement and hurt, so best to maintain your distance. Anger, ridicule, avoidance, and denial are just some of the ways that clients use to defend themselves against the dangers of closeness, whether with partners or parents, professionals or practitioners. It is therefore vital that social workers see the importance of engaging with their clients emotionally as well as contractually.

Although a psychologist and a counsellor, Carl Rogers has remained an influential figure for many social workers. His writings as a person-centred counsellor rose to prominence in social work's literature during the 1970s and 1980s. In particular, his belief that the presence of *empathy, genuineness,* and *warmth* in the professional relationship were critical to successful outcomes lodged in the minds of social work's more humanistically inclined practitioners. Rogers (1957) referred to these three elements as the 'core conditions' of the helpful relationship. He believed that the core conditions were not only necessary but could even be sufficient for therapies to be successful.

Together, the core conditions help establish the *therapeutic alliance*, also known as the *working alliance* between practitioner and client. In their major review of therapeutic changes that work, Castonguay and Beutler (2006) examined three key variables – the relationship, treatment techniques, and participant characteristics. They report that a good relationship between therapist and client is critical in predicting successful outcomes. Specifically, the researchers found that therapy is likely to be beneficial if a *strong working alliance* is established and maintained during the course of treatment.

Practitioners who work *collaboratively* with clients also do well. Supporting Rogers's earlier findings, the three principles most associated with good outcomes are: practitioners should relate to clients in *an empathic way*; practitioners should show *warmth* and *acceptance*; and practitioners should adopt an attitude of *congruence* and *authenticity* (Castonguay and Beutler 2006: 359).

In similar vein, Reid and Epstein (1972: 127) also required their task-centred workers to be responsive. A responsive worker is one whose communications help clients feel understood, who expresses interest in what clients have to say about themselves and their lives, who listens attentively, and who conveys appreciation and interest, who expresses warmth and goodwill, who accepts and does not judge. 'Perhaps the most critical component of responsiveness,' they write, 'is the communication of empathic understanding' (Reid and Epstein 1972: 129).

Empathy requires the social worker to recognise and understand the client's own interpretation of their world and their experience of it. It involves, writes Jordan, 'getting alongside my clients, feeling with rather than for them. I did not feel impelled to offer them false reassurance or to disarm them. I was not over-anxious to present myself as nice and helpful. I was aware of people's right to make their own choices and their own mistakes' (Jordan 1979: 10). For Jordan, good social work combines *empathy* and *realism*. 'The most precious gift we can offer anyone,' said Thich Nhat Hanh, a Buddhist, 'is our attention.'

Feeling empathically understood helps clients recognise and explore their own thoughts and feelings (Howe 2012). This sets them on a road which leads them to recover control over the meaning and content of their own lives.

It seems, then, that social workers who establish good-quality relationships with their clients are half-way there in terms of delivering effective treatments, appropriate services, and valued support. Relationships matter.

Working well

The approach here brings together several of our earlier appreciations of the value of clear thinking, structured interventions, and evidence-based practice. All interventions which have a strong theoretical base recognise the importance of making the 'work' element explicit. However, the kind of work to be done will vary a lot in character, especially between the more psychodynamic and person-centred approaches on the one hand, and the brief solution, task-centred, and cognitive-behavioural approaches on the other. Helping clients to reflect and gain insight demands as much work and effort as getting clients to keep to task and practise new behaviours. It's just that the kind of work to be done varies a great deal between theories.

One of the major benefits of approaching practice in a structured and systematic fashion is the confidence and sense of purpose it gives to both the social worker and her client. Practitioners who know where they are and where they are going, and who involve their clients in planning the therapeutic journey, are more likely to be effective and well-regarded.

Interventions that are orderly and systematic are those which are clear about the goals to be achieved and what steps have to be taken to achieve them. Workers who are systematic and purposeful are also likely to be the most explicit in their use of theory, particularly the more evidence-based and scientific theories. It is no accident that evidence-based interventions happen to be some of the most systematic and structured interventions. It is their structured approach to helping and problem solving that goes some way towards explaining their attraction for clients as well as their success in bringing about change.

Most of these interventions combine helping clients to improve their perception and understanding of what's going on, getting them to adopt mental states that are forward-looking and positive, encouraging them to explore and identify the steps that seem most likely to get them from problem to solution, and then spurring them on to take those steps. These interventions are good at keeping clients to task.

Many social work methods recognise the value of these rational, *step-wise* approaches when helping clients meet needs and solve problems. Task-centred practices, solution-focused therapies, possibility thinking, strengths-based approaches, and, of course, cognitive behavioural therapies all involve clear and strict practice running orders. And because clients are required to take an active part in these practice processes, they, too, see and begin to appreciate the benefits of logical thinking, systematic planning, and structured problem-solving. The organized way social workers set about solving problems itself offers a powerful model for clients who might otherwise flounder in confusion.

For most of these approaches, the practice running order goes something like this: explore the problem; assess the character and condition of the problem; identify and agree the target problem to be resolved; formulate the problem to be tackled in concrete, possibly behavioural terms; set and specify the goal of the intervention in terms which can be observed or measured; carry out the intervention; evaluate its outcome.

Task-centred practices provide a good example of this way of working. The:

> …model is designed to be carried out in a step-wise progression; the client's problems are explored, a target problem is identified, a task is formulated, durational limits are set, work on the task is carried out, and termination is effected. The practitioner is expected to concentrate his efforts on completing a particular step before moving on to the next. (Reid and Epstein 1972: 125)

If there are time limits involved in the method – and there usually are – these must be kept. Time limits help both worker and client to keep the work in focus, meet deadlines, and build purpose and pace into the intervention.

Taking a purely systematic approach, these methods of intervention and the techniques they employ should work independent of the person using them. The implication is that the technique is doing the work and bringing about the change. Any worker using the technique and following the stated intervention sequence would achieve the same results with the same client. The client simply needs to know and accept the nature and philosophy, order and purpose of the intervention for it to work, assuming the technique has evidence to support its efficacy. Work pays.

Feel secure then explore

In practice, the research evidence tells us that the most effective interventions are those in which good relationships and evidence-based techniques are both present. A successful practitioner is one who is responsive *and* systematic in her dealings with clients. Techniques don't work so well if there is no therapeutic alliance between worker and client. Even the most 'systematic' and traditionally technical methods acknowledge the importance of the worker being attuned, warm, and empathic.

Bowlby (1988) said that unless clients feel safe, secure, and trusting in relationship with their practitioner, they find it difficult to put their minds to work. If clients remain anxious, then thinking about problems and how to resolve them isn't easy. Good workers therefore act as a 'safe haven' for clients. And the more confident clients are in the presence and availability of the 'safe haven', the easier they find it to think about troublesome things and how they might be tackled. Reflection, exploration, play, curiosity, imagination, and the energy to problem solve are not possible when we feel anxious and unsafe. For clients, the recipe for therapeutic success is therefore *feel secure then explore*.

The technique of Motivational Interviewing (MI) offers a nice example of clients first needing to feel secure before they can go on to explore, problem solve, and change. In developing MI, Miller and Rollnick (2002) took a range of therapeutic insights from cognitive psychology, self-efficacy models, and models of how we set about making changes and then married them with the more person-centred thinking of Carl Rogers (1959).

> We define motivational interviewing as *a client-centred, directive method for enhancing intrinsic motivation to change by exploring and resolving ambivalence.* (Miller and Rollnick 2002: 25, emphasis original)

In collaboration with the client, the idea is to strengthen his or her motivation for, and commitment to change toward a specific goal. 'Change talk' explores and picks up on the client's own ideas and arguments for change and then supports them. These ideas and arguments are drawn out of the client in the context of an empathic, collaborative relationship. In essence, MI is a strengths-based approach that believes clients are capable of change if they really believe change is possible. Practitioners therefore focus on success, both past and present.

MI is a technique that works well with people who have problems of addiction and people who feel stuck trying to change behaviours that are harmful, unacceptable, or self-defeating.

The approach is collaborative. Social workers are not cast as experts. They are guides (Hohman 2012: 4). MI is person-centred. Empathy, warmth, and congruence are valued. In particular, *empathy* facilitates change and its absence frustrates it.

In addition to the presence of these 'core conditions', the intervention is also very goal directed. The first thing clients have to do is express a willingness and desire to change, even though they are finding change difficult. MI attempts to capitalize on people's motivation to change.

Clients rate their own determination to change on a scale of 0 to 10. They are asked to specify in concrete behavioural detail how they would like things to be different. The pros and cons of changing or staying the same are considered. Using these scaling techniques, clients might be asked 'On a scale of 0 to 10, how important is the need to change for you?' Similar ratings can be made for their confidence and readiness to change.

This is then followed by the key question. 'So, what are you going to do now?' or 'What, if anything do you plan to do?' The answer to this question leads to an agreement about what's going to be done. Rollnick et al. (2008: 57) offer a few suggestions, albeit in a health setting which then go to encourage 'change talk':

'Why do you want to make this change?' [desire].
'If you did decide to make this change, how would you do it? [ability]
'What are the three most important benefits that you see in making this change? [reasons]

'How important is it to you to make this change?' [need]
'What do you think you will do?' [commitment]
'What are you already doing to be healthy?' [taking steps]

Both Hohman (2012) and Teater (21012) offer useful outlines of MI's character for social workers. They describe MI's four basic principles:

1. *Express empathy* and have a genuine interest in the client's feelings, experiences, and perspective. Listen carefully. Listen well. As social workers reflect back in a non-judgemental way what they believe the client is thinking and feeling, the client will feel accepted.
2. *Develop discrepancy*; that is, listen for discrepancies in current behaviour, between what is said and what is done, between present values and future goals. 'We confront clients', writes Hohman (2012), 'not in a negative or shaming way, but by holding up a mirror to examine the ambivalence they may be experiencing… [for example]… the client may state that she likes being around other adults in the bar, and she realizes that leaving her children alone does not fit with her desire to be a good mother' (p. 19).
3. *Roll with resistance*; that is, avoid arguing for change. The more workers push for change, pointing out how sensible and logical it would be, the more clients tend to become defensive, digging in their heels. Exhortation rarely works. Instead of arguing, it is much better to reflect back what the client has just said or done. This is not to agree with what has been said or done, but rather to state in a neutral manner where the client believes themselves to be. Rolling with the resistance sees clients move from a defensive stance to an engaged response.
4. Support self-efficacy and hold a genuine belief in the client's ability to make and carry out changes. Clients are reminded that the decision to change is ultimately theirs.

Talk about change between worker and client has a distinct character. The positive tone of the interview is captured by talk which emphasizes client beliefs such as 'I need to change', 'I want to change', 'I can change', 'I will make changes', 'I am taking specific actions to change', and so on.

MI, like many modern technically based interventions, recognises that most of us are helped to move forward and tackle life's challenges when we feel recognised, accepted, and understood. With the support and encouragement of an empathic other, we gain in strength. We begin to believe that we do have the capacity to change and so feel motivated to give change a shot. Practitioners who are skilled at weaving together love and work, empathy and structure, therapeutic alliances and technical know-how, are effective practitioners. People become motivated to change when their social workers bring warmth, recognition, hope, and purpose to the relationship.

Clients grow more resistant and less cooperative the more confrontational or challenging the style of communication. Demands that they need to change lead to defensive postures in which reasons for not changing, or why change is not possible or necessary, increase. Resentment mounts. 'There is something in human nature that resists being coerced and told what to do. Ironically, it is acknowledging the other's right and freedom not to change that sometimes makes change possible' (Rollnick et al. 2008: 7).

Clients actually become less resistant the more social workers listen, empathize, and come across as wanting to understand their clients' thoughts and feelings, histories, and circumstances.

> …change talk and resistance are substantially influenced by counselling style. Counsel in a directive, confrontational manner, and client resistance goes up. Counsel in a reflective, supportive manner, and resistance goes down while change talk increases. (Miller and Rollnick 2002: 9)

Workers should therefore roll with the resistance and avoid arguing for change.

Miller and Rollnick (2002) recognise four basic client-centred skills in MI. These are the ability to ask *open-ended questions*, make *affirmative* statements, *reflect* what the client has said and done, and offer *summaries*.

Open-ended questions allow clients to respond with what's on *their* mind rather than the mind of the social worker. The ability to ask open-ended questions is an important communication skill for the motivational interviewer. For example, 'Tell me about a typical day when you drink.' 'Tell me how you've been managing since your arthritis has got worse.' 'How would you like things to be different?' Clients can also be asked what they think are the pros and cons for changing or staying the same.

Affirmations are statements that recognise and support a client's past and current achievements: 'In spite of your ex-partner breaking into the house and stealing your money, you still managed to get Kelly to school and take Ruben to the clinic to have his immunisation. I can see that you're determined to do the best for your kids whatever happens.'

Reflections take place when social workers repeat, rephrase, or paraphrase what clients have said (Hohman 2012: 20). Reflections can be simple, complex, and even 'double sided', for example when clients feel ambivalent about their situation.

> 'On the one hand, it has been important for you to take care of her [daughter with a terminal illness] yourself since you love her so, and on the other hand, you are feeling overwhelmed and tired with all that you have to do'... Double-sided reflections are important because they help our clients hear their ambivalence. The goal of MI is to work toward resolving ambivalence. (Hohman 2012: 21)

Summaries are very important, in social work in general and MI in particular. They review where things are at and they pull threads together. They provide clients with opportunities to make links and see connections. The following example, noting which skills are being used, is given by Rollnick et al. (2008):

> PRACTITIONER: Tell me a little about your drinking. [open question]
> PATIENT: Well, I do drink most days, but not that much, really.
> PRACTITIONER: You're a pretty light drinker? [reflection]
> PATIENT: Well, I'm not sure about that. I can hold it pretty well, more than most.
> PRACTITIONER: You can drink a fair amount and it doesn't seem to affect you. [reflection]
> PATIENT: Yeah, that's right. I can drink quite a bit.
> PRACTITIONER: And you do sometimes. [reflection...]

PATIENT: Sure, I'll have five or six beers after work on the way home.
PRACTITIONER: …What do you think about drinking that much? [open question]
PATIENT: I don't really think about it that often.
PRACTITIONER: Sometimes you do, but not often. [reflection]
PATIENT: Well, sometimes I think, you know, I'm getting older, and I ought to cut back.
PRACTITIONER: What have you noticed? [open question]
PATIENT: These stomach pains, like I've been getting, and I'm not as sharp sometimes in the mornings. But don't misunderstand, I don't have a problem with drinking.
PRACTITIONER: It hasn't really caused any problems for you. [reflection]
PATIENT: Well, I wouldn't say that… (Rollnick et al. 2008: 79–80)

Workers should always be interested in the client's own concerns, beliefs, hopes, values, and motivations. It is much more effective to elicit the client's thoughts about the situation and how it might be changed than to tell them what to do and how to do it.

Social workers can't force people to change. They can only help if clients want to move on. MI is directive. It encourages people to talk about reasons to change their behaviour. It is a technique based on 'change talk'. Throughout clients' strengths are identified and promoted. Therefore MI is compatible with and perfectly willing to combine with CBT, strengths-based approaches, brief solution-focussed therapies, and task-centred practices. What they all have in common, of course, are clear behavioural goals and time-limits designed to motivate clients.

In 2012, Louise Casey was appointed by the UK government to 'turn around' 120,000 of the country's most damaged and damaging families. The Troubled Families Programme works with those lost in violence, mental illness, abuse, neglect, prison, teenage pregnancies, drugs, alcohol, poverty, and debt. A year into the Programme, Casey was interviewed by Decca Aitkenhead, a journalist. During the conference prior to the interview, Casey reports early success and feels the Programme is on target to meet its goal of turning around the majority of families. But, wonders Aitkenhead, what are the ingredients of success? Valuing both relationship and structure, love and work, and echoing the hopes of this book, this is part of Casey's reply:

> All of what we do turns on something very simple: the relationship between the worker and the family... None of us changes because we are given a report or an analysis. We have to feel we want to change and know how to change. The difference in family interventions is that they make people believe in themselves... What's missing here is love... I think we need to bring back... some emotional exposure, the ability to be human, the ability to empathise, not to be fearful of empathy. (Aitkenhead, *Guardian* 30 November 2013: 49)

In social work, good relationships and clear structures, connecting and moving forward, thought and feeling, clarity and compassion go hand in hand. Good social workers get to the heart of the matter as they keep their clients in mind. It turns out that the smartest workers are also the most emotionally literate workers (Howe 2008). If you want your interventions to be effective, then make sure that your practices are emotionally intelligent *and* cognitively wise. Social work always has been, and should continue to be, a matter of the heart as well as the head.

13
Freedom and Equality

How to Balance Individual Choice and the Collective Good

Introduction

In these final stages in our quest to find the *compleat* social worker, we need to engage with some of social work's more profound political and philosophical challenges. In this chapter and the next, we consider how social workers have recognised the fundamental role that politics and philosophy, ideology and values play in everyday practice. We begin with two major concepts – freedom and equality – that tend to pull thinking and practice in opposite directions, not just for social workers but for social policy and political theorists alike.

It seems sound to argue that so long as individuals are not interfering with the freedoms of other people, they should be free to choose what they do and how they do it.

Equality, particularly equality of opportunity, values treating people the same and giving everyone a fair chance to make the best of themselves and their lives. This seems eminently reasonable.

The tension between these two political values is met when one person's freedom limits another person's opportunities to engage on an equal footing, or when treating all people equally and fairly necessarily means that some people's freedoms to do what they want have to be curtailed. For example, people with a profound physical disability might be unable to work. In order to live they will need money and help with supported housing. The only way to pay for these is by taxing people who are in work and earn an income. People who earn an income are therefore not completely free to do as they choose with every penny of what they earn; they have no choice but to pay their taxes.

Similar clashes occur when freedom is in the political ascendancy. The freedom to spend your money on private health care might mean that you are able to access medical services more quickly than people who have to rely on the National Health Service. Here there is an inequality of access to certain medical services between those who pay privately and those who use public health services. This might not seem fair.

Social workers regularly get caught up in these debates between freedom and equality. It seems right that clients should be free to have a strong say in the types of service which best suit their needs, but wrong that parents should be entirely free to raise their children in any manner they choose. It seems reasonable to argue that children should have equal opportunities to learn, be physically healthy, and enjoy psychological wellbeing, but parents will vary in the provisions and stimulations they provide, particularly in the early years, as they exercise their freedom whether or not to buy books, play with their children, feed them well, and relate in an emotionally intelligent way. At the point when the state decides to intervene to ensure a child's safety and preserve their equalities of opportunity, the parents' freedoms are forfeited.

Liberty and freedom

Libertarians believe that maximizing people's freedoms is the best way to unleash talent and increase motivation. Libertarianism is the political philosophy most likely to sponsor innovation and growth, diversity and development. If personal effort and hard work result in success, then those who achieve success should be allowed to enjoy the fruits of their labours without penalty. Penalizing success by the overtaxation of income or the imposition of too many legal restrictions on what people are allowed to do frustrates creativity. It holds back entrepreneurship.

Neoliberals prefer free market economics to state involvement, personal freedoms to governmental restrictions, the private to the public sector. Free market economies value and reward independence and hard work. So being in work is better than being on welfare, hence the push to get the unemployed back in the workplace.

> Perhaps the most important thing to grasp about the different theories gathered together under the banner of neoliberalism is that they have in common a central emphasis on the market as the organising principle of social life… social life and social relationships are viewed through the prism of economic categories. (Penna and O'Brien 2013: 137)

Neoliberalism is also the politics of personal responsibility. Libertarians who champion the virtues of freedom argue that it should be up to individuals to decide how to live their lives. So, for example, over recent years there has been a shift in adult care services from the paternalistic delivery of services towards giving clients greater choice and the ability to take control over key aspects of their lives. The state, it believes, should resist interfering in the lives of its citizens as much as possible. Social workers should therefore only intervene when there is good cause.

In fact, as we saw in chapter 2, many recent reforms of public services have been shaped by the idea of 'personalization' and person-centred planning. The belief is that people should be given greater choice and control over how best to meet their needs, all set within a human rights framework (Department of Health 2010b: 5). Clients can be given their own budgets to spend on their needs and care. Parents, by and large, should be free to raise their children as they see fit without the 'nanny' state interfering. People should make their own plans for old age and not automatically expect the state to pick up the bill for any care they might need.

In this political vision, the state's approach to welfare is therefore minimalist (Dickens 2010). Purchasing services from the private sector is acceptable. And those who cannot afford to buy services have the option of turning to charities and voluntary organizations which, under neoliberal politics, are expected to play a much bigger role in meeting people's welfare needs.

However, freedom and personal responsibility have consequences. If you fail, then on your own head be it. Failure, whether it's the abuse of drugs and alcohol, not having a job, getting pregnant in your teens, or committing crimes, hints at moral weakness which should not be rewarded. For too long the Welfare State has supported weakness and fecklessness. It is time to value freedom and reward responsibility.

The role of the state in the lives of those who are a risk to themselves or a risk to others is therefore twofold (Dickens 2010: 44–6). In the case of those who through no fault of their own need help to manage their lives, the state offers a safety net and a rescue service. In the case of those who break the law, don't play fair, or who refuse to pull their weight, the response is one of control and punishment. A hard-line, punitive approach is taken towards those who transgress.

The politics of freedom bloomed in the nineteenth century. This was a time when the poor and needy were divided into the deserving (the injured, ill, young, and old) and undeserving (the drunken, unemployed, criminal, neglectful, violent, bad, and mad).

Modern libertarian attitudes hint that they still find merit in these divisions. Neoliberal and paternalistic ideologies replace the dream of ending poverty in the name of social justice with 'the more functionalist goal of managing poverty to contain its deleterious effects on society and the economy' (Schram 2013: 67).

Equality and welfare

In practice, most societies recognise that unbridled freedom is likely to lead to a measure of brutishness. This is the paradox of freedom (Popper 1945). Too much freedom eventually leads to too little. If people are allowed to do what they like, the strong invariably exploit and abuse the weak. Thus, the self-interest and selfishness of some can cause deprivation and misery for others. When there are no rules and few constraints, only the strong, unprincipled, immoral, or privileged are likely to do well. The weak and vulnerable, the very old and the unwell, the dependent and unemployed, the caring and decent will struggle. All too often, unregulated freedom leads to inequality and injustice.

> Equality may demand the restraint of the liberty of those who wish to dominate; liberty – without some modicum of which there is no choice and therefore no possibility of remaining human as we understand the word – may have to be curtailed in order to make room for social welfare, to feed the hungry, to clothe the naked, to shelter the homeless, to leave room for the liberty of others, to allow justice or fairness to be exercised. (Berlin 1990: 12–13)

As we noted earlier, the mid-nineteenth century was a time of great individual and political freedom. The free rein given to the market certainly helped power industrial enterprise. But while it led to great wealth for some, it also meant increasing poverty for others. More and more people left the countryside to work in factories. This growing pool of cheap labour of men, women, and children, drove wages down and down. Vast numbers lived in overcrowded, poor-quality housing. The poorest struggled to feed themselves. And if you were unlucky enough to be old or ill, injured or disabled, then you were on your own, without work and entirely dependent on family or friends, felony or philanthropy. There was no Welfare State. Taxes were minimal and when they did exist, they were used to support only a limited range of state activities including paying for the navy and supporting the army.

However, as we observed in the opening chapter, it was becoming apparent that the growing mass of the poor also meant growing restlessness and discontent. There was always the fear by the rich that the poor might rise up, that revolutions might be fomented. People could only tolerate so much before desperation set in. And in fairness to many of the nineteenth century's rich and privileged, there was also genuine concern and compassion felt for the plight of the poor and the working classes.

Even the more full-blooded libertarians, the champions of the free market and personal responsibility, sensed that it was risky to leave so many people on or below the breadline. If misery was to be mitigated and dissent avoided, then some fairer ways of distributing the country's increasing wealth had to be introduced, if only to maintain the existing order.

Little by little the state began to provide better supports and provisions for those who were struggling to survive. Schools were built to educate the children of the working classes. By the early twentieth century, very modest pensions for the injured and old began to be introduced. There was legislation for better and safer working conditions. Housing standards improved. And to pay for all this, taxes of one kind or another were introduced. The price the rich and powerful were prepared to pay was a loss of some income and a slight increase in the rights of the lower classes.

Throughout the twentieth century, the idea and practice of a Welfare State slowly began to develop. Collective action and the idea of shared citizenship meant that by everyone pulling together and contributing something, everyone would be better off.

Governments took an increasing interest in people's behaviour and wellbeing. Laws, statutes, and policies grew to protect children, support families, improve housing, supervise offenders, treat those with a mental illness, provide residential care for the old and frail, and develop services for people with a disability.

People who championed the idea that the state should support, look after, and help those who struggled and got into difficulty became known as *communitarians* – people who believed communities adopting a caring, compassionate approach to their most vulnerable members were communities in which a strong sense of equality, belonging, commitment, and contentment were likely to be felt. It was thought that the best responses to social need and economic disadvantage were in the form of collective action.

The declared aim of this Welfare State was to protect people 'from the cradle to the grave' (Beveridge 1942). It was thinking of this kind which ushered in the social democratic state whose primary value was that of the removal of disadvantage and the promotion of equality – equality of opportunity, equality of treatment, equality of results (Banks 2012: 63). In this kind of state, less blame was laid at the feet of struggling individuals and more responsibility placed on the state to improve resources, services and opportunities for all citizens, including those in need.

The main mechanism to achieve these aims was the redistribution of wealth. Those with the most money were required to pay the highest taxes to help support the *universal* services of health, welfare, and education. A healthy, well-educated citizenry enjoying general wellbeing was seen as most likely to produce a stable, smooth-running society.

Although social work has a long history, the growth of the Welfare State gave the profession a huge boost to its extent and compass. The profession was also taking inspiration from many of the ideas being developed by post-war sociologists and psychologists.

For example, there was recognition that many troubled parents and children were themselves the products of disturbed, poor, and unhappy families. These parents and their families needed support, help, and guidance. Many people suffering mental ill-health and behavioural problems might also be better understood in terms of their biology, upbringing and stressful social environments.

Seeing people's problems and behaviour in these ways began to suggest that rather than wait until clients got into serious difficulty, it was much more sensible to help them before they become a risk to themselves or others. This approach encouraged social workers to think more about early interventions and preventative work, to nip things in the bud, and to help people become more psychologically resilient so that they were better equipped to deal with any future problems that might come their way.

The more extreme critics argued that most of the problems suffered by the poor were in fact problems of inequality – economic, social, political. Theirs was a critique of western capitalism. Their analysis demanded a radical change in the social and economic order. For radicals, most clients of social workers should not be seen as a problem for society. For most clients, it was society and all its manifest and entrenched inequalities that was a problem for them. Lack of jobs, run-down housing, deprived environments, inequalities of opportunity, overcrowded schools, minimum wages, and entrenched discrimination make it difficult to cope, and not coping is stressful. Long-term stress is not good for your mental health, physical health, parenting capacities, or relationships. Clients really need support and understanding. They need help and treatment. They need money and services. They need equality of opportunity and treatment. They need more power and control.

The clash of imperatives and living with moral uncertainty

However, for the neoliberal New Right of the 1980s, all of this welfarist talk was getting too much. It seemed to them that too many excuses were being made for delinquent children being the products of broken homes, neglectful parents being sufferers of poor mental health, drug addicts being the innocent casualties of a cruel world, and homeless families being the victims of a tough economic climate. All the talk was of understanding people's weaknesses. Their strengths and personal responsibilities were being ignored. Social democracy was promoting a 'dependency culture' and social work was one of the prime suspects charged with encouraging this culture (Rogowski 2012: 924).

For the new political Right, it seemed that the ideological pendulum had swung too far in the direction of equality, community, and collective responsibility. The politics of communitarianism were making too many people dependent on the Welfare State. Welfare and equality were sapping the nation's moral fibre. The emphasis on collective action and social control was undervaluing individual liberty and personal responsibility. There was no incentive to improve one's life. It was all too easy. It was therefore time to remind society that freedom and being responsible for your destiny were not only bracing but also much more likely to lead to change, improvement, and success. Social workers needed to shift their focus from the bigger issues of social justice and poverty to ones of individual behaviour, rights, and responsibility. Strong pressures were exerted to depoliticize social work. Any glint of a structural analysis or hint of a radical agenda was frowned upon.

According to this analysis, the Welfare State had become too intrusive. The best way to tackle rising crime rates, fecklessness, dysfunctional families, and the growing number of people on benefits was to make fewer excuses for those who were difficult or in difficulty. It was time to reduce the size of the Welfare State and revive ideas of individual freedom and personal responsibility. Success and change should be rewarded, not failure, deficiency, and weakness.

So from the 1980s to more or less the present day, there has been a resurgence of the politics of liberty, freedom, and personal responsibility. Neoliberal thinking has swept through governments, economics, personal behaviour, and social policy.

Social work, of course, hasn't been immune from these changes in the political climate (Harris 2008). The direction of social work policy and practice began to shift from focusing on the weaknesses of clients to promoting their strengths. There was less talk of why clients fail and more encouragement to help clients help themselves. The political emphasis changed from one of redistributing wealth to encouraging employment. Psychological causation was replaced by personal motivation. And as political philosophies shifted from people seeing themselves as victims to defining themselves as responsible, so clients were re-designated as 'consumers' and 'services users'.

Clients were discouraged from harking back to a deprived past and instead helped to take a more positive look and see a better future. Social excuses were out; individual strengths were in. 'Tell me what you can do, not what you can't do.' The focus was now on what can be changed rather than on what can't be fixed.

Riding this neoliberal wave were rafts of new social work theories and methods. They included solution-focused approaches, task-centred practices, strengths-based interventions, and motivational interviewing. Not only should people be treated as responsible for what happens to them in life, they should be credited with possessing strengths, answers, and expertise which the Welfare State for far too long had ignored. Independence, and not dependence, is the only long-term answer.

Individually, liberty and equality are fine principles by which to live. Each promotes many goods. More often than not we are quite content to back one or the other, but, as we have seen, in practice we find that all too frequently they clash head on.

It might seem reasonable to argue that parents should be free to spend their income how they choose. For example, rich parents might choose to buy their children a private education. However, if private education also buys children an advantage over their state school counterparts, making it more likely that they get places at the top universities and secure better-paid jobs, then freedom of choice comes into conflict with equalities of opportunity. Similarly, is it right that money can buy you private health care if that care is delivered faster and more thoroughly than state-provided health?

Equality argues that people should be treated the same unless there are *relevant* grounds for treating them differently. It is broadly true that race, gender, religion, sexual orientation, disability, and age are not seen as relevant grounds for treating people differently. This would be true in the case of giving children equal opportunities to enjoy a sound education, allocating all families decent housing, and providing good quality medical care for all those who need it.

But sometimes these same categories *might* be seen as relevant grounds for treating people differently, for example in the case of old people needing more help with transport and mobility, or recognising that women who have children might not be able to compete on a level playing field when it comes to job promotion. In these cases, equality is achieved by treating people differently because there are relevant grounds for doing so.

Thus injustice, said Aristotle, arises as much from treating unequals equally as from treating equals unequally (Peters 1966: 123).

In social work, the clash between these moral imperatives can be just as tricky. On the face of it, parents should be free to raise children as they see fit. The state should not interfere. But what does the situation look like from the child's point of view?

Clearly different parenting practices can lead children to experience different life prospects. Embedded in many parenting practices are a range of implied inequalities – inequalities of opportunity if your parents don't bother to send you to school every day, of health if your parents fail to keep immunization appointments, of emotional development if parents abuse or neglect you.

If children's needs are to be met and if children are to be given an equal chance to succeed along with their peers, there might be times when parental freedoms have to be overridden by other values, including ones of fairness and equality. Should a parent be free to reject medical treatment for their child if doctors believe the intervention will save the child's life? Should a parent be allowed to have contact with a child they have harmed who is now in foster care?

Similar moral dilemmas arise in adult care. A daughter's 90-year-old mother wants to stay put in her own home, but even with the help of the social care services, the daughter is exhausted caring for her parent. Whose freedom, whose autonomy do we respect? And in order for some very old and frail people to stay warm in winter and not die of cold, should people in work be required to pay taxes on their income? In any state with a modicum of welfare decency, not being entirely free to spend every penny of your income as you choose is the price that most of us are prepared to pay to iron out some of the inequalities that any society is bound to throw up. This is how Isaiah Berlin put it:

> Both liberty and equality are among the primary goals pursued by human beings through many centuries; but total liberty for wolves is death to the lambs, total liberty of the powerful, the gifted, is not compatible with the rights to a decent existence of the weak and the less gifted. (Berlin 1990: 12)

In practice, we have to steer a tricky course between the two. Neither freedom nor equality is an absolute value. Neither outbids the other in all situations. As moral imperatives they have to be discussed and debated, argued about, and negotiated in each unique situation. Even when cases raise obvious worries, it is not always clear what to do.

For example, in a case of child neglect we might know what *is* the case, but not necessarily what we *ought* to do. As the eighteenth-century Scottish philosopher, Hume (1967), observed, we cannot argue from an *is* to an *ought*, from an empirical observation to a moral action. What *is* the case doesn't tell us what we *ought* to do.

As we shall see in the next chapter, to make choices we have to hold values which direct us to courses of action which we think are best, the most effective, or the proper thing to do. Moral values cannot be thought about in the same way as empirical facts. Facts and values must not be confused. Nor can we derive values from facts.

So, the child *is* being neglected but *ought* we to remove him? Can the neglectful parent be helped and supported? Can he or she be taught to improve their skills of feeding, interacting, protecting, and stimulating their child? How to act based on what we see requires us to wrestle with a range of moral dilemmas and fine judgements. Different principles pull us in different directions. Parental autonomy versus child wellbeing; privacy and freedom versus social failure and state intrusion.

Social workers have no choice but to make such practical judgements, whether in cases of mental illness, child protection, or adult care, on a daily basis. Moral trading is therefore unavoidable:

...if we allow that Great Goods can collide, that some of them cannot live together, even though others can – in short, that one cannot have everything, in principle as well as in practice... then... 'What is to be done?' How can we choose between possibilities? What and how much can we sacrifice to what? There is, it seems to me, no clear reply... But claims can be balanced, compromises reached: in concrete situations not every claim is of equal force – so much liberty and so much equality; so much for sharp moral condemnation, and so much for understanding a given human situation; so much for the full force of the law, and so much for the prerogative of mercy... So we must engage in what are called trade-offs – rules, values, principles must yield to each other in varying degrees in specific situations. (Berlin 1990: 17)

But as a social worker, don't expect any thanks for agonizing over these dilemmas. If you back freedom and autonomy someone is sure to tell you that you should have been on the side of welfare and equality. If you rail against prejudice and discrimination, you will surely be accused of being politically correct to the point of madness.

14
Facts and Values
What is Known and What Ought to be Done

Introduction

If they are to do their job well, social workers need to know many things, including lots of facts. They need to know facts about the law and facts about departmental policies and procedures. They need to gather facts about clients' situations and compile facts by enquiring, observing, and researching. When they go to court or write a report or apply for a resource, they will be asked to present the facts of the case.

However, facts rarely speak for themselves. They have to be interpreted. They have to be judged. They have to be seen in context. Whenever social workers make decisions, make judgements or mount arguments, they have to shift from stating what is the case (matters of fact) to deciding what ought to be done (matters of opinion). Expressions of opinion and arguments about what ought to be done involve values. Values may be professional or personal, but they all fall under the purview of moral philosophy and not natural philosophy, which is to say the empirical sciences.

Social work is an intriguing business inasmuch as it asks its practitioners to be skilled in matters of fact as well as matters of opinion. Social workers have to be good at gathering facts, knowing things, and applying knowledge. On the other, they have to make judgements and take decisions. Social workers have to show nimbleness and finesse as they constantly move between facts and values, between what is *true* and what is *right*, between *science* and *ethics*. Most social work situations demand ethical sensitivity and technical flexibility. Making a judgement is therefore unavoidable. Dingwall et al. (1983) give an example arising out of child protection work.

Child protection raises complex moral and political issues which have no one right technical solution. Practitioners are asked to solve problems every day that philosophers have argued about for the last two thousand years and will probably debate for the next two thousand… These difficulties, however, are not a justification for avoiding judgements… What matters is that we should not disguise this and pretend it is all a matter of finding better checklists or new models of psychopathology – technical fixes when the proper decision is a decision about what constitutes a good society. How many children should be allowed to perish in order to defend the autonomy of families and the basis of the liberal state? How much freedom is a child's life worth? (Dingwall et al. 1983: 244)

Facts

Put somewhat simply, social workers hold two kinds of knowledge: knowledge *that*, and knowledge *how*. 'Knowledge that this is the case' includes knowing a wide range of facts – about the law, policies, procedures, rules, resources, systems, responsibilities, clients, behaviours, neighbourhoods, human development, theories, and methods.

Trevithick (2013: 120) recognises five types of factual knowledge (knowledge *that*) which are important to social workers: (i) law and legislation; (ii) social policy; (iii) agency policy, procedures, and systems; (iv) information relating to particular problems; and (v) information relating to specific groups of people. She distinguishes these types of factual knowledge from knowledge associated with practice. Practice knowledge covers *how* knowledge and skills are applied in practice, and so includes all of social work's theories and methods of intervention (Trevithick 2013).

People can be said to be doing some jobs simply by virtue of being in the role connoted by that job. These are *role-jobs* (Downie and Loudfoot 1978). For example, being appointed mayor of the city doesn't imply the display of any particular skills. Simply being elected mayor means that the person elected is now in the job of being mayor. This is not to say some people don't carry out their duties of mayor without flair or commitment.

Similarly, some element of being in the job of a social worker will be present as soon as you are appointed to the *role* of social worker.

The job might give you the right to intervene in the lives of others should a situation demand it. And with such rights come duties, rules, and responsibilities. The social worker must know these rights and rules, duties and responsibilities if she is to be recognised as being in the role of social worker. It would be possible to be seen to be doing the job of social worker entirely in terms of these official roles. We get a sense of this when people say 'I'm just doing my job' or 'I am only following the rules.' However, as these roles involve social workers dealing with people in complex and often stressful situations, it is unlikely that simply being in the role and following the rules would be sufficient to be seen as doing the job well. Bureaucratically sound yes, but professionally appropriate, no.

'Knowing *how*' refers to skills and techniques. It is possible to think about jobs in terms of how much they are defined by, and made up of particular skills and their performance. Some jobs are defined entirely by the presence of certain well-performed skills. Without the possession of these particular skills, an individual would not be recognised as doing that kind of job. For example, to be recognised as a musician requires the possession of a certain level of musical skill and ability. Someone who picks up a violin and just scratches away tunelessly wouldn't be seen as a musician. To become skilled at an activity normally requires many hours of practice, and possibly some natural talent. We therefore don't talk about a musician's job in terms of a role but rather in terms of the presence of certain music-making skills.

To the extent that in order to be seen to be doing social work, you need to possess certain skills and you need to perform them well, then social work might be defined as a *skill-job* (Downie and Loudfoot 1978). Developing skills in human relationships, leadership, report writing, case presentations, and decision making generally involve a lot of practice, good supervision, and constructive feedback. Skilled social workers know *how* to do the job. However, in most cases, people first have to be appointed to the role of social worker, including its statutory responsibilities, before they can be in a position to exercise their skills.

Knowledge of facts and 'knowing *that*' on their own would not define a competent social worker. It is what is done with the factual knowledge – laws, procedures, theories, methods – that matters. 'Knowing *how*' to do things is as important, if not more so, than simply being appointed to the role of being a social worker. But knowing how to do something and being skilful at doing it still does not say whether it should be done in the first place. Deciding whether a thing should be done involves making a judgement and making judgements involves values.

Values

Knowledge and facts give us information about what is the case and ideas about what to do. But however knowledgeable is the social worker or however gifted with technical skills, she still has to make practical judgements about how she ought to act in given situations.

> No amount of knowledge of what is the case can ever establish for us what we ought to do about it. The need for practical judgment of what we ought to do, granted our knowledge, is inescapable; and therefore there are radical limitations to the possibility of expertise. (Downie and Loudfoot 1978: 122)

Whenever the social worker moves from saying 'I now know this and that' about a case to then wonder 'But what *ought* I to do?', she is shifting from matters of fact to questions of value. So, following the philosopher Hume (1967), whose arguments we first met in the previous chapter, we cannot derive an *ought* from an *is*. The decisions we take, the judgement we make, the choices we pursue are based on our values.

Although talk of ethics and values has been present from the moment the social work profession came into being, current thinking has refined our understanding of these issues. Values are now seen as a defining feature of the profession, holding much of what is done ethically together. Ethics and values underpin and support what we do across all client groups whatever methods of intervention we employ. As professional judgements and matters of discretion enter the frame, so our minds must turn to moral matters.

> Social work embraces work in a number of sectors (public, private, independent, voluntary); it takes place in a multiplicity of settings (residential homes, neighbourhood offices, community development projects); practitioners perform a range of tasks (caring,

The Compleat Social Worker

controlling, empowering, campaigning, assessing, managing); and the work has a variety of purposes (redistribution of resources to those in need, social control and rehabilitation of the deviant, prevention or reduction of social problems, and empowerment of oppressed individuals and groups). Faced with such diverse roles and settings, some argue that it is the values of social work that hold it together. (Banks 2012: 2)

The philosophical ideas which inform and define what we mean by ethics and values in social work are, not surprisingly, sophisticated and thought-provoking. Fortunately there are a number of excellent books on the subject which will help us to think our way through these moral challenges (Banks 2012; Beckett and Maynard 2013; Dickens 2013; Gray and Webb 2010; Parrot 2010). Let's tease out some key ideas.

Ethics are about matters of right and wrong in our conduct and behaviour. They look at our character in terms of qualities which are good and qualities which are bad. They consider how we should behave in relationships.

Values, not surprisingly, are about what is regarded as valuable and worthwhile. Professional values consider how practitioners should treat their clients. In their actions, social workers should be mindful of promoting the good society. Professionals should strive to act in a worthy manner.

Moral philosophy provides social work with a number of basic *principles*. These are often guided by Immanuel Kant's dictum that we should only behave in ways that we would wish others would behave towards us (Kant 1785/1964). We should never treat other people as means to an end but always as ends in themselves.

One of the most important principles is *respecting the individual* as a rational, self-determining being and treating him or her with dignity, respect, and worth. This fits nicely alongside the growth of service user involvement in service design and delivery. Other universal principles include *treating people fairly and equitably* in terms of ensuring their welfare and wellbeing, and *promoting social justice*.

Promoting social justice has been a key feature in many people's idea of what social work should be about. The idea supports equality of treatment and access to services. Society's resources should be distributed according to individual need. People who are disadvantaged by poverty or poor health, learning disability or old age should, in fairness, be given extra resources so that they, too, might enjoy a decent life, equal opportunities and reasonable wellbeing.

For example, the concept of independent living, supported by a number of important values, is premised on the following four basic principles:

1. That all human life, regardless of the nature, complexity, and/or severity of impairment is of equal worth.
2. That anyone, whatever the nature, complexity, and/or severity of their impairment, has the capacity to make choices and should be enabled to make those choices.
3. That people who are disabled by societal responses to any form of accredited impairment – physical, sensory, or cognitive – have the right to exercise control over their lives.
4. That people with perceived impairments and labelled 'disabled' have the right to participate fully in all areas – economic, political, and cultural – of mainstream community living on a par with non-disabled peers. (SCIE 2004, cited in Wilson et al. 2011: 588)

The idea of *person-centred planning* when working with clients who have a learning disability takes much of its inspiration from respecting human rights and believing in social justice. Whereas 'personalization' recognises people's rights to choose the services and resources they deem best for them, person-centred planning 'is concerned with how people with learning disabilities learn and how they can make difficult decisions for themselves' (Buchanan 2013: 254).

The White Paper, *Valuing People* (Department of Health 2001), recognises the importance of giving people with a learning disability more choice and control. Supported by the four basic principles of Rights, Independence, Choice, and Inclusion, the individual client is placed at the centre with family and friends acting as full partners. Furthermore, 'person-centred planning' requires workers to continue paying attention and listening to what their clients have to say to help them get what they want out of life (SCIE 2005; Wilson et al. 2011: 588).

Oppression and discrimination, too, should be challenged whenever they are met. 'Practitioners who work from an anti-oppressive standpoint,' writes Burke (2013: 416), 'reject taken-for-granted ideas about the nature of inequality, power and privilege. Through practices fostering conditions characterized by care, mutuality and equality they can, with others, contribute to the difficult process of changing systems which preserve inequality and social exclusion.'

Social justice exists when societies operate fairly, freely, and equally allowing people to live safely, develop well, and achieve their potential. In such societies, people not only expect to be treated fairly, equally, and supportively but they, in turn, are expected to play their part in bringing about and maintaining a fair and just society (Smith 2008). However, in reality, those who support the idea of a socially just society recognises that very often many of society's policies, laws and institutions benefit the rich and powerful at the expense of the poor and weak who are social work's traditional constituents. This is unjust. Whenever social workers meet injustice and unfairness, they should speak out and act. Indeed, for Fine and Teram (2013) fighting moral injustice and championing social fairness are the very essence of social work.

Values such as the need to promote fairness and social justice have given rise to what Giddens refers to as *emancipatory politics* (Giddens 1991; Ferguson 2001). Structurally-based social work, too, taps deep into the politics of social justice. Structurally-based social work and radical critiques look at the economic, political, and social contexts of people's lives. They are mindful of issues of gender, sexual orientation, race, age, and disability. Structural social work prefers not to blame the individual but critically look at existing social arrangements. Thus, emancipatory politics attempts to expose and make people aware of inequality and injustice, oppression and discrimination (Mullaly 2007; Fook 2012). It seeks the emancipation of clients from inequality and oppression so that along with everyone else, they, too, can enjoy a fair life whatever their age, ability, ethnicity, or gender.

However, like most principles, respect, freedom, equality, justice, and fairness can and do clash. Values collide. Moral imperatives can and do come into conflict. Social work is a profession which poses an unusually high numbers of *ethical dilemmas* for its practitioners. This reflects the complexity and uncertainty present in the work (Gray and Webb 2010). But it also reflects the diversity, plurality, and richness of human life which refuses to be reduced to simple formulae, contained by bureaucratic boxes, or confined by rigid rules.

We met an example of colliding values in the previous chapter when we were looking at freedom and equality. But there are other examples. Client confidentiality is important, but there will be cases in which the rights of another might mean that confidentiality should be broken. A parent mentions that he 'accidently' scalded the baby when he was drunk. In value terms, the protection of the child is likely to outbid the value of client confidentiality. An old person with dementia wants to continue living at home on her own but the social worker isn't sure that she will be safe. Does the worker put safety first and arrange residential care or does she continue to respect the client's right to choose and increase the amount of home support made available?

For social workers one of the most frequently met clashes is when the principle of respect for the individual as a self-determining being comes up against the need to control a socially troublesome or troubled individual by limiting their freedom to act. There is rarely a clear-cut right choice in these situations and social workers simply have to make a practical judgement, albeit one based on careful, considered reflection and thought. As Banks (2012: 18) reminds us, laws only tell us what we can do, not what we ought to do.

In practice, many of our decisions are made only after we have spent some time reflecting and ruminating, usually with one or more of our colleagues. Should a boy who is failing to attend school, who is menacing the neighbourhood, and refusing to see the educational psychologist be removed from home against the wishes of the boy and his father? Should a 15-year-old girl with a learning disability who lives with her alcoholic mother be supported in keeping her baby? Should an elderly man be free to refuse the efforts of the environmental health office to clean up his house even though the agencies feel that the squalor in which he lives is a risk to the health of the man and his neighbours? Decisions in each of these cases are matter of judgements which can only be arrived at through critical reflection and reflexive thought. *Discourse ethics* have proved helpful in these cases insofar as they remind us that there are many forces at work limiting who can speak and how they are heard.

Discourse ethics was developed by the German social theorist, Jurgen Habermas (e.g. Habermas 1990). His work has been of interest to a number of social work scholars (Gray and Webb, Houston 2010). Discourse ethics holds precious the idea that everyone should have a fair hearing, and that a person's wealth, power, position, authority, or influence should have no bearing on the worth or weight of what is said and heard. What a person says enters the arena of discourse and there it is given a fair and full hearing.

Banks (2012: 45) helpfully reports Habermas' rules of discourse in the following list:

1. Every subject with the competence to speak and act is allowed to take part in a discourse.
2. a. Everyone is allowed to question any assertion whatsoever.
    b. Everyone is allowed to introduce any assertion whatever into the discourse.
    c. Everyone is allowed to express his [sic] attitudes, desires and needs.
3. No speaker may be prevented, by internal or external coercion, from exercising his rights as laid down in (1) and (2). (Habermas 1990: 89)

This reminds us that we must allow clients to speak, be heard and understood whether it is during the course of an investigatory visit, an interview, a review, a conference, a court, or a meeting to plan where to go next.

Seeing the world from the other's point of view is a key social work skill. However, clients are unlikely to risk too much 'speech' until they feel that the relationship with the worker is a safe one, one that can be trusted (see chapter 12). Here, ethics and values, and relationship-based social work go hand in hand. Which leads us to the next take on ethics and values.

Recently a good deal of interest has been taken in what is known as *virtue ethics* or *relationship-based ethics* (Banks 2012). This is a philosophical approach which potentially has great relevance for social work. Principle-based ethics, discussed above, provide the worker with a number of universal values, such as respect for persons and confidentiality, which should be followed in all cases at all times.

In contrast, virtue ethics pays more attention to the qualities that workers possess as they engage with each one of their clients (Houston 2003; Clark 2006). Rather than base actions and decisions on rational, abstract, and universal principles, virtue-based ethics sees social workers acting on what they believe to be right, proper, and caring. Social workers should do the right things for the right reasons. The *character* of the social worker matters. It is important what kind of person he or she is. So the question is 'What kind of social worker should I be?' rather than 'What should I do?' (Houston 2012: 656).

To practice ethically, and ultimately effectively, social workers need to possess one or more of a number of key virtues. These include such things as kindness, truthfulness, care, compassion, empathy, courage, integrity, impartiality, openness, and honesty. Beckett and Maynard (2013) explain the idea of virtue rather nicely:

> Let's be honest, if we were to ask you whether a person of your acquaintance – let's call him Karl – struck you as being a good person, you would be unlikely to say, 'Yes he is, because he always does his duty'. Nor would you say, 'Yes he is, because he always works out the consequences of everything he does, and makes sure he only does the thing that has the best outcome for most people'. More likely you would say something like: 'Yes he is, because he is brave, loyal, generous and kind'. In other words, your view on whether or not Karl is a good person would be based on your estimation of his virtues (and on their opposite, his vices) rather than on an analysis of the principles of action that he applies. (Beckett and Maynard 2013: 31)

We also meet the idea of the virtuous social worker when we ask clients what they think makes a good social worker (Houston 2003; Howe 1993; Rhodes 1986; Mayer and Timms 1970). Clients tell us they value warmth and friendliness, understanding and acceptance, reliability and a willingness to listen, open-mindedness and 'being straight', shows of support and acts of kindness, offers of hope, and a sense of purpose.

These are the kind of virtues which, if possessed by everyone, would make for a good and decent society. If workers believe that these are good character traits, then they should present them in their practice. And if these virtues are present in the worker–client relationship, then that practice is likely to possess a certain kind of ethical soundness. Thus, observes Webb (2010: 119), if we are to develop good social workers, then along with many other things, we should also be promoting their moral education and training their character.

But there is yet another ethical position, one that seems to suit social work particularly well. *Care ethics* is another form of relationship-based ethics. Care ethics recognises and values the virtues present in close, caring, protective family relationships, particularly between mothers and their children. Care ethics differs from virtue ethics in the sense that it emphasizes what takes place in the caring relationship (Gray 2010). It is only indirectly concerned with an individual's character and inherent virtues. 'Care is an activity *and* an attitude' (Featherstone and Morris 2013: 348, emphasis original).

Vulnerability is part of our lot as human beings. There will be times when any one of us will feel fragile or vulnerable. These are the times when we look to others for care and protection, acceptance and understanding, love and recognition. Recognising and responding to other people's needs is the starting point for an ethics of care (Tronto 1993). In this sense, care ethics reflects a feminist approach to the subject of values in social work.

> The morality associated with an ethic of care is tied to concrete circumstances rather than being an abstract philosophical concept. Moreover, the morality is best expressed not as a set of principles but as an activity – the activity of caring. (Featherstone 2010: 74)

Caring relationships are ones in which relatedness, receptivity and responsiveness are present (Noddings 2003; Featherstone 2010). Abstract principles are replaced by personal relationships. Recognition and value is given to interdependence, vulnerability, and mutual care. There is less talk of respecting persons and more interest in caring about this woman, Jane, or this man, John. Whereas abstract notions of justice talk about rights and rules, ethics of care centre on the concrete business of people relating one to another and feeling mutually responsible (Featherstone and Morris 2013).

Actions and behaviours which promote interdependence between people generally cement relationships and create a sense of belonging and wellbeing. They are life-sustaining, physically and emotionally. Care promotes mutual love and respect. It is an integral part of citizenship and the idea of the civil society (Featherstone and Morris 2013: 245). Intuition also runs through the idea of care. Helping in social work, believes Jordan (1978), is as much to do with caring and sharing as it is to do with looking for technical fixes.

The idea of care takes the other's needs as the starting point for what must be done. Care, according to Tronto (1993) consists of four connected phases and their ethical implications:

1. *Caring about,* demanding *attentiveness.*
2. *Taking care of,* involving *responsibility.*
3. *Care giving,* requiring *competence.*
4. *Care receiving,* implying *responsiveness.*

Care, therefore, is an active ethic, involving thought and action (Featherstone 2010: 77). In this sense, an ethics of care is much more than a set of principles or desirable feelings. It is a practical business in which people value each other in the context of caring relationships. To give and receive care humanizes us. It makes us feel worthwhile. It makes us moral beings. It helps us feel that we belong. In fact, much of our moral development as children and our growing ability to care for others is the result of us being lovingly cared for by others (Hollway 2006; Howe 2012).

Knowledge, skills, and values

As Beckett (2006: 18) reminds us, social workers acquire knowledge, deploy skills, and hold values, but knowledge, skills, and values are three very different things.

> Knowledge can tell us what our choices are and what their consequences might be. Skills set limits on what choices are practicable. But when it comes to making the choice itself, this will be determined by values. (Beckett 2006: 19)

There are links as well as limits between these three domains. You can read as many books as you like about how to drive a car, but not until you try driving one will the skill of car driving be achieved. In fact, you could learn to drive a car without ever reading a book that tells you about steering wheels, clutches, accelerators, brakes, and engines. But what you do with your driving skills is another matter and can, occasionally, raise matters of value.

The skill of driving might be thought of as value-neutral. But the uses to which you put your driving skill involves choice and choices involve values. Robbing banks and escaping at great speed in a 'get away' car is likely to be judged immoral, and certainly illegal. Volunteering to drive old people with mobility problems to a day centre seems a morally decent thing to do. But what about driving for pleasure or for short journeys to the local shops? As well as get you about speedily and efficiently, cars also pollute the atmosphere, emit greenhouse gases, cause accidents, decrease opportunities for exercise, and increase the risk of obesity. Few things we do are, in fact, entirely value-neutral.

And if this is true for something as simple as driving a car, how much more complex when we consider the work and actions of social workers. In social work it is not enough to know the law, procedures, rules, circumstances, theories, methods, research findings, and form filling. You need skills. You need to know how to observe, listen, engage, connect, encourage, structure, empathize, direct, advocate, collaborate, battle, write, present, explain. Indeed, as we argued at the beginning of this chapter, without these skills being present, you could say that individuals, whatever they happen to know, could not be said to be doing social work.

So, social workers need to *know* many things. They need to be able to *do* many things, with skill. But however much they know and no matter how good their skills, they also have to decide what *ought* to be done. Judgements have to be made and decisions taken. And here questions of value arise.

Alice is 91 and lives on her own. She is frail and has arthritis in her feet and hands. This means that things like cooking and washing are difficult. Recently she has shown some confusion, and her doctor has diagnosed the presence of Alzheimer's disease, albeit not yet severe. Over the last month she has twice scalded herself trying to drain a pan of boiling potatoes. She has help at home every day for short periods as well as receiving a hot meal which is delivered at lunchtime. The social worker observes Alice at home. She talks with her, her relatives, home help and family doctor. The social worker has now amassed a lot of facts and information about Alice's situation. There are risks and a moderate probability that she could have a serious accident. The social worker has a good relationship with Alice and has shown great skill in bringing all the facts together.

But Alice is adamant that she does not want to move into residential care. Given the rising risks, at what point, if any, do those risks outweigh Alice's wish to stay at home? Does the presence of Alzheimer's and her impaired capacity to reason and think mean that she should forfeit her right to remain in her house, given that relatives, neighbours, home help services, and doctors say they are unwilling to keep up their support given the amount of help and supervision they say she needs? Cases such as Alice and the value questions they raise pose everyday challenges for adult social care workers.

When working with Alice, the ethical social worker blends professional principles with personal virtues in the context of a caring relationship. She respects Alice and her rights. She shows kindness and compassion, patience and perception. And as she strives to see and hear the world from Alice's point of view, the social worker begins to know the woman. A relationship forms in which the social worker viscerally begins to care *about* as well as care *for* Alice. Clients are tuned into each one of these ethical frequencies. It is when they feel recognised, understood, and valued that clients begin to trust, engage, and show a willingness to collaborate.

Similar dilemmas are faced by child and family social workers. They, too, gather facts, accumulate evidence, read the research, refer to the law, consider procedures and, ideally, relate with skill to their clients. But as in so much of social work, no amount of knowledge about what is the case can tell you what ought to be done.

Kristina is 22. She suffers bipolar disorder and has panic attacks. She became pregnant in her late teens. Although some concerns were expressed by both the midwife and health visitor about Kristina's ability to concentrate on her baby boy, Ryan, and feed and change him when needed, he managed to get through his first year without any social services involvement.

When Ryan was aged two, he was joined by his half-sister Alicia. From the outset it was apparent that Kristina was struggling. She was not taking her medication. The children suffered severe neglect. Alicia's nappy rash, missed immunization appointments, and failure to gain much body weight resulted in the baby's admission to hospital. Neighbours also reported that on many occasions Kristina would go drinking in the local pub with her partner leaving the children in the care of a young man who would invite his mates around to take drugs. The police were regularly involved as were children's social services. There were incidents of domestic violence, starving children and an empty fridge, food poisoning, Kristina feeling depressed and listless, and finally unexplained injuries to both Ryan and Alicia, including a broken rib and bruises on the little girl dating back several weeks.

The upshot was that the children were removed and eventually placed together for adoption. Kristina was admitted to psychiatric hospital with a complex diagnosis which included bipolar disorder.

18 months later, Kristina is no longer in hospital. She is on medication but her mental health social worker still has concerns that she sometimes doesn't take her pills. Kristina is now in the final trimester of her third pregnancy. She has been drinking and taking some cocaine while pregnant and there are worries about the health of the foetus. The father of the baby, with whom Kristina is currently living, is a known drug dealer who has a history of domestic violence.

The hospital, local doctor, and mental health worker have brought all of these facts to the attention of the children's services social worker. The health professionals do not think that Kristina is fit to look after the new baby and suggest removal at birth with a view to adoption. The mental health worker thinks that if Kristina gets herself off the drink and drugs, takes her medication, and receives support she will be able to cope. Kristina has said she wants to keep the baby and will do anything it takes to be a good mother, including leaving her violent partner (the father of the baby), taking her medication, going to parenting skills classes, and giving up the drugs and alcohol.

It is two weeks before the baby is due. The social worker and her department are now in possession of a huge file of facts. There is a conflict of opinion between the health and mental health professionals. So, what should the worker and her department do? Remove the baby or not? Of course, if the baby is removed, the ultimate decision will be that of a court, but nevertheless there is an impending decision that cannot be avoided, with risks and reassurances weighing in the balance.

This is typical of the many cases in which social workers are damned when they do and damned when they don't. If the child is removed and ultimately placed for adoption, it will never be known whether the mother would have actually coped and the baby thrived.

If the baby is left with the mother and in the event does suffer neglect and abuse and dies, in retrospect it will seem obvious that the pre-birth facts were sufficiently clear and weighty to make any decision not to remove look foolish and incompetent.

Such cases offer examples of what philosophers call 'moral luck' (Nagel 1979; Williams 1981). In these cases, moral judgements are made on consequences and outcomes, not well-rehearsed intentions. If I choose to drive home drunk, weaving erratically along the road, I could be arrested and found guilty of dangerous driving. However, if the same drunken action on my part leads to me running someone over and killing them, then the crime could be one of manslaughter which carries a much more severe penalty. The same action, drunken driving, has the potential to lead to very different consequences, radically different outcomes, and significantly different judgements. It is simply a matter of luck whether I career home without killing someone.

In our social work example, the competent social worker, having taken full and proper account of all the risk and protective factors, intends the best possible outcome for the child, given all that she knows. The science, the research and the empirical evidence informing child protection work can never be exact, so predicting outcomes can never be 100 per cent accurate. And so even the most skilled and best informed workers can make carefully weighed decisions with which others might disagree. Some might believe that by removing the child, the human rights of the mother have been trammelled and the baby, if she had been left with her parent, would have been safe. Or, alternatively, the worker decides to return the baby to the care of her mother where she subsequently suffers neglect or even death. The retrospective judgement by others in this case is that it now seems clear to anyone with an ounce of common sense that there were enough worrying signs to make any decision to return the baby a risky one.

Social workers are exposed to the seeming unfairness and apparent illogic of moral luck on a regular basis. However, intending good but causing harm happens in all walks of life. Doctors immunize toddlers knowing that the statistics are highly favourable in terms of future health benefits, but very occasionally a child might react adversely to the injection and die. Should the doctor have known that the risk was present and high in these rare, but particular cases? A schoolteacher takes a group of children on a school educational outing, having completed all the required risk assessment forms. But a child trips, falls in the stream, and drowns. Who, if anyone, is to blame?

Social work is a morally hazardous place. This partly accounts for its importance, its difficulty, and its stimulation. But when practised well, it is also a morally uplifting place where respect is shown and personal virtues abound. And because social life is a messy place, social workers are well served by a variety of value systems – the pursuit of universal and rational principles, ideas of the virtuous person, and the ethics of care, a position discussed with some elegance by Houston (2012) in his paper on value pluralism. Good social workers know many things, and one of the things they know is that facts alone are not enough. An appreciation of their work's moral character makes good social workers peculiarly sensitive, humane, and empathic. This is why values and virtues flow as a key part of the profession's lifeblood.

15
On the Whole and Taking Everything into Consideration

Introduction

We are now getting close to our idea of the *compleat* social worker. The previous 14 chapters have been looking at some of the divisions that have pulled social work apart. But rather than look for a simple reconciliation between the two sides, we have gone for synergy. Nature *interacting dynamically* with nurture offers far more possibilities than simply arguing that perhaps both views have merit. Feelings inform thought every bit as much as thought helps manage feelings. Social work's techniques can only take hold if there is a social work relationship.

There have been many spirited attempts to identify the things that social work's many approaches have in common. The idea of a common base has repeatedly attracted some of the profession's best minds. For example, the systems theorists of the 1970s sought to bring social work together within the compass of various grand, integrated models. Harriett Bartlett wrote a classic book in 1970 called *The Common Base of Social Work Practice* in which she tried to understand the profession as a whole. Others quickly followed in her wake including Howard Goldstein with *Social Work Practice: A Unitary Approach* (1973) and Allen Pincus and Anne Minahan who wrote *Social Work Practice: Model and Method* (1973).

These integrated, unitary models left little out. They attempted to capture every theory, method and client group in one unifying model. These were intellectually stimulating times in which social work was busy trying to pull itself together not only theoretically and practically but also professionally and organizationally.

More recently, ecological perspectives, which also take a holistic view, have had an energizing effect on social work theory and practice.

Ecology is the study of organisms as they relate to, and interact with their surrounding or 'home' environment, including other organisms. The Greek for 'house' is *oikus* from which we derive the prefix *eco*, hence ecology – the study of the house, home, environment – and economy, the management of a household or an environment.

Bronfenbrenner (1979) was one of the first to introduce the concept of ecology to human development and behaviour. Social ecology explores the connections, supports, cooperations, interdependences, reciprocities, and shared responsibilities which exist between people in groups and communities. The richer and more dense these connections the greater the 'social capital', that is the bonds that keep people together and support social wellbeing.

Rich social capital helps people cope better with old age, disability, poverty, illness. Jack (2000) argues that the key role for social workers practising ecologically therefore is to strengthen community, family, and kin networks. So although the model takes a social ecological perspective rather than an individualistic psychological one, nevertheless it recognises that healthy psychological development is more likely to take place in communities where there are strong bonds, a sense of belonging and rich social capital.

More specifically, Bronfenbrenner (1979) felt that in order to understand children's development, we had to look at the interactions between their genes, family, friends, neighbourhood, schools, class, wealth, society, and culture. All were relevant, all had a part to play.

> One of the reasons ecological theory is so useful for social work practice is that it provides a holistic organising framework within which to locate all the different elements of people's lives and the connections between them. This serves to remind social workers that the problems they encounter, rather than having a single cause, are more likely to be the product of combinations of factors at multiple levels of influence… (Jack 2013: 130)

Thus, a key insight when taking an ecological view is to recognise the importance of informal relationships and social supports in people's lives. Such relationships and supports provide individuals with advice, practical help, and emotional succour. Promoting social support networks reduces family stress. Lowering family stress decreases the risks of children being abused (Jack 1997). Jack therefore sees a link between strong social capital and healthy child development.

> …research dating back at least fifty years has demonstrated that trust, networks, norms of reciprocity within a child's family, school, peer group and larger community have wide-ranging effects on the child's opportunities and choices and hence, on his behaviour and development (Putnam 2000: 296)

Environments which feel unsafe and in which other people's behaviour is less predictable are stressful. These are places in which crime is common and mental health problems are high. Social ecological models recognise the importance of feeling safe and secure, and of having a sense of belonging and social solidarity. Socially supportive communities are ones in which people feel greater commitment and experience less stress.

Recent efforts to create more coherent, less divided views of social work have also brought together an interesting, sometimes surprising range of ideas. So, for example, we meet models which feel comfortable incorporating critical, reflexive, and evidence-based thinking. We find practices that recognise the importance of a strong value-base upon which rests the social work relationship. And running through all of these attempts to bring ideas together is the realization that effective social workers are good at giving their work order and structure. Practitioners who share with their clients a clear sense of place, purpose, and direction, who know where they are in the social work process, these practitioners create relationships in which others feel safe, relaxed, and motivated.

Before we attempt in the final chapter to bring these elements fully together in the idea of the *compleat* social worker, it is worth acknowledging that this present book is only one of a number of recent attempts to celebrate what social workers have in common rather than what keeps them apart. It is not possible to report in detail each and every one of these excellent projects, but readers will find much to inspire them in Kate Wilson and colleagues' innovative book *Social Work: an Introduction to Contemporary Practice* (2011), Steve Goodman's *Social Work Reclaimed* (2011), Pamela Trevithick's *Social Work Skills and Knowledge: a Practice Handbook* (2012), and Brid Featherstone, Susan

White and Kate Morris's *Re-imagining Child Protection: Towards Humane Social Work With Families* (2014).

But to help us on our way before we actually get to meet the *compleat* social worker, let's first have a brief look at a number of other landmark texts that have sought to recognise the best in social work. Each one nicely illustrates the open-mindedness as well as the critical acumen that continues to define the profession's best thinkers and most effective practitioners.

Pragmatic social work

For some commentators, social work practice is simply too complex to be captured by any one theory, ideology, or body of knowledge. 'In practising social work', believe Evans and Hardy (2010), 'you will need to be able to draw on a range of ways of understanding people in their various social situations, as well as understand your own impact on and relationship with them... Limiting yourself to one perspective curtails your ability to help' (pp. 13–14). And so Evans and Hardy are drawn towards taking a pragmatic approach.

They explain that as a philosophy, pragmatism is a broad church which accommodates diverse perspectives. Knowledge 'is seen as a practical vehicle for problem-solving' (Evans and Hardy 2010: 169). Pragmatism is happy to turn to the sciences for evidence of what works but it will push for practical solutions even when such evidence is thin.

In wanting to get the job done, 'pragmatists look to make use of methods which appear best suited to the task in hand... In this respect, they have no fixed theoretical or methodological allegiances, reflecting their belief that neither knowledge or the purposes to which it is put is static, and so theory and method have to change to reflect these variable contexts' (Evans and Hardy 2010: 169–79).

Thus, the pragmatic social worker is one keen to find solutions to problems. She is willing to reach for evidence but also recognises that good judgements require sound values. She is happy to change her mind when events require it and reflect on her own actions when things get stuck. In short, the pragmatic social worker sees practice as both an art and a science (see chapter 11).

Constructive social work

Parton and O'Byrne (2000) in their book *Constructive Social Work* thought hard and long about social work's perennial, enduring character. Like so many others before them, they recognised that social workers operate in a world where there is uncertainty and ambiguity.

Inspired by the idea that reality is social constructed, they explain that as we talk and use language, so we construct meaning – about who we think we are, what's going on, why things happen the way they do, what can and can't be done, and so on. As we talk and describe things first this way and then that, we are exploring different ways of thinking about and understanding things, including our own and other people's behaviour. We look for and find new meanings. Thus, purposeful talk between social workers and clients can and does change perceptions, meanings, understandings, realities, and, ultimately, behaviour.

This leads to the thought that much of what social workers do, and achieve, is a *process*, one that takes place as workers and clients interact and communicate. Indeed, the social worker's expertise is in engaging the client, forming a relationship, and facilitating the social process.

The constructive approach is described as affirmative and reflexive. Workers have to listen hard as well as talk collaboratively. Listening is something active and creative, not something passive (Jordan 1979: 19). And as worker and client talk, there is reflection, challenge, and doubt. There are ideas, wonderings, and criticisms. There is recognition of strengths and what is positive in a life or a situation. There is talk about what is possible rather what is impossible and can't be done.

However, the talk has to be of a particular kind. Weaknesses and deficiencies are not mentioned. There are no diagnostic labels attached to clients and their behaviour. All too easily, diagnostic labels define, delimit, and determine the client's reality. The labels take control of the client's story. Whatever knowledge and ideas the worker does introduce must be seen as shared information, a possible resource, a way of thinking about things which otherwise puzzle and frustrate.

Constructive social workers have a bias towards exploring solutions rather than accounting for problems. Indeed, following de

Shazer (1985) and brief solution-focussed approaches, there is little interest taken by the constructive social worker in what causes problems. Instead, talk about change and what might be possible is encouraged. So, not 'What caused the two of you to argue last night?' but 'How did you end it?' (Parton and O'Byrne 2000: 57). The talk is about what can be done, how it can be done, and let's get on and do it.

> Solutions are therefore built by the dialogue between service user and worker, talking in detail about the exceptions the person has noticed, about how they did that, about the difference it makes, about what others notice and say about it. The conversation builds on the positives, focusing on what the future without the problem will be like and focusing on the user's strengths and abilities, their confidence and their willingness to work hard at progressing. (Parton and O'Byrne 2000: 71)

In all of this, conversation and collaboration are key. The process of talking leads to new ideas, new possibilities, and the vision of a better future. The authors stress the ethical basis of practice, one which is reflexive, respectful, and empowering. In the conversational space that the worker sponsors, clients are encouraged to explore ideas and think of solutions. Practice is therefore premised on the relationship and the values which support it.

This outline of the constructive social worker helps us on our way as we look at practices that are pragmatic, grounded, reflexive, and flexible. These are approaches which systematically seek out the 'best', the most critically aware, and the most collaborative in social work's theories, research, and methods.

Critical best practice

The idea of 'best practice' in social work, as the superlative suggests, is one in which the evidentially, theoretically, and ethically best ideas are brought together, in a bespoke fashion, on a case-by-case basis (Jones et al. 2008).

It is rare for any practice to run in a neat, straight, textbook line. Best practice recognises that, in reality, the world is full of twists and turns. Unexpected things happen. There can be a pull and tension between the duties of the social worker and the choice, freedom, and individuality of the client. Best practice explores the best ways in which to act *under the circumstances*, drawing on values, relationship-based work, support networks, material advice, and evidence-based interventions where appropriate.

The 'best practice' approach lays great emphasis on tuning into the client's world and trying to understand what their experiences mean for them. It is important that the client's voice is heard, for them to tell their own story. All too often their voice is ignored, their views silenced. But what do clients have to say? What is their experience? What ideas do they have about their needs and how they should be met? What are their thoughts about creating better services? And with attentive listening comes better understanding.

Giving clients their voice can be particularly effective when they speak together – in support groups, campaigning groups, political arenas, community projects. Listening to clients who have learning disabilities can be very informative. Allowing those who have a mental illness to give voice to their feelings and thoughts on the prospects of going into psychiatric hospital is important. And trying to stay with an aggressive father who feels angry and powerless as all three of his children are taken off to hospital for examination is not easy, but may be a vital first step in working with the family.

The ability to tune in is also helped by practising in a critically reflexive way (Brechin et al. 2000). Critical practices involve being critically aware of yourself – what you say, think and feel – as you talk with others. Whether client or worker, our psychological make-up comes into play in all kinds of ways. Our emotions can de-rail us or make us unreasonable. Our thoughts can get stuck in a groove. Our beliefs are a product of our background or training or prejudices. As we saw in chapter 6, when we engage with others, we have to pay attention not only to the outer world and what's going on there, but also to the inner world of our own and other people's thoughts and feelings (Schofield 1998; Cooper and Lousada 2005; Winnicott 1964).

Critical best practices require that we should treat other people fairly and with respect. The practitioner should recognise how the law, circumstances, social context, resources, and the respective roles and positions of worker and client affect what people, including the social worker, think and feel. Issues of power, inequality and constraint are recognised, but, just as important, the strengths of the client have to be used and acknowledged (Jones et al. 2008: 24). Hence critical best practice's interest in, but not slavish adoption of solution-focussed and strengths-based approaches. For example, a social worker within the context of a long-term supportive relationship with a mother, mentioned that 'The mother would focus on the daughter's "got seven spellings wrong out of ten" and I'd say, "Brilliant you got three right, get four right next week"' (Ferguson 2008: 154).

The book edited by Karen Jones, Barry Cooper and Harry Ferguson (2008) provides many excellent examples of 'best practice' across all client groups. 'Best practitioners' represent a type of *compleat* social worker in so far as they draw on, and integrate a wide range of knowledge-bases, interventions and skill sets on a case-by-case basis. The following example, taken from the book, helpfully illustrates this flexible, creative, empathic, feet-on-the-ground way of working (Keeping 2008).

Celia Keeping is an Approved Social Worker. One of her duties is to organize assessments of mentally ill patients with a view to making a compulsory admission to hospital. We join the case as Celia is about to meet Jane, a patient, in her friend's flat. Also present are Jane's GP and a psychiatrist. Celia has chosen the case because it:

> … focuses on the importance of *emotional engagement* within the social work encounter. Whether the core task is statutory assessment, practical assistance or therapeutic support, attention to the quality and nature of the emotional relationship between social worker and service user is intrinsic to best practice. As I hope to show…conscious and thoughtful emotional engagement on the part of the practitioner with the inner world of the service user is vital to the development of a meaningful, insightful and powerful relationship. (Keeping 2008: 71–2, emphasis in original)

Jane had arrived at the flat in an ambulance. Previously she had been staying in a nursing home where she had been diagnosed with Myalgic Encephalomyelitis (M.E.) or Chronic Fatigue Syndrome. The home, however, discharged her saying that they could no longer cope with her high levels of anxiety and difficult behaviour. Her mother, who had also been looking after Jane, said the same.

When Celia and the two doctors arrived at the flat they found Jane to be extremely anxious, panicky, and distressed. She was unable to move except by crawling around on all fours. Celia recognised that the sudden appearance of three formal figures must have provoked feelings of shock, powerlessness, and panic in Jane's mind. Jane also knew that she might be compulsorily admitted into hospital – that is, 'sectioned' under the Mental Health Act. In the face of her highly distressed and odd behaviour, there was the distinct temptation by Celia just to 'get on' and do the assessment, rather than engage and understand Jane – the danger of 'doing' rather than 'being', as Keeping nicely puts it.

The situation was therefore fraught and in a state of crisis. Jane was homeless and unable to look after herself. She was 'falling apart' and feeling psychotic. Jane, her family, and friends felt a range of emotions including distress, fear, panic, guilt, anger, and blame. Celia felt that it was important to 'contain' these emotions in the manner described by Wilfred Bion (1962).

One of the key emotional tasks for practitioners working in highly charged situations is to be honest about what might happen but also to recognise, acknowledge, hold, and contain the difficult feelings flying around, including those which the social worker herself feels. However, instead of being caught up in the emotional maelstrom, the worker tries to contain the anxieties on behalf of the client and others so that everyone feels less aroused, and a little more secure and able to reflect. Containing, processing, and psychologically 'holding' strong feelings gives the client a space, a brief moment to stop and think rather than run and panic. The social worker is then in a position to explore with the client, and others, where to go next in the face of the crisis.

There may be no ideal path which to take, but making an empathic and emotional connection with Jane at least allows the possibility of finding some way forward under the difficult circumstances. This is how Celia describes her position:

> The powerful feelings evoked in me could be seen partly as a vivid form of the communication through which Jane was conveying the horror of her predicament. It was therefore vital for me to listen to and reflect upon those feelings. To undertake the emotional labour involved in meeting another person on this level

demands attention and energy, but for me it constitutes the heart of critical best social work practice. (Keeping 2008: 80)

It was clear to Celia, the social worker, that Jane's situation was desperate. Resources were limited. She couldn't stay with her friend. Her mother could no longer cope. After talking at length with Jane and consulting with her two medical colleagues, the decision was made to compulsorily admit Jane to hospital under Section 2 of the Mental Health Act. The decision to deprive Jane of her liberty weighed heavily on Celia, but it was her role and responsibility to make the assessment and consider the extent that the client, her mental state, and physical behaviour were posing a risk to herself. Jane was kept in hospital for the next four months.

Since this admission, which took place five years earlier, Celia has remained involved with Jane as her care coordinator, giving her emotional and practical support. Psychologically 'holding' Jane has allowed her to explore, recognise, and build up her emotional strengths. Jane now lives in a supported house which she shares with four others. Social worker and client continue to talk about the day Jane went to hospital. In conversation, Celia reminded Jane that she 'sectioned her'. Jane remembered:

Yes, you did! I hated you – who is this woman coming into my life and taking over? I did need to go into hospital but I couldn't see it then – I couldn't see that there was anything wrong with me – you can't if you're ill. But it did help. I got really physically well... (Keeping 2008: 81)

I remember saying to Mum: 'I can't find Jane. I don't know where she's gone.' I lost my centre. My vision – it was awful – those things I kept seeing – so frightening... I feel better now – I'm in touch with my centre, my core now – it's still fragile but it's there – it's the stuff around the centre that's difficult between me and the world, but I'm in touch with myself now. So much better... (Keeping 2008: 83, 85)

Jane still has problems, good days and bad, but the continuity of care provided by Celia and the feeling of being 'held' – by the structure of the supported housing and the emotional relationship with her worker – have been important to Jane. But let's give the last word on this case to the excellent Celia:

> As social workers we are governed by various legislative, organisational and bureaucratic structures, which aim to deal with welfare issues in a technical/managerial way. Human pain is a complex and messy business however and requires more than a one-dimensional 'doing' approach to practice. The process of engaging with the psychological and emotional life of service users requires close attention, resilience, courage and a willingness to face our own sometimes painful responses. However it is my experience that through this act of emotional engagement we are able to offer a source of help which can enrich both our own lives and the lives of those with whom we work. (Keeping 2008: 86)

The models and ideas of social work outlined above beseech social workers constantly to reflect on their actions, their thoughts, and their feelings. The good social worker never forgets to keep her client's world in mind as together they struggle to find meaning, make sense, and recover control.

16
The Compleat Social Worker

Introduction

We began the book by recognising that social workers practice in the middle ground, between the individual and society. They need to know something of individuals and their psychological make-up. They need to know something of the social context and environment in which clients live their lives. Practitioners work with people on the margins, who are vulnerable, disadvantaged, and failing to cope. They meet the troubled and troublesome. They face inequality and injustice.

For some, social workers offer a safety net buffering them from uncertainty, crisis and insecurity (Webb 2006: 38). Social workers get involved when people hit a 'fateful moment' and are looking for support (Webb 2006: 15). Marriages break down, partners get divorced, parents abuse their children, old people become frail, children need care, adults become clinically depressed, a child is born with a learning disability – these are all fateful moments, times of need, concern, fear, confusion and uncertainty.

Faced with these needs and problems, social workers search for the right thing to do. They think about how best to help people, and how to protect them and others. To help them understand their clients' needs and problems, social workers have to know something of the law, sociology, social psychology, human development, psychology, philosophy, and politics. Different schools of thought and intervention make strong cases to do things their way, to become skilled in the techniques of their approach, whether that approach is one of cognitive behavioural therapy, social learning theory, crisis intervention, motivational interviewing, critical theory, psychodynamic casework, radical structuralism, or a strengths-based approach.

However, Gould (2003) reminds us that 'social work is an inherently complex and fuzzy activity' and that 'the process of social work cannot be modelled algorithmically. Despite the claims of evidence-based practice, the core business of social care cannot be characterised in terms of technical rationality' (Gould 2003: 46).

> If we… build organisational noise into our argument we find that linear rational planning and calculative judgement are unattainable in settings where knowledge is limited, resources constrained, time pressing and where practitioners simply don't think that way. (Webb 2006: 133)

There are, therefore, rarely clear-cut, right and wrong answers, suggest Taylor and White (2000), and the pursuit of 'dependable scientific knowledge may well prove elusive and that other approaches which foreground understanding rather than explanation and prediction may be more fruitfully explored' (p. 5).

These distinctions are helpful. Implicit in much of what follows in our notion of the *compleat* social worker is the idea that a struggle shared with clients and colleagues to understand is more useful than seeking certainty and the 'right' explanation.

In social work there is so much to know and understand, far more than any one individual can possibly absorb. Nevertheless, in order to be a *compleat* social worker, practitioners must have a sense of the intellectual landscape even if they cannot be expert in all the local geographies. To be interested in people is to be interested in the human condition and all the thought that has gone into that interest. This is why we must never cease to be curious.

The dichotomized debates we have been exploring in this book are one way in which people have prodded their curiosity, and deepened their insights. But recognising that people and their social worlds are far too complex and involved to submit to being understood entirely by one side or the other leads most of us to adopt a more inclusive, dynamic approach, an approach which characterizes this book's ideas of the *compleat* social worker.

As we have seen, this embracing attitude is in tune with the times. Epigeneticists marry nature *and* nurture. The social world is one of order as well as conflict. There is continuity *and* change. We live at the subjective centre of our own experience even as our behaviour is being observed objectively by others. We are creatures who feel as well as think. And when we are loved we feel safe, safe enough to live, work, and play.

However, as we meet clients, consider needs, and face problems, we need guides to help us structure what we see, think, and do. From social work's beginnings over a hundred and fifty years ago, some of the profession's smartest thinkers have grappled with the challenge of how to find firm ground upon which to build social work. This final chapter takes advantages of their efforts. In fact, some of the most elegant thinking on this subject has taken place over the last ten to 15 years. It is these thoughts and reflections along with the insights and arguments we have been exploring over the previous 15 chapters which give us an idea of what the *compleat* social worker might look like.

Of course, rendering and simplifying matters runs the risk of not getting things quite right. However, if this sketch of the rounded social worker does manage to excite some interest, the reader is encouraged to go on and visit some of the fully worked pieces referenced in the following paragraphs.

We shall consider the part the following play in doing social work:

1. Curiosity and an interest in people.
2. Ethics, values, and practical judgment.
3. Empathy, process, and structure.
4. Relationship-based work.
5. Evidence-based and pragmatic practices.
6. Critical thinking and reflexive practice.

Forged together, these elements shape the idea of the *compleat* social worker and good practice.

Curiosity and an interest in people

When we meet clients we must be genuinely interested in them and their lives. We must try to understand, with them, how things have got to be the way they are. Clients must feel that we truly want to 'get it'. This doesn't mean we condone all that they've done or that we don't have views of our own. We have to be 'up-front' and 'straight' about our position. We are allowed to question and challenge. But so long as it is clear to clients that we must work together if we are to understand and make sense, then an honest and challenging relationship is likely to be the most helpful.

The worker–client relationship has to be the place where workers and clients think of ways to sort things out and move forward. As we saw in chapter 12, not until clients feel secure can they explore. This is Crittenden talking about working with parents who have abused or neglected their children:

> In order to understand parents' intent, we will need to get 'inside' their adaptive strategies. That is, understanding how they develop over childhood… we will need to think and feel like someone using their strategy if we are to understand parents who harm their children… without understanding them as they understand themselves, we may not be able to help. (Crittenden 2008: 120)

And this is Banks pulling her thoughts together:

> It is… important that social workers take account of the unique circumstances of each person's life, recognize and respect diversity, express care and compassion, exhibit empathy, and act in ways that honour the trust placed in them by the people with whom they work. (Banks 2012: 95)

There *is* an awful lot to know about people and society. This is why social workers should never lose their interest in what sociologists and psychologists, philosophers and novelists have to say about people, society, and human experience. They fuel our interest and curiosity. Maintaining a healthy curiosity in the human condition helps sustains a caring interest in, and compassionate concern for those with whom we work. We all know when someone is trying hard to see and feel things from our point of view.

Ethics, values, and practical judgement

Social workers engage with people who are vulnerable, in a state of need, and unable to solve their own problems. They work with those who are disadvantaged and live on the margins of society. In order to work fairly and decently with clients, social workers need to be guided, even inspired by a strong sense of what is morally the right and proper thing to do, and recognise 'what is good and bad or right and wrong in our society' (Hugman 2013: 385).

The primary values of social work derive from philosophy's classic writings on the founding principles which underpin all moral principles. They include respecting human beings, their rights and dignity. A clear idea of social justice is especially relevant to social work. These values must be present if social work is said to be being done.

These universal values sponsor a wide range of ethically sound social work practices. Social workers should never exploit their clients. Discrimination, inequality, and injustice hover over the lives of service users. Discrimination on non-relevant ground should never be tolerated. Worker–client relationships should therefore endeavour to be democratic and collaborative. A respect for persons is a prerequisite for any society that aspires to be fair and good, and inasmuch as social workers wish to promote a society that is fair and good, respect for persons remains one of its basic principles.

However, given social work's particular character and purpose, other value systems seem peculiarly relevant. The idea of the virtuous person receives uncanny support from clients whose views, when sought, give high praise for workers who are available, reliable, fair, empathic, and honest. As we saw in chapter 14, virtue ethics provides social workers with a strong mandate to be true to their own selves, to be caring, concerned, compassionate, and kind; to be interested, involved, and inspiring. Such virtues are personal and particular, but their presence matters, and none more so than to clients.

The point of the ethically principled, virtuous social worker is to relate well and engage effectively. The idea of an ethics of care, which rests happily on the moral bed of principles and virtues, suits social work particularly well. To care we must be interested and empathic. Curiosity and concern along with empathy and understanding allow us to care about what we do and care about what we feel. Caring about, and caring for others is the lifeblood of so much of social work that care ethics seems tailor-made for our profession. It is the presence of care and compassion that raises our game from one of doing a job to that of following a vocation.

And finally, having gained a strong moral compass, although it might not make decision making easier, it does make the task clearer. In social work there is no escaping the need to make decisions, often difficult decisions. In spite of all the complexity, the presence of 'multiple discourses', and the clash of moral imperatives, decisions have to be made. These require 'practical wisdom' which can lead to 'good judgement'. (Banks and Gallagher 2009; Banks 2012: 89)

Social workers whose moral reasoning, virtuous character, and caring ethic is strong will think and feel their way to decisions based on values that are clear and defensible. Others might reach different judgements, but so long as the social worker can explain and articulate the moral reasoning and ethical basis that led to her decisions, she will find herself on professionally firm ground.

Empathy, structure, and process

Empathy crops up time and time again as a key ingredient in practices found to be effective and successful (Castonguay and Beutler 2006; Miller and Rollnick 2002; Howe 2012). For Baron-Cohen 'Empathy is like a universal solvent. Any problem immersed in empathy becomes soluble' (2011: 127).

Agosta (2010) says we are designed to be affected by each other's feelings. Those who are gifted at understanding how the world might look and feel from the other's point of view, and are skilled at communicating that understanding are society's natural healers. However, we all have the capacity to become better empathizers. Making an effort to see the world and how it might feel from the other's point of view makes us more empathic. The more we know of the other's history, experiences, condition, circumstances, hopes and fears, the more empathic and understanding we are likely to become (Howe 2012).

But as well as clients valuing the experience of feeling understood, they also like to feel that they know where they are with the social worker. They like to know the purpose of the visit or interview. It helps to have the outline and purpose of each meeting spelt out. Practices that offer *clear structures* provide clients with a strong sense of direction. Clients appreciate plans which include 'end goals, specific tasks to reach the goal, suggestions for maintaining the change and relapse prevention strategies' (Teater 2013: 452; Miller and Rollnick

2002). Reviews and recaps of what has happened are then provided before the next stage is begun.

Spelling things out, confirming what is going to happen next, and why, reduces feelings of unpredictability and makes people feel less helpless and more involved. Being invited to take an active part in the content and direction of events increases control and lowers stress.

In other words, social workers who are clear, up-front and collaborative in their approach, help clients feel anchored. Social workers who practice in ways that are clearly structured and who understand the social work process and are prepared to share it, give clients a reassuring sense of time, place, and direction. It is when we don't know what's happening or why it's happening that we feel stressed and anxious. Social workers who give their practice structure and shape and share this with their clients lower resistance and increase cooperation.

Patient-centred doctors, like client-centred social workers, also believe that good communication sponsors good relationships, and good relationships have a positive effect on health-related outcomes (Griffin et al. 2004).

When treated in an open and democratic way, patients reveal more about their condition and symptoms. This helps doctors make better diagnoses. Moreover, listening to patients' Ideas, Concerns and Expectations (ICE) also encourages them to be more willing to collaborate and comply with the treatment, hence the increased rates of positive outcomes in cases where doctors have followed the ICE practice and structure (Matthys et al. 2009). The same holds true for social work.

For their take on practice, Gallagher and Sykes (2008) also offer an acronym – ETHICS. When exploring problems, making decisions, and forming judgements, social workers should: Enquire about facts; Think through options; Hear views; Identify principles; Clarify meaning; Select action. This, too, encourages a structured and collaborative approach to practice.

Empathy helps connect social worker and client. To be understood affirms our right to be without necessarily condoning what we do. Structure helps us know where we are going. We feel less at sea. Combined, *empathy* and *structure* offer the possibility of meaningful help and therapeutic success.

Relationship-based work

It is not until the client feels that their social worker is interested in them, cares about them, is honest with them, and is striving to see and feel the world from their point of view that a purposeful relationship can form (also see de Boer and Coady 2007). This relationship has been variously called the therapeutic, helping, or working alliance. Unless it has been established, both client and worker will find the going heavy.

The relationship is the medium in which work of a more technical, supportive, protective, risk-assessing, service-minded, legal, awareness-raising, political, or procedural kind takes place. If there isn't a good working relationship, techniques don't work as well and resistances build up. Remember from chapter 12 that clients must feel secure before they can explore. Emotional safety and understanding must be in place before work can be done, reflections made, and changes planned.

In the Preface to their splendid book on contemporary social work, Wilson et al. (2011) hold the belief 'that relationships are at the heart of effective social work and that the essential and distinctive characteristic of social work is its focus on the individual and the social setting and context' (p. xiv).

Relationship-based practices require workers to recognise the uniqueness of each and every client and that good relationships with clients are the basis on which effective social work is carried out. One of the key themes running through the book by Wilson et al. (2011) is the understanding that we are creatures who feel as well as think. As we noted in chapter 8, we have to be ever aware of our emotional as well as our rational selves. So much of what we say and do is governed by our emotional make-up. Complex and stressful situations all too easily trigger feelings of anxiety and pain, fear and hurt, guilt and shame, anger and contempt. When we feel emotionally aroused and bothered, thinking rationally is difficult. This is true for both worker and client.

In contrast, some of us deal with emotional arousal by cutting ourselves off from our feelings. As we deny our feelings, we become more rigidly rational and inflexibly logical. Arguments become cold and legalistic. They become divorced from the stress and distress out of which they are really emerging. But the strong feelings haven't gone away. They lie beneath the surface churning away in some unconscious cauldron, occasionally erupting in an extreme outburst or pushing the individual to drink, drugs, or detachment as desperate ways to escape the hurt, fears, and pain which threaten to destabilize the brittleness and fragility of the life that is being lived.

Whether the client feels overwhelmed by powerful feelings or defensively detached from them, 'getting in touch' with our emotions is the first step in managing them better. This is best done on the context of a good relationship where it becomes safe to think about feelings, where the worker is able to 'contain' the client's anxieties and help them begin to process them more consciously and reflectively. But this can only happen if the worker is able to offer a secure base from which the client can begin to explore.

Social workers therefore need to be emotionally intelligent (Howe 2008; Ingram 2013). There is the added bonus, too, that the empathic and emotionally intelligent social worker is also a resilient worker, less liable to burn out, and more likely to remain creative.

Also implicit in any relationship-based practice is the social worker's use of self. 'As a social worker one of the biggest challenges you will face is being able to simultaneously focus in professional encounters on what is happening for the service user and what is happening to you' (Wilson et al. 2011: 9). To be aware of, and reflect on how the client is affecting you as well as how you are affecting the client is a basic skill. Indeed, it is often entirely appropriate to share such reflections with the client. This is all part and parcel of helping clients to develop their own reflective, regulatory capacities. When mind can think about mind, self-regulation, and interpersonal competence increase.

The social work relationship therefore allows and facilitates rapport, the delivery of services, decisions, and evidence-based practices. Indeed, without a good relationship being in place, it is doubtful whether any service or treatment would be effective. In this sense, relationship-based social work is *the* evidence-based practice upon which all other evidence-based practices must rest if they are to be effective. Thus, for Bentall, 'good relationships… are a universal therapeutic good' (2009: 260), while for Siegel 'Whatever the individual approach or clinical technique employed, the therapeutic relationship is one of the most powerful determinants of positive outcome…' (2010: xi).

Evidence-based and pragmatic practices

We have been bumping into evidence-based thinking off and on throughout this book. Evidence-based interventions are those associated with positive outcomes. They are part of the drive to find scientific evidence of what interventions work in practice and then apply them in all future situations of that kind.

In chapter 7 we noted that the most robust and rigorous evidence has been generated by randomized controlled trials (RCTs). Although social work has not produced much evidence of this kind, it is a reminder that when the profession can tap into research that is clear about what works, what works best, for whom, in what circumstances, over what time scale, and against which outcome indicators, then it would seem remiss not to use it. What little there is seems to have come out of a limited number of theoretical stables, including cognitive behavioural therapies (CBT), task-centred practices, strengths-based approaches, motivational interviewing, attachment theory, self-help manuals, and preventative programmes.

However, what most observers and critics note is that social work is a wide-ranging, value-saturated business that doesn't always lend itself to neat, one-dimensional, standardized interventions with neat packages of evidence to support them. This is not to say that when social workers come across a discrete problem for which there is evidence supporting what works, then they shouldn't use it. On the contrary. We know that CBT works well for clients who are depressed, anxious, or phobic. We know there is strong evidence to back the use of behavioural modification for children with behavioural problems or who are poor school attenders. It's just that so much of the work that comes the way of social workers doesn't arrive in neat bundles. The demands and dilemmas faced by practitioners are rarely simple and they never stand still. In conclusion, writes Plath (2013):

> ... the current state of research in social work falls far short of the requirements of an evidence-based practice culture. (p. 231)

This should certainly encourage governments, policy makers, and academics to carry out more research and generate more evidence. But given the nature of social work, there is probably a natural limit on how much unambiguous evidence can be produced. Our discussions of uncertainty, language, and meaning in earlier chapters go some way to explain why this might be so.

So given that social workers deal with a complex mix of needs, problems, client groups, service provision, policy changes, statutory demands, human behaviour, value dilemmas, and environmental stresses, many now argue that social work should have a more relaxed view of what might count as evidence (Plath 2006; Shaw 2011). Given its subject matter, this wider take on evidence has edged beyond the boundaries of scientific and quantitative research and begun to take in qualitative information, the idea of practice wisdom, and professional judgement.

This wider stance, suggests Plath, invites slightly different questions: What aspects worked well? What aspects didn't work well? Why? For whom? From whose perspective? What were the relevant factors impacting on the situation? In what context did or didn't things work well? (Plath 2013: 232–3). The social worker and her organization still need to explore the evidence, but the evidence looked at is likely to be more relevant, more realistic, more rooted.

> Social workers are concerned with the range of factors and conditions that impact the quality of life and wellbeing of clients and communities. Generally, multiple outcomes can emerge from social work interventions tailored in response to the presenting issues. Just how effective these outcomes are depends on the values and perspectives of the stakeholder making the assessment. For the client, it may be an intangible sense of feeling more positive about life. For the social worker it may be the degree to which goals established at the start of the intervention have been met. For the organisation, effectiveness may be reflected in the proportion of clients returning with the same issue. (Plath 2013: 233)

All of this suggests that the *compleat* social worker and her organization need to be aware of, and up to date with research which relates to their field. But the use of such evidence requires a flexible mind and a pragmatic attitude set within practices which are structured and disciplined.

In chapter 15 we saw that pragmatic approaches and critical best practices do acknowledge that social workers need to be research aware (Shaw 2003; Jones et al. 2008). However, they also recognise that because social work has to deal with psychosocial complexities that rarely stand still, flexible minds and collaborative practices are the only way to remain connected and engaged with people whose lives all too easily feel as if they are running out of control. Which leads us on to the final element in the make-up of the *compleat* social worker – the need to reflect critically and reflexively.

Critical thinking and reflexive practices

This final component in the make-up of the *compleat* social worker appears in the guise of a professional overseer. Whenever we become involved in lives that are fragile or distressed, in need or in pain, it is particularly important that we become ultra-aware and extra-sensitive to what we see and the way we see it, what we think and why we think it, and what we do and why we do it. We therefore have to reflect on what we see, think and do critically, reflectively, and reflexively. We must strive to see the bigger picture – of clients' lives, professional practices, theoretical assumptions, research epistemologies, departmental procedures, policy constraints, structural limits, and political climates in which we all have to live and operate.

There are some similarities, here, with the practice of mindfulness (Kabat-Zinn 2013; Siegel 2010). We possess mindfulness in those moments when we become fully aware of the present and how we see it and experience it. It contrasts with those many moments when we feel caught up in events. The ability to stay with the moment and critically reflect helps social workers remain empathic and connected, less stressed and more resilient (Hick 2009; Kinman and Grant forthcoming). The critically reflexive, mindful worker sees more clearly and more widely. Her options increase. Her potential to be creative becomes greater.

These things can be done in your own head, but it is usually much easier and much better to do them with colleagues and supervisors. A version of reflective and mindful practice, of course, can be done with clients. Clients, after all, have the canniest, most telling view of what you're seeing and saying, thinking, and doing.

Donald Schon (1991) was an early advocate of our need to reflect on what we do in practice. He recognised that working with people is never easy or straightforward. There are rarely simple solutions to the problems presented. Instead, and in the case of social work:

> ... more complex and fluid understandings are required that acknowledge the uniqueness of the individual and the inter-subjective dimensions of social work situations. For Schon, the development of such understanding requires practitioners to embrace the breadth of knowledge that can inform professional practice and to reflect both *on* practice, i.e. after the event, and *in* practice, i.e. during the event. (Wilson et al. 2011: 13, emphasis original)

Critical reflection involves workers reflecting on experience and what they're doing. They need to think about the contexts in which clients, their needs and problems, arise (Taylor 2013). It implies a structural approach in which problems are as likely to be the result of inequalities of power and money as they are of individual weakness and inadequacy. Critically reflective practices are therefore likely to be emancipatory practices (Fook 2012: 47). Reflective practices are also good when working with complex cases.

Reflexivity includes reflection but it also demands that the worker examines the assumptions, the context, and the purpose of what is being thought, seen, and done. Here, the knowledge and technical assumptions on which practice is taking place also become ripe for analysis. How does attachment theory shape our thinking about parenting and child development (Taylor and White 2000: 198)? Is a medical model actually steering our thoughts about old age and physical disability? Is a young man with mental health problems best understood in terms a neurological dysfunction, a troubled childhood, being unemployed and living in a deprived neighbourhood, or being the victim of a long-term drug habit? Individual workers, agencies, and cultures can easily get locked into one way of thinking about people, their problems and needs. A reflexive stance demands that these habitual views are made explicit and subject to critical review.

> ... we are suggesting that you listen much more carefully to your own practice talk and that of others. How do you say things? Why do you say them in that way? How do you try to achieve

compliance from service users? How does resistance manifest itself and how do you deal with it? What are the situations in which you feel 'powerless' with clients? Are there times when clients' voices are silenced or not listened to? (Taylor and White 2000: 117)

In their assessments and analyses, social workers have to be critical, that is, their view should be wide and their gaze deep. A family might not be coping. There might be neglect. The parents' own histories might be troubled. But they also live in a house which is too small and damp. They spend a lot on heating. They have got behind with the rent. The mother suffers depression and has been prescribed pills but no thought has been given to other kinds of help and support. The critical practitioner therefore has to be political, 'not in the party political sense but in the sense that it engages about how scarce resources are allocated and where the power to make decisions about them is located. Critical practice, therefore, deploys social work values in challenging inequalities and social justice' (Adams et al. 2009a: 334).

Thus, in complex situations, we will find many points of view being present and many explanations being pushed. The professionals involved are as likely to be choosing and framing the facts to suit their interests every bit as much as clients. Whenever, professionally or personally, we attempt to justify, explain, or advance a view of the world, we tend to present our arguments in a story-like or narrative form. We tell things in a particular way using certain words that convey particular meanings. We set the scene, we identify players, we see problems, we find connections, we attribute causes, we offer explanations, we reach conclusions, we present the 'truth'.

Clients give their stories whenever they are interviewed by practitioners, but practitioners also tell and frame these stories, give their take on the situation whenever they find themselves in supervision, at a case conference, justifying a decision, or explaining their position to a client. And some of the most potent 'storytellers' whose version of events can spread far and wide are case records, departmental forms, computer files, court reports, and written assessments. They can easily take on a life and authority of their own, to be recycled, without question again and again.

However, trying to establish the right 'truth' is unlikely to be successful, for in a sense there are no fundamental truths that lie bedrock-like beneath all others. There will be facts but how these get presented and explained will differ from person to person. X-rays show that a young child *does* have a broken femur, but how did it happen? Old people do suffer dementia, but at what point, if any, do they lose control over the right to make their own decisions? Understanding a fuel bill might be difficult if you have a learning disability, but if you are going to live independently these are skills that you have a right to acquire.

Taylor and White (2000) give many examples which nicely illustrate the use of 'plausible accounts' to justify views and actions. For example, a ward sister argues that a 91-year-old female patient, frail and confused after a fall at home, is a social and not a medical problem. The elderly woman is therefore described as a bed-blocker. The patient's physical state, reluctance to have home help, and unwillingness to admit her own vulnerability are defined as personality traits and matters of social and not medical concern.

But as you listen to the social worker, the GP, the relatives, the neighbours, you hear other views, other accounts, other 'truths' as different 'realities' are constructed to support a position, a hope, a defence. The one 'voice' that often goes unheard in these presentations is that of the patient and client. The challenge is for each participant to begin to recognise that there are 'multiple accounts' and no one truth.

Rather than each participant digging in their heels and blocking other ways of seeing things, the only way forward is to explore, recognise, and appreciate the existence of the many accounts in the manner recommended by Habermas (1990) and described by Banks (2012) in chapter 14. Then working collaboratively, clients and professionals can fashion new shared accounts that offer ways of moving forward. Social work can therefore be seen as a 'sense-making' activity (White 1997: 740).

> An alternative approach is to see assessment as a 'construction of professional narrative' in which the worker enters into a more collaborative dialogue with service users, takes account of complexities and changes, resists traditional labels, and may co-create new narratives and labels which better frame the service user's view of themselves. An essential aim of a professional narrative is to construct a narrative about the service user which works

to empower them (in the professional context of the worker). (Fook 2012: 148)

As Fook (2012: 148) continues, she identifies the following as the main elements that should compose the professional narrative: (i) the service user's perspective/story; (ii) the perspective of other players; (iii) contexts and changes; (iv) how the narrative will be interpreted and enacted in the professional context of the worker; before finally (v) constructing a narrative to be effective in this context.

So, discussion and dialogue are preferable to bombast and bluster. By attempting to get participants to be reflexive, more reasoned, and reasonable, shared understandings can be reached. Language carries meaning. Talk carries language. Thus, if new and shared meanings are to be created between social workers, their clients, and other professionals, then talk matters. However, if talk that matters is to take place, then social workers must establish working relationships with their clients and other colleagues.

The social worker herself, of course, cannot lie outside this reflexive attitude. There is 'no view from nowhere' (Nagel 1986). As social workers we must therefore concern ourselves 'with the (tacit) assumptions we are making about people, their problems and their needs when we apply knowledge about child development, mental health, learning disability and so forth' (Taylor and White 2000: 35).

None of this reflexive talk rules out facts and theories. It doesn't prohibit the use of particular evidence-based interventions and techniques. It doesn't deny the presence of values and the need to make judgements. It just requires their presence and presumptions to be raised, acknowledged, discussed, and possibly questioned. The theoretical biases present in any explanation need to recognised, not to be awkward but simply for everyone to be clear about how a need is being framed or a problem shaped. Social workers should not be afraid to provoke *constructive controversies* amongst their colleagues and in their organisations (Johnson et al. 2000).

Constructive controversy encourages that alternative constructions are laid out and rendered visible so, hopefully, more robust decision making takes place. (Doherty and White 2013: 220)

Many of the deeper ambiguities and uncertainties are discovered when critically reflective practitioners examine and disturb the underlying and often hidden assumptions that define a case, influence an assessment, inform a judgment, or govern an agency's response (Fook 2013; Knott and Scragg 2013). Personal reflection, good supervision, and teamwork have the potential to provoke workers into thinking more critically about what they do and how they do it. And out of such provocations, social workers might learn to practise more sensitively, more collaboratively, less judgementally, less prejudicially.

The idea of being a *compleat* social worker is a demanding one. It asks a lot of practitioners, indeed clients. There are so many things to think about and attend to: empathy, listening, collaborating, being virtuous, keeping up to date with evidence-based findings, promoting social justice. Each one of these is a good thing and you wouldn't want to take any one of them out of the idea of being a social worker. But sustaining any one, never mind all of them is hard. So much emotional and cognitive effort required to do the job well risks burnout and compassion fatigue (Kinman and Grant 2011, forthcoming).

Social workers hope to foster good lives and better lives. But the very pursuit of practices to bring about those good lives and better lives can come at some personal and professional cost. A refined version of this thesis, extended to all areas of modern life in neoliberal, capitalist societies, has been described by Lauren Berlant (2011) in her book *Cruel Optimism*.

Optimism is present when people still hold on to the idea of the good life (money, health, emotional wellbeing, success, happiness, ideal families, contented old age) in spite of so many aggressive forces (political, economic, social) making the chances of achieving anything like the good life for most people if not remote, then hard going.

> Cruel optimism is the condition of maintaining an attachment to a significantly problematic object… But… the fear is that the loss of the promising object/scene itself will defeat the capacity to have any hope about anything. (Berlant 2011: 24)

Hope and optimism, the idea that things can get better, gets most of us, including our professional selves as social workers, through the day even as we face uncertainy, setbacks, and muddle. To give up on hope and optimism would take away so many reasons for living, so many reasons for doing what we do as social workers. But there is a danger that the price to be paid for hope and optimism is burnout and compassion fatigue.

The only way to overcome the cruelty of this vital optimism is to be reflective, to be critically reflexive, to be aware, and to be realistic even as you hold on to the vision and hope of a better life for these children, that family, this old woman, that disabled man. With good supervision, group support, team togetherness, shared reflection, pauses for breath, and an emotionally intelligent department, critically reflexive practitioners have the chance to re-value, re-imagine and, with hope and realism held in precarious balance, sustain what they do.

Encouraging social workers to recover their commitment to social justice, Marston and McDonald (2012) recognise that political and structural changes can take place at multiple points and many levels. No longer the single 'heroic' social worker battling structural inequality and social injustice, but a shared effort directed at both the local issues and societal wrongs. We have to acknowledge, they say, 'the potential for political change within local organisational settings, while remaining cognisant of how practice settings have changed dramatically over the last twenty to thirty years' (Marston and McDonald 2012: 1036). They conclude that:

> In the face of evidence of growing social inequality, social workers undoubtedly need individual hope to inspire collective action. What might seem to be unrealistic hope can begin in considering the possibility that tiny cracks might yet break open the dam and contingent openings are sites of unexpected force – for better or worse (Tsing 2004). (Marston and McDonald 2012: 1036)

Critically reflective practices recognise that we construct our understandings and approaches to the world as we relate with others. Out of the tangle of mixed feelings and muddled happenings, we seek order. We try to make sense of what has happened, what is happening, and what might happen next. These attempts to get the past, present, and future into some kind of narrative sequence reveal our struggle to understand our own and other people's thoughts, feelings, and behaviour.

> Some stories, such as those which support depression, seem both fixed and hopeless and lack any awareness of personal strengths. A deep belief in one's own uselessness or unlovability or irredeemable guilt may act as a prison from which there is no simple release. Implicit in the concept of a better story is that such truths are never final but ultimately provisional and open to revision… Lack of certainty may be the first step towards hope. (Pocock 1995: 167–8, cited in White 1997: 751).

The more we can make sense and find meaning, the more we feel in control of what is going on. Feeling in control is empowering. Making sense and feeling in control lower our levels of stress. It is being at the mercy of unregulated thoughts, feelings, and events that is the problem and that *is* stressful.

Completing the journey

So there we have it; the idea of the *compleat* social worker. The portrait is inevitably a personal one, the journey to find her perhaps a little quirky. The hope is that the book as a whole and each chapter in particular will provoke thought and stimulate debate and encourage you to explore your own ideas of what defines a good and effective social worker.

Of course, what makes for a well-regarded, effective practitioner will differ a little from individual to individual, but I sense a growing consensus that because social work does have to deal with so many worlds it does demand a special kind of practitioner, one who is endlessly curious about the human experience.

To feed that curiosity, the *compleat* social worker is one who must remain fascinated by both the social sciences and the arts, the psychological sciences and the humanities. The empathic worker is one who appreciates that for those in distress, a sense of structure and predictability is important. Empathy and structure are key pillars in building sound therapeutic alliances and offering relationship-based practices. Unless the relationship is sound, the technique, any technique, remains unstable and without grip. But if the relationship is good, interventions, technical skills, and evidence-based practices can take hold.

Of course, the idea of a *compleat* social worker is full of ironies and paradoxes. 'Compleat' in the sense being used here does not mean perfect or finished. Rather, it suggests someone whose curiosity is forever restless; someone who understands that human behaviour and social life is never straightforward or simple; someone who can live with incomplete knowledge and uncertain outcomes; someone who can make practical judgements knowing, as Downie and Loudfoot (1978: 122) recognised, that in human affairs there will always be radical limits on professional expertise.

Because the *compleat social worker* is someone who is always thinking about what people do and why they do it, about society and its reactions, and about how best to help and what might be done, for them social work can never be dull. Difficult, yes. Demanding, true. But never dull.

Bibliography

Adams, R., Dominelli, L. and Payne, M. (eds.) (2009a). *Practising Social Work in a Complex World* (2nd ed.). Basingstoke: Palgrave Macmillan.

Adams, R., Dominelli, L. and Payne, M. (2009b). In R. Adams, L. Dominelli and M. Payne (eds.), *Practising Social Work in a Complex World* (2nd ed.). Basingstoke: Palgrave Macmillan, pp. 1–12.

Agosta, J. G. (2010). *Empathy in the Context of Philosophy*. Houndmills: Palgrave Macmillan.

Aitkenhead, D. (2013). What's missing is love. *Guardian*, 30 November, pp 49–50.

Allen, J., Fonagy, P. and Bateman, A. (2008). *Mentalizing in Clinical Practice*. Washington, DC: American Psychiatric Publishing.

Allis, C., Jenuwein, T. and Reinberg, D. (2007). *Epigenetics*. Cold Spring Harbour, NY: Cold Spring Harbor Laboratory Press.

Asbury, K and Plomin, R. (2013). *G is for Genes: The Impact of Genetics on Education and Achievement*. Chichester: Wiley.

Bailey, R. and Brake, M. (eds.). *Radical Social Work*. London: Edward Arnold.

Baldwin, M. (1997). Day care on the move. *British Journal of Social Work*, 27: 951–8.

Baldwin, M. (2012). Participatory action research. In M. Gray, J. Midgley and S. A. Webb (eds.), *The Sage Handbook of Social Work*, London: Sage, pp 467–81.

Bamber, M., Brooks, J., Cusack, S., Edwards, J., Gardner, M., Gridley, K., Howard, L., Marshall, N., Salmon, L. and Wood, J. (2012). Personalization in practise. In M. Davies (ed.), *Social Work with Adults*. Basingstoke: Palgrave Macmillan, pp. 77–90.

Banks, S. (2012). *Ethics and Values in Social Work* (4th ed.). Houndmills: Palgrave Macmillan.

Banks, S. and Gallagher, A. (2009). *Ethics in Professional Life: Virtues for Health and Social Care*. Basingstoke: Palgrave Macmillan.

Baron-Cohen, S. (2011). *Zero Degrees of Empathy: a New Theory of Human Cruelty*. London: Allen Lane.

Bartels, M. (2007). An update on longitudinal twin and family studies. *Twin ResearcBartlett, H. (1970). *The Common Base of Social Work Practice*. New York: National Association of Social Workers.

Bateman, A. and Fonagy, P. (2006). *Mentalization-based Treatment for Borderline Personality Disorder: a Practical Guide*. Oxford: Oxford University Press.

Bateman, A. and Fonagy, P. (2011). *Handbook of Mentalizing in Mental Health Practice*. Arlington, VA: American Psychiatric Publishing Inc.

Bateson, M. and Martin, P. (2000). *Design for Life: How Behaviour Develops*. London: Vintage.

Baumrind, D. (1967). Child care practices anteceding three patterns of preschool behaviour. *Genetic Psychology Monographs*, 75(1): 43–88.

Beck, A., Rush, A. J., Shaw, B. and Emery G. (1987). *Cognitive Therapy of Depression*. New York: Guilford Press.

Beck, U. (1992). *Risk Society*. London: Sage.

Becker, H. S. (1963). *Outsiders: Studies in the Sociology of Deviance*, New York: Free Press.

Beckett, C. (2006). *Essential Theory for Social Work Practice*, London: Sage.

Beckett, C. and Maynard, A. (2013). *Values and Ethics in Social Work* (2nd ed.). London: Sage.

Bentall, R. (2009). *Doctoring the Mind: Why Psychiatric Treatments Fail*. London: Allen Lane.

Berger, P. and Luckman, T. (1967). *The Social Construction of Reality: a Treatise on the Sociology of Knowledge*. New York: Doubleday.

Berlant, L. (2011). *Cruel Optimism*. Durham: Duke University Press.

Berlin, I. (1990). *The Crooked Timber of Humanity*. London: Fontana.

Beveridge, W. (1942) *Report of the Inter-Departmental Committee on Social Insurance and Allied Services* ('The Beveridge Report'). London: HMSO.

Bion, W. R. (1962). *Learning from Experience*. London: Heinemann.

Bion, W. R. (1963). *Elements of Psycho-Analysis*. London: Heinemann.

Bower, M. (2005). Psychoanalytic theories for social work practice. In M. Bower (ed.), *Psychoanalytic Theory for Social Work Practice*. London: Routledge, pp. 3–14.

Bowlby, J. (1988). *A Secure Base: Clinical Applications of Attachment Theory*. London: Routledge.

Brechin, A., Brown, H. and Eby, M. (2000). *Critical Practice in Health and Social Care*, London: Sage.

Britton, R. (2005). Re-enactment as an unwitting professional response to family dynamics. In M. Bower (ed.), *Psychoanalytic Theory for Social Work Practice*. London: Routledge, pp 165–74.

Bronfenbrenner, U. (1979). *The Ecology of Human Development: Experiments by Nature and Design*. Cambridge, MA: Harvard University Press.

Brookner, A. (1982). *Look at Me*. London: Triad Grafton.

Brown, G. (1998). Loss and depressive disorders. In B. P. Dohrenwend (ed.), *Adversity, Stress, and Psychopathology*. San Diego, CA: Academic Press, pp. 358–70.

Brown, G. and Harris, T. (1978). *Social Origins of Depression: a Study of Psychiatric Disorder in Women*. London: Tavistock.

Buchanan, I. (2013). Social work and learning disabilities. In M. Davies (ed.), *The Blackwell Companion to Social Work* (4th ed.). Oxford: Wiley-Blackwell, pp. 283–9.

Burke, B. (2013). Anti-oppressive practice. In M. Davies (ed.), *The Blackwell Companion to Social Work* (4th ed.) Oxford: Wiley-Blackwell, pp. 414–16.

Burrell, G. and Morgan, G. (1979). *Sociological Paradigms and Organisational Analysis.* London: Heinemann.

Callon, M. (1986). Some elements of a sociology of translation: the domestication of the scallops and fishermen of St. Brieuc Bay. In J. Law (ed.), *Power, Action and Belief: A New Sociology of Knowledge?* London: Routledge and Kegan Paul, pp. 196–223.

Caspi, A., Sugden, K., Moffitt, T., Taylor, A., Craig, I., Harrington, H. and Poulton, R. (2003). Influence of life stress on depression: moderation by a polymorphism in the 5-HTT gene. *Science*, 301: 386–9.

Castonguay, L. G. and Beutler, L. E. (2006). Common and unique principles of therapeutic change: what do we know and what do we need to know? In L. G. Castonguay and L. E. Beutler (eds.), *Principles of Therapeutic Change That Work.* Oxford: Oxford University Press, pp. 353–69.

Challis, D. and Davies, B. (1986). *Case Management in Community Care.* Aldershot: Gower.

Cicchetti, D. (2015). *Developmental Psychopathology: Risk, Disorder, and Adaptation* (3rd ed.). Chichester: Wiley.

Clark, C. (2006). Moral character in social work. *British Journal of Social Work,* 36: 75–89.

Cohen, S. (1985). *Visions of Social Control.* Cambridge: Polity Press.

Cooper, A. and Lousada, J. (2005). *Borderline Welfare: Feeling and Fear of Feeling in Modern Welfare.* London: Karnac Books.

Cournoyer, B. R. and Powers, G. T. (2002). Evidence-based social work: the quiet revolution continues. In A. R. Roberts and G. J. Greene (eds.), *Social Workers Desk Reference,* New York: Oxford University Press, pp. 798–807.

Cree, V. E. and Wallace, S. (2009). Risk and protection. In R. Adams, L. Dominelli and M. Payne (eds.), *Practising Social Work in a Complex World* (2nd ed.). Basingstoke: Palgrave Macmillan, pp. 42–56.

Crittenden, P. (2008). *Raising Parents: Attachment, Parenting and Child Safety.* Cullompton: Willan Press.

Cupitt, D. (1985). *The Sea of Faith.* London: BBC Books.

Davenport-Hines, R. and Sisman, A. (2013). *One Hundred Letters from Hugh Trevor-Roper.* Oxford: Oxford University Press.

Davies, M. (1994). *The Essential Social Worker.* Aldershot: Ashgate.

Davies, M. (ed.) (2012). *Social Work with Adults.* Basingstoke: Palgrave Macmillan.

Davies, M. (2013). Maintenance theory. In M. Davies (ed.), *The Blackwell Companion to Social Work* (4th ed.). Oxford: Wiley-Blackwell, pp. 449–50.

Department of Health (2001). *Valuing People: a New Strategy for Learning Disability for the 21st Century*. London: The Stationery Office.

Department of Health (2010a). *A Vision for Adult Social Care: Capable Communities and Active Citizens*. London: Department of Health.

Department of Health (2010b). *Practical Approaches to Safeguarding and Personalisation*. London: Department of Health.

de Boer, C. and Coady, N. (2007). Good helping relationships in child welfare: learning from stories of success. *Child and Family Social Work*, 12: 32–42.

de Shazer, S. (1985). *Keys to Solution in Brief Therapy*. New York: Norton.

Dickens, J. (2010). *Social Work and Social Policy: an Introduction*. London: Routledge.

Dickens, J. (2013). *Social Work, Law and Ethics*. London: Routledge.

Dickens, J., Howell, D., Thoburn, G. and Schofield, G. (2007). Children starting to be looked after by local authorities in England: an analysis of inter-authority variation and case-centred decision-making. *British Journal of Social Work*, 37: 597–617.

Dingwall, R., Eekelaar, J. and Murray, T. (1983). *The Protection of Children: State Intervention and Family Life*. Oxford: Blackwell.

Doherty, P. and White, S. (2013). Knowledge for reflexive rractice. In M. Gray, J. Midgley and S. A. Webb (eds.), *The Sage Handbook of Social Work*. Sage: London, pp. 211–23.

Donzelot, J. (1979). *The Policing of Families*. London: Hutchinson.

Douglas, M. (1992). *Risk and Blame: Essays in Cultural Theory*. London: Routledge and Kegan Paul.

Downie, R. S. and Loudfoot, E. M. (1978). Aim, skill and role in social work. In N. Timms and D. Watson (eds.), *Philosophy in Social Work*. London: Routledge and Kegan Paul, pp. 111–26.

Duffy, M. Gillespie, K. and Clarke, D. (2007). Post-traumatic stress disorder in the context of terrorism and other civil conflict in Northern Ireland: randomise control trial. *British Medical Journal*, 334(7604): 1147–50.

England, H. (1986). *Social Work as Art*. London: Allen and Unwin.

Erikson, E. H. (1950). *Childhood and Society*. New York: W. W. Norton.

Evans, T. (2010). *Professional Discretion in Welfare Services: Beyond Street-level Bureaucracy*. Farnham: Ashgate.

Evans, T. and Hardy, M. (2010). *Evidence and Knowledge for Practice*. Cambridge: Polity Press.

Featherstone, B. (2010). Ethic of care. In M. Gray and S. Webb (eds.), *Ethics and Value Perspectives in Social Work*. Basingstoke: Palgrave Macmillan, pp. 73–84.

Featherstone, B. and Morris, K. (2013). Feminist ethics of care. In M. Gray, J. Midgley and S. A. Webb (eds.), *The Sage Handbook of Social Work*, London: Sage, pp. 341–54.

Featherstone, B., White, S. and Morris, K. (2014). *Re-imaging Child Protection: Towards Humane Social Work With Families*. Bristol: Policy Press.

Ferguson, H. (2001). Social work, individualisation and life politics. *British Journal of Social Work*, 31(1): 41–55.

Ferguson, H. (2008). Best practice in family support and child protection: promoting child safety and democratic families. In K. Jones, B. Cooper and H. Ferguson (eds.), *Best Practice in Social Work: Critical Perspectives*, Basingstoke: Palgrave Macmillan, pp. 14–63.

Fine, M. and Teram, E. (2013). Overt and covert ways of responding to moral injustices in social work practice: heroes and mild-mannered social work bipeds. *British Journal of Social Work* 43(7): 1312–29.

Flaskas, C. (1997) Reclaiming the idea of truth: some thoughts on theory in response to practice. *Journal of Family Therapy*, 19(1): 1–20.

Fook, J. (2000). Deconstructing and reconstructing professional expertise. In B. Fawcett, B. Featherstone, J. Fook and A. Rossiter (eds.), *Practice and Research in Social Work: postmodern feminist perspectives*. London: Routledge, pp. 105–20.

Fook, J. (2012). *Social Work: a Critical Approach for Practice*. London: Sage.

Fook, J. (2013). Critical reflection in context: contemporary perspectives and issues. In J. Fook and F. Gardner (eds.), *Critical Reflection in Context: applications in health and social care*. London: Routledge, pp. 1–11.

Fook, J., Ryan, M. and Hawkins, L. (1997). Towards a theory of social work expertise. *British Journal of Social Work*, 27: 399–417.

Forrester, D. (2012), Evaluation research. In M. Gray, J. Midgley and S. A. Webb (eds.), *The Sage Handbook of Social Work*. London: Sage, pp. 440–53.

Foucault, M. (1975): *Discipline and Punish: the Birth of the Prison*. Harmondsworth: Penguin.

Freidson, E. (1986). *Professional Powers*. Chicago: University of Chicago Press.

Freud, S. (1914). *Remembering, Repeating and Working Through*, Standard Edition XII. London: Hogarth Press and Institute of Psychoanalysis.

Frost, L. and Hoggett, P. (2008). Human agency and social suffering. *Critical Social Policy*, 28(4): 438–60.

Gallagher, A. and Sykes, N. (2008). A little bit of heaven for a few? A case analysis. *Ethics and Social Welfare*, 2(3): 299–307.

Gallagher, M. (2010). *Engaging with Voluntary Service Users in Social Work: Literature Review 2: Children and Families*. Available at http://www.socialwork.ed.uk/_data/assets/pdf_file/0017/44225/review_2_children_and_families.pdf. Accessed 25 July 2013.

Gibson, F. (2011). *Reminiscence and Life Story Work: a Practice Guide* (4th ed.). London: Jessica Kingsley.

Giddens, A. (1991), *Modernity and Self-identity.* Cambridge: Polity Press.

Gilbert, P. (2010). *The Compassionate Mind: Compassion Focused Therapy.* London: Constable.

Goldstein, H. (1973). *Social Work Practice: A Unitary Approach.* Columbia: University of South Carolina Press.

Goldstein, H. (1992). If social work hasn't made progress as a science, might it be an art? *Families in Society*, 73: 48–55.

Goldstein, H. (1999). The limits and art of understanding in social work practice. *Families in Society*, 80: 385–95.

Goodman, S. (2011). *Social Work Reclaimed.* London: Jessica Kingsley.

Gould, N. (2003). The caring professions and information technology – in search of a theory. In E. Harlow and S. Webb (eds.), *Information and Communication Technologies in Welfare Services.* London: Jessica Kingsley, pp. 29–48.

Gray. M. (2010). Moral sources and emergent ethical theories in social work. *British Journal of Social Work*, 40: 1794–811.

Gray, M. and Webb, S. (eds.) (2013). *The New Politics of Social Work.* Basingstoke: Palgrave Macmillan.

Gray, M., Plath, D. and Webb, S. (2009). *Evidence-based Social Work: a Critical Stance.* London: Routledge.

Gray, M. and Webb, S. (2008). Social work as art revisited. *International Journal of Social Welfare*, 17: 182–93.

Gray, M. and Webb, S. (eds.) (2010). *Ethics and Value Perspectives in Social Work.* Basingstoke: Palgrave Macmillan.

Gray, M. and Webb, S. (2010). Conclusion: practising values in social work. In M. Gray and S. Webb (eds.), *Ethics and Value Perspectives in Social Work.* Basingstoke: Palgrave Macmillan, pp. 219–23.

Graybeal, C. T. (2007). Evidence for the art of social work. *Families in Society*, 88(4): 513–23.

Gredig, D., Shaw, I. and Sommerfeld, P. (2012). Mapping the Social Work Research Agenda. In M. Gray, J. Midgley and S. A. Webb (eds.), *The Sage Handbook of Social Work.* London: Sage, pp. 391–407.

Griffin, S., Kinmonth, A., and Veltman, M. (2004). Effect on health-related outcomes of interventions to alter the interaction between patients and practitioners: a systematic review of trials. *Annals of Family Medicine*, 2(6): 595–608.

Habermas, J. (1990). *Moral Consciousness and Communicative Action.* Cambridge, MA: MIT Press.

Harris, J. (2008). State social work: constructing the present from moments in the past. *British Journal of Social Work*, 18, 662–79.

Healy, K. (2000). *Social Work Practices.* London: Sage.

Heath, L., Tindale, R. S., Edwards, J., Posavac, E., Bryant, F., Henderson-King, E., Suarez-Balcazar, Y. and Myers, J. (eds.) (2013). *Applications of Heuristics and Biases to Social Issues.* New York: Springer.

Hebb, D. O. (1949). *The Organization of Behavior*. New York: Wiley and Sons.

Heidegger, M. (1971). The origin of the work of art. In *Poetry, Language, Thought*. New York: Harper Collins and Row.

Heston, L. L. (1966). Psychiatric disorders of foster home reared children and schizophrenic mothers. *British Journal of Psychiatry*, 112: 819–25.

Hick, S. F. (2009). *Mindfulness and Social Work*, Chicago, IL: Lyceum Books.

Hinchliffe, S. (2004). Living with risk: the unnatural geography of environmental crises. In S. Hinchliffe and K. Woodward (eds.), *The Natural and the Social: Uncertainty, Risk, Change*. (2nd ed.). London: The Open University Press, pp. 115–51.

Hofman, S. G., Asnaani, A., Vonke, I., Sawyer, A. T., and Fang, A. (2012). The efficacy of Cognitive Behavioural Therapy: a review of meta-analyses. *Cognitive Therapy and Research*, 36: 427–40.

Hohman, M. (2012). *Motivational Interviewing in Social Work Practice*. New York: Guilford Press.

Hollis, F. (1972). *Casework: a Psychosocial Therapy* (2nd ed.). New York: Random House.

Hollway, W. (2006). *The Capacity to Care*. London: Routledge.

Hood, R. (2014). Complexity and integrated working in children's services. *British Journal of Social Work*, 44(1): 27–43.

Houston, S. (2003). Establishing virtue in social work: a response of McBeath and Webb. *British Journal of Social Work*, 33(6): 819–24.

Houston, S. (2010), Further reflections on Habermas's contribution to discourse in child protection: An examination of power in social life. *British Journal of Social Work*, 40(6): 1736–53.

Houston, S. (2010). Discourse ethics. In M. Gray and S. Webb (eds.), *Ethics and Value Perspectives in Social Work*. Basingstoke: Palgrave Macmillan, pp. 95–107.

Houston,S. (2012). Engaging with the crooked timber of humanity: value pluralism in social work. *British Journal of Social Work*, 42: 652–68.

Howe, D. (1979). Agency function and social work principles. *British Journal of Social Work*, 9(1): 29–47.

Howe, D. (1987). *An Introduction to Social Work Theory*. Aldershot: Gower.

Howe, D. (1992). Child abuse and the bureaucratisation of social work. *Sociological Review*, 40(3): 491–508.

Howe, D. (1993). *On Being a Client: Understanding the Process of Counselling and Psychotherapy*. London: Sage.

Howe, D. (2005). *Child Abuse and Neglect: Attachment, Development and Interventions*. Houndmills: Palgrave Macmillan.

Howe, D. (2008). *The Emotionally Intelligent Social Worker*. Houndmills: Palgrave Macmillan.

Howe, D. (2011). *Attachment Theory Across the Lifecourse: a Brief Introduction*. Houndmills: Palgrave Macmillan.

Howe, D. (2012). *Empathy: What It Is and Why It Matters*. Houndmills: Palgrave Macmillan.

Howe, D., Sawbridge, P. and Hinings, D. (1992). *Half a Million Women: Mothers Who Lose Their Children by Adoption*. London: Penguin.

Hugman, R. (2013). Ethics. In M. Davies (ed.), *The Blackwell Companion to Social Work* (4th ed.). Oxford: Wiley-Blackwell, pp. 379–86.

Hume, D. (1967). *A Treatise on Human Nature*. Oxford: Oxford University Press.

Hupe, P. and Hill, M. (2007). Street-level bureaucracy and public accountability. *Public Administration*, 85(2): 279–99.

Hutchinson, A. (2013) Care management. In M. Davies (ed.), *The Blackwell Companion to Social Work* (4th ed.). Chichester: Wiley-Blackwell, pp. 321–32.

Ingram, R. (2013). Locating emotional intelligence at the heart of social work practice. *British Journal of Social Work*, 43(5): 987–1004.

Irvine, E. E. (1974). *Literature and the Study of Human Experience*. Northampton MA: Smith College School for Social Work.

Jack, G. (1997). An ecological approach to social work with children and families. *Child and Family Social Work*, 2(2): 109–20.

Jack, G. (2000). Ecological influences on parenting and child development. *British Journal of Social Work*, 30: 703–20.

Jack, G. (2013). Ecological perspective. In M. Gray, J. Midgley and S. A. Webb (eds.), *The Sage Handbook of Social Work*. London: Sage, pp. 129–42.

Jensen, J., Lundin-Olsson, L., Nyberg, L. and Gustafson, Y. (2002). Fall and injury prevention in older people living in residential care facilities: a cluster randomized trial. *Annals of Internal Medicine*, 136 (10): 733–41.

Johnson, D., Johnson, R. and Tjosvold, D. (2000). Constructive controversy: the value of intellectual opposition. In M. Deutsch and P. Coleman (eds.), *Handbook of Conflict Resolution: Theory and Practice*. San Francisco, CA: Jossey-Bass Publishers, pp. 65–85.

Johnson, T. (1972). The *Professions and Power*. London: Macmillan.

Jones, E. (1974). *The Life and Work of Sigmund Freud*. New York: Basic Books.

Jones, K., Cooper, B. and Ferguson, H. (eds.) (2008). *Best Practice in Social Work: Critical Perspectives*. Basingstoke: Palgrave Macmillan.

Jones, M. A. (1985). *A Second Chance for Families: Five Years Later*. New York: Child Welfare League of America.

Jordan, B. (1978). A comment on 'Theory and practice in social work'. *British Journal of Social Work*, 8: 23–5.

Jordan, B. (1979). *Helping in Social Work*. London: Routledge and Kegan Paul.

Juffer, F., Bakermans-Kranenburg, M. J. and van Ijzendoorn, M. H. (eds.) (2008). *Promoting Positive Parenting: an Attachment-based Intervention*. Abingdon: Psychology Press.

Kagan, J. (1994). *Galen's Prophecy: Temperament in Human Nature*. New York: Harper Collins.

Kahneman, D. (2012), *Thinking, Fast and Slow*. London: Penguin.

Kant, I. (1785/1964). *Groundwork of the Metaphysics of Morals*. New York: Harper and Row.

Keeping, C. (2008). Emotional engagement in social work: best practice and relationships in mental health work. In K. Jones, B. Cooper and H. Ferguson (eds.), *Best Practice in Social Work: critical perspectives*. Basingstoke: Palgrave Macmillan, pp. 71–87.

Kabat-Zinn, J, (2013). *Full Catastrophe Living: How to Cope with Stress, Pain and Illness Using Mindful Meditation*. London: Piatkus.

Kemshall, H. (2002). *Risk, Social Policy and Welfare*. Buckingham: Open University Press.

Kendrick, M. J. and Hartnett, F. M. (2005). Choosing values: the consequences for people's lives. In P. O'Brien and M. Sullivan (eds.), *Allies in Emancipation: Shifting from Providing Services to Being of Support*. Melbourne: Thomson Dunmore Press.

Kinman, G. and Grant, L. (2011). Exploring stress resilience in trainee social workers: the role of emotional and social competencies. *British Journal of Social Work*, 41(2): 261–75.

Kinman, G. and Grant, L. (forthcoming). *Resilience for Social Work Practice*. Basingstoke: Palgrave Macmillan.

Kirk, S. A. (1999). Good intentions are not enough: practice guidelines for social work. *Research on Social work Practice*, 9(3): 302–10.

Knott, C. and Scragg, T. (2013). *Reflective Practice in Social Work* (3rd ed.). London: Sage.

Latour, B. (2005). *Reassembling the Social: an Introduction to Actor–Network Theory*. Oxford: Oxford University Press.

Lavalette, M. (ed.) (2011). *Radical Social Work Today: Social Work at the Crossroads*. Bristol: Policy Press

Law, J. (1986). On the methods of long-distance control: vessels, navigation and the Portuguese route to India. In J. Law (ed.), *Power, Action and Belief: A New Sociology of Knowledge*. London: Routledge and Kegan Paul.

Law, J. and J. Hassard (eds.) (1999). *Actor Network Theory and After*. Chichester: Wiley-Blackwell.

Lazarus, R. S. (1982). Thoughts on the relations between emotion and cognition. *American Psychologist*, 37: 1019–24.

Lee, N. and Hassard, J. (1999). Organization unbound: actor–network theory, research strategy and institutional flexibility. *Organization* 6(3): 391–404.

Lee, P. (1937). *Social Work as Cause and Function*. New York: Columbia University Press.

Leece, J. (2012). The emergence and development of the personalization agenda. In M. Davies (ed.), *Social Work with Adults*. Basingstoke: Palgrave Macmillan, pp. 10–23.

Lehrman, D. S. (1970). Semantic and conceptual issues in the nature-nurture problem. In L. Aronson, E. Torbach, D. Lehrman, and S. Rosenblatt (eds.), *Development and Evolution of Behavior*. San Francisco, CA: W. W. Freeman, pp. 17–52.

Lipsky, M. (1980). *Street-level Bureaucracy*. New York: Russell Sage.

Lively, P. (2013), *Ammonites and Leaping Fish: a Life in Time*. London: Fig Tree/Penguin Books.

Macdonald, G. and Kakavelakis, I. (2004). *Helping Foster Carers Manage Challenging Behaviour: Evaluation of a Cognitive-Behavioural Training Programme for Foster Carers*. University of Exeter: Centre for Evidence-based Social Services.

Macdonald, K. (1997). *The Sociology of the Professions*. London: Sage.

Marston, G. and McDonald, C. (2012). *British Journal of Social Work*, 42(6): 1022–38.

Martinez-Brawley, E. and Zorita, M-B. (1998). At the edge of the frame: beyond science and art in social work. *British Journal of Social Work*, 28: 197–212.

Marx, K. (1852). *Eighteenth Brumaire of Louis Bonaparte*. New York: Die Revolution.

Matthys, J., Elwyn, G., van Nuland, M., van Maele, G., de Sutter, A., de Meyere, M. and Deveugele, M. (2009). Patients' ideas, concerns and expectations (ICE) in general practice: impact on prescribing. *British Journal of General Practice*, Jan. 1: 59 (558): 29–36.

Mayer, J. and Timms, N. (1970). *The Client Speaks: Working-class Impressions of Casework*. London: Routledge and Kegan Paul.

Miller, W. R. and Rollnick, S. (2002). *Motivational Interviewing: Preparing People for Change* (2nd ed.). New York: Guilford Press.

Mullaly, B. (2007). *The New Structural Social Work* (3rd ed.). Toronto: Oxford University Press.

Mullender, A. (2009). Persistent oppressions: the example of domestic violence. In R. Adams, L. Dominelli and M. Payne (eds.), *Practising Social Work in a Complex World* (2nd ed.). Basingstoke: Palgrave Macmillan, pp 33–41.

Munro, E. (2002). *Effective Child Protection*. London: Sage.

Murdoch, I. (1968), *The Nice and the Good*, Harmondsworth: Penguin.

Nagel, T. (1979). *Mortal Questions*. New York: Cambridge University Press.

Nagel, T. (1986). *The View from Nowhere*. New York: Oxford University Press.

Neil, E. (2007). Coming to terms with the loss of a child: the feelings of birth parents and grandparents about adoption and post-adoption contact. *Adoption Quarterly*, 10(1): 1–23.

Neil, E., Cossar, J., Lorgelly, P. and Young, J. (2010). *Helping Birth Families: Services, Costs and Outcomes.* London: BAAF.

Neisser, U. (1967). *Cognitive Psychology.* New York: Appleton-Century-Crofts.

Nicholson, W. (1993). *Shadowlands.* London: Paramount Pictures.

Noddings, N. (2003). *Caring: A Feminine Approach to Ethics and Moral Education* (2nd ed.). Berkeley, CA: University of California Press.

Oatley, K. (1998). Emotion. *The Psychologist,* June, pp. 285–8.

Office of National Statistics (ONS) (2014). *Personal Income and Wealth,* London: www.ons.gov.uk/rel/wealth/was/wealth-in-gerat-britian-wave-3/2010-2012/report.

Olds, D., Kitzman, H., Hanks, C., Cole, R., Anson, E. et al (2007). Effects of nurse home visiting on maternal and child functioning: age 9 follow-up of a randomized trial. *Pediatrics,* Oct, 120(4): e832–45.

Oliver, M. (1989) *The Politics of Disablement.* Basingstoke: Macmillan.

Owsley, R. (2002). Heidegger and German Expressionism. Available at: http://www.unt.edu/heidegger/papers.htm (date accessed by M. Gray and S. Webb 2008: 12 December 2006).

Parker, J. (2013). Assessment, intervention and review. In M. Davies (ed.), *The Blackwell Companion to Social Work* (4th ed.). Chichester: Wiley-Blackwell, pp. 311–20.

Parrot, L. (2010). *Values and Ethics in Social Work Practice.* Exeter: Learning Matters.

Parsons, T. (1951), *The Social System.* New York: The Free Press.

Parton, N. (1996). Social work, risk and 'the blaming culture'. In N. Parton (ed.), *Social Theory, Social Change and Social Work.* London: Routledge, pp. 98–114.

Parton, N. (1998). Risk, advanced liberalism and child welfare: the need to rediscover uncertainty and ambiguity. *British Journal of Social Work,* 28: 5–27.

Parton, N. (2003). Rethinking Professional Practice: the contributions of social constructivism and the feminist 'ethics of care'. *British Journal of Social Work,* 33(1): 1–16.

Parton, N. and O'Byrne, P. (2000). *Constructive Social Work: towards a new practice.* Basingstoke: Palgrave Macmillan.

Parton, C. and Parton, N. (1989). Child protection: the law and dangerousness. In O. Stevenson (ed.), *Child Abuse: Public Policy and Professional Practice,* Hemel Hempstead: Harvester Wheatsheaf, pp. 54–73.

Pease, B. (2013). A history of critical and radical social work. In M. Gray and S. Webb (eds.), *The New Politics of Social Work.* Basingstoke: Palgrave Macmillan, pp. 21–43.

Penna, S. and O'Brien, M. (2013). Neoliberalism. In M. Gray and S. Webb (eds.), *Social Work Theories and Methods* (2nd ed.). London: Sage, pp. 137–46.

Perrow, C. (1972). *The Radical Attack on Business*. New York: Harcourt Brace Janovich.

Peters, R. S. (1966). *Ethics and Education*. London: George Allen and Unwin.

Philp, M. (1979). Notes on the form of knowledge in social work. *Sociological Review*, 27: 83–111.

Piketty, T. (2014). *Capital in the Twenty-First Century*. Cambridge, MA: Harvard University Press.

Pincus, A. and Minahan, A. (1973). *Social Work Practice: Model and Method*. Itaca, IL: F. E. Peacock Publishers.

Plath, D. (2006). Evidence-based practice: current issues and future directions. *Australian Social Work*, 59 (1): 56–72.

Plath, D. (2013). Evidence-based practice. In M. Gray and S. Webb (eds.), *Social Work Theories and Methods* (2nd ed.). London: Sage, pp. 229–40.

Plomin, R., Asbury, K. and Dunn, J. (2001). Why are children in the same family so different? Non-shared environments a decade later. *Canadian Journal of Psychiatry*, 46: 225–33.

Plomin, R., DeFries, J., Knopik, V. and Neiderhiser, J. (2013). *Behavioral Genetics* (6th ed.). New York: Worth Publishers.

Plomin, R., DeFries, J. and Loehlin, J. (1977). Genotype–environment interaction and correlation in the analysis of human behaviour. *Psychological Bulletin*, 84: 309–22.

Pocock, D. (1995). Searching for a better story: harnessing modern and postmodern positions in family therapy. *Journal of Family Therapy*, 17: 149–73.

Popper. K. (1945). *The Open Society and its Enemies*. London: Routledge and Kegan Paul.

Putnam, R. D. (2000). *Bowling Alone: the Collapse and Revival of American Community*. New York: Touchstone.

Rabiee, P. (2013). Exploring the relationships between choice and independence: experiences of disabled and older people. *British Journal of Social Work*, 43(5) 872–88.

Rapoport, L. (1968). Creativity in social work. *Smith College Studies in Social Work*, 38(3): 139–61.

Reason, P. and Bradbury, H. (2008). *Handbook of Action Research: Participative Inquiry and Practice* (2nd ed.) London: Sage.

Rees, J. (2009). *Life Story Books for Adopted Children: a Family Friendly Approach*. London: Jessica Kingsley.

Reid, W. and Epstein, L. (1972). *Task-Centred Casework*. New York: Columbia University Press.

Reid, W. and Shyne, A. (1969). *Brief and Extended Casework*. New York: Columbia University Press.

Rhodes, M. (1986). *Ethical Dilemmas in Social Work Practice*. Boston, MA: Routledge and Kegan Paul.

Rickman, H. P. (1967). *Understanding and the Human Studies*. London: Heinemann Educational.

Ridley, M. (2003). *Nature via Nurture: Genes, Experience and What Makes Us Human*. London: Fourth Estate.

Rogers, C. (1957). The necessary and sufficient conditions of therapeutic personality change. *Journal of Consulting Psychology*, 21: 95–103.

Rogowski, S. (2012). Social work with children and families: challenges and possibilities in the neo-liberal world. *British Journal of Social Work*, 42: 921–40.

Rollnick, S., Miller, W. R. and Butler, C. C. (2008). *Motivational Interviewing in Health Care*. New York: Guilford Press.

Ronen, T. and Freeman, A. (eds.). *Cognitive Behavior Therapy in Clinical Social Work*. New York: Springer.

Ruch, G. (2012). Where have all the feelings gone? Developing reflective and relationship-based management in child-care social work. *British Journal of Social Work*, 42: 1315–32.

Rutter, M. (2005). *Genes and Behavior: Nature–Nurture Interplay Explained*. Chichester: Wiley-Blackwell.

Ryan, T. and Walker, R. (2007). *Life Story Work: a Practical Guide to Helping Children Understand their Past* (3rd ed.). London: British Association for Adoption and Fostering.

Sackett, D. L., Straus, S. E., Richardson, W. S., Rosenberg, W. and Hayes, R. B. (2000). *Evidence-based Medicine: How to Practice and Teach EBM*. (2nd ed.). New York: Churchill-Livingstone.

Saleeby, D. (ed.) (2008). *The Strengths Perspective in Social Work Practice* (5th ed.). Boston: Allyn and Bacon.

Salovey, P. and Mayer, J. (1990). Emotional intelligence. *Imagination, Cognition and Personality*, 9: 185–211.

Sands, R. and Nuccio, K. (1992). Postmodern feminist theory and social work. *Social Work*, 37(6): 480–94.

Santayana, G. (1905). *The Life of Reason*. New York: Scribner.

Sapolsky, R. M. (1996). *Why Zebras Don't Get Ulcers*. New York: W. H. Freeman.

Schofield, G. (1998). Inner and outer worlds: a psychosocial framework for child and family social work. *Child and Family Social Work*, 3(1): 57–67.

Schofield, G. and Thoburn, J. (1996). *The Voice of the Child in Child Protection*. London: Institute for Public Policy Research (69).

Schon, D. (1991). *The Reflective Practitioner*. Aldershot: Arena.

Schram, S. (2013), Welfare professionals and street-level bureaucrats. In M. Gray, J. Midgley and S. Webb (eds.), *The Sage Handbook of Social Work*. London: Sage, pp. 67–80.

Schutz, A. (1962–6). *Collected Papers: Vols I–III*. The Hague: Martinus Nijhoff.

Schwartz, J. M. and Gladding, R. (2011). *You Are Not Your Brain: the 4-step*

Solution for Changing Bad Habits, Ending Unhealthy Thinking, and Taking Control of Your Life. New York: Avery.

SCIE (2004). Improving the use of social research in social care. *Knowledge Review 7*. Bristol: The Policy Press.

Sennett, R. (2008). *The Craftsman*. New Haven: Yale University Press.

Shaw, I. (1999). Evidence for practice. In I. Shaw and J. Litman (eds.), *Evaluation and Social Work Practice*. London: Sage, pp. 14–40.

Shaw, I. (2003). Qualitative research and outcomes in health, social work and education. *Qualitative Research*, 3(1): 57–77.

Shaw, I. (2011). *Evaluating in Practice*. Aldershot: Ashgate.

Sheldon, B. (2011). *Cognitive Behavioural Therapy: Research and Practice in Health and Social Care*. Abingdon: Routledge.

Sheldon, B. and Macdonald, G. (2009). *A Textbook of Social Work*. London: Routledge.

Sheppard, M. (1995). Social work, social science and practice wisdom. *British Journal of Social Work*, 25(5): 265–94.

Sheppard, M. (2006). *Social Work and Social Exclusion*. Aldershot: Ashgate.

Siegel, D. (2010). *The Mindful Therapist*. New York: W. W. Norton.

Skidelsky, E. (2014). *I Spend, Therefore I Am* by Philip Roscoe: a review, Guardian, 23 Jan. p. 7.

Skinner, K. (2010). Supervision, leadership and management: Think piece. In Z. van Zwanenberg (ed.), *Leadership in Social Care*. London: Jessica Kingsley.

Smith, P. (2008). *Moral and Political Philosophy*. Basingstoke: Palgrave Macmillan.

Smith, R. (2005). Welfare versus Justice – again. *Youth Justice* 5(3): 1–16.

Snow, C. P. (1959/1964), The Rede Lecture, 1959. In C. P. Snow, *The Two Cultures: and a Second Look*. Cambridge: Cambridge University Press, pp. 1–21.

Social Work Task Force (2009) *Building a Safe, Confident Future: the Final Report of the Social Work Task Force* November. Available at http://publications:dcsf.gov.uk.DCSF-01114-2009.

Spector, T. (2012) *Identically Different: Why You Can Change Your Genes*. London: Phoenix.

Stanley, N., Graham-Kevan, N. and Borthwick, R. (2012). Fathers and domestic violence: building motivation for change through perpetrator programmes. *Child Abuse Review*, 21(4): 264–74.

Stanley, N., Fell, B., Miller, P., Thomson, G. and Watson, J. (2012) Men's Talk: Men's understanding of violence against women and motivations for change. *Violence Against Women*, 18(11): 1300–18.

Stefansson, H., Ophoff, R., Steinberg, S., Andreassen, O., Cichon, S., Rujescu, D. and Collier, D. (2009). Common variants conferring risk of schizophrenia. *Nature*, 460: 744–7.

Stein, M. (2004). *What Works for Young People Leaving Care?* Barkingside: Barnardos.

Stein, M. (2006). Research review: young people leaving care. *Child and Family Social Work*, 11(3): 273–9.

Stein, M., Pinkerton, J. and Kelleher, J. (2000). Young people leaving care in England, Northern Ireland and Ireland. *European Journal of Social Work*, 3: 235–46.

Sullivan, W. P. (2012). Strengths perspective. In M. Gray, J. Midgley and S. A. Webb (eds.), *The Sage Handbook of Social Work*. London: Sage, pp. 176–90.

Taylor, B. J. (2012). Intervention research. In M. Gray, J. Midgley and S. A. Webb (eds.), *The Sage Handbook of Social Work*. London: Sage, pp. 424–39.

Taylor, C. (2013). Critically reflective practice. In M. Gray and S. Webb (eds.), *The New Politics of Social Work*. Basingstoke: Palgrave Macmillan, pp. 79–97.

Taylor, C. and White, S. (2000). *Practising Reflexivity in Health and Welfare*. Buckingham: Open University Press.

Teater, B. (2013). Motivational Interviewing (MI). In M. Davies (ed.), *The Blackwell Companion to Social Work* (4th ed.). Chichester: Wiley-Blackwell, pp. 451–4.

Teater, B. and Baldwin, M. (2014). Singing for successful ageing: the perceived benefits of participating in the Golden Oldies Community-Arts Programme. *British Journal of Social Work*, 44(1): 81–99.

Thomas, P. (2013). Social work practice and people with physical and sensory impairments. In M. Davies (ed.), *The Blackwell Companion to Social Work* (4th ed.). Oxford: Wiley-Blackwell, pp. 259–65.

Thomas, S. and Wolfensberger, W. (1999). An overview of Social Role Valorization. In R. J. Flynn and R. A. Lemay (eds.), *A Quarter Century of Normalization and Social Role Valorization: Evolution and Impact*. Ottawa: University of Ottawa Press, pp. 125–57.

Timms, N. and Timms, R. (1977). *Perspectives in Social Work*. London: Routledge & Kegan Paul.

Tollefsbol, T. O. (2011). *Handbook of Epigenetics: the New Molecular and Medical Genetics*. London: Academic Press.

Tompkins, S. S. (1962). *Affect, Imagery and Consciousness Volume 2: The Negative Affects*. New York: Springer-Verlag.

Tonkiss, F. (1998). Continuity/change, In C. Jenks (ed.), *Core Sociological Dichotomies*. London: Sage, pp. 34–48.

Tronto, J. (1993). *Moral Boundaries*. London: Routledge.

Trevithick, P. (2012). *Social Work Skills and Knowledge: a practice handbook*. (3rd ed.). Maidenhead: Open University Press.

Trevithick, P. (2013), Practice perspectives. In M. Gray, J. Midgley and S. A. Webb (eds.), *The Sage Handbook of Social Work*. London: Sage, pp. 113–28.

Tsing, A. (2004). *Friction: An Ethnography of Global Connection*. Princeton, NJ: Princeton University Press.

Turner, L. M. (2013). Encouraging professional growth among social work students through literature assignments: narrative literature's capacity to inspire professional growth and empathy. *British Journal of Social Work*, 43(5): 853–71.

Tversky, A. and Kahneman, D. (1974). Judgement under uncertainty: heuristics and biases. *Sciences*, 185: 1124–31.

Valk, M. (1979). Poetry can help: the work of Kenneth Koch. *British Journal of Social Work*, 9: 501–7.

Valk, M. (1979). The therapeutic imagination: a comment. *British Journal of Social Work* 9(1): 87–91.

Walsh, D. F. (1998). Structure/agency. In C. Jenks (ed.), *Core Sociological Dichotomies*. London: Sage, pp. 8–33.

Walton, I. (1653/2000). *The Compleat Angler*. Oxford: Oxford Paperbacks.

Webb, S. (2006). *Social Work in a Risk Society*. Basingstoke: Palgrave Macmillan.

Webb, S. (2010). Virtue ethics. In M. Gray and S. Webb (eds.), *Ethics and Value Perspectives in Social Work*. Basingstoke: Palgrave Macmillan, pp. 108–19.

Weber, M. (1964). *The Theory of Social and Economic Organizations*. New York: The Free Press.

Webster, J. D. (2002). *Critical Advances in Reminiscence Work: From Theory to Application*. New York: Springer.

Westmarland, N. and Kelly, L. (2013). Why extending measurements of 'success' in domestic violence perpetrator programmes matters for social work. *British Journal of Social Work*, 43(6): 1092–100.

White, S. (1997). Beyond Retroduction? Hermeneutics, reflexivity and social work practice. *British Journal of Social Work*, 27: 739–53.

Williams, B. (1981). *Moral Luck*. Cambridge: Cambridge University Press.

Williams, R. (1965). *The Long Revolution*. Harmondsworth: Penguin.

Wilson, K., Ruch, G., Lymbery, M. and Cooper, A. (2011). *Social Work: an Introduction to Contemporary Practice* (2nd ed.) Harlow: Pearson Longman Education.

Winnicott, C. (1964). *Child Care and Social Work*. London: Bookstall Publications.

Wolfensberger, W. (1983). Social Role Valorization: a proposed new term for the principle of normalization. *Mental Retardation*, 21(6): 234–9.

Woodroofe, K. (1962). *From Charity to Social Work in England and the United States*. London: Routledge and Kegan Paul.

Ziemkendorf, M. (2013). *Actor–Network Theory*. Munich: GRIN Verlag.

Author Index

Subject Index